Divorce in China

Institutional Constraints and Gendered Outcomes

Xin He

NEW YORK UNIVERSITY PRESS

New York

NEW YORK UNIVERSITY PRESS
New York
www.nyupress.org

References to Internet websites (URLs) were accurate at the time of writing. Neither the author nor New York University Press is responsible for URLs that may have expired or changed since the manuscript was prepared.

Library of Congress Cataloging-in-Publication Data

Names: He, Xin, author.
Title: Divorce in China : institutional constraints and gendered outcomes / Xin He.
Description: New York : New York University Press, 2021. | Includesbibliographical references and index.
Identifiers: LCCN 2020015051 (print) | LCCN 2020015052 (ebook) | ISBN 9781479805532 (cloth) | ISBN 9781479805549 (ebook) | ISBN 9781479805587 (ebook)
Subjects: LCSH: Divorce—Law and legislation—China. | Divorce—China.
Classification: LCC KNQ558 .H495 2021 (print) | LCC KNQ558 (ebook) | DDC 346.5101/66—dc23
LC record available at https://lccn.loc.gov/2020015051
LC ebook record available at https://lccn.loc.gov/2020015052

New York University Press books are printed on acid-free paper, and their binding materials are chosen for strength and durability. We strive to use environmentally responsible suppliers and materials to the greatest extent possible in publishing our books.

Manufactured in the United States of America

10 9 8 7 6 5 4 3 2 1

Also available as an ebook

CONTENTS

Preface

Gender Bias in Chinese Courts

The Saleswoman's Case: On a chilly winter morning in 2013, a plain-looking woman arrived at a courthouse in the Pearl River Delta. In her early forties, she worked as a salesperson in a local department store. She was alone and without a lawyer, or a citizen representative, or a relative. Under her arm a bag contained her marriage certificate, identity documents, and court summons. A few minutes later, her husband, a tall, slender, stern-faced bus driver, also arrived alone.

This divorce hearing was peaceful and orderly at first. China's civil procedures have four formal stages for hearing: court investigation, court debate, court mediation, and court announcement (He and Ng 2013b). At the court investigation stage, when the judge asked the woman why she wanted a divorce, her plain-looking face turned pained. The pitch of her originally soft voice escalated, and her calm statements turned emotional.

> PLAINTIFF: He has beaten me savagely (暴打、毒打)... more than
> six hundred times! I have always wanted a divorce, but our son was
> young. Now that our son has reached eighteen years old, I can't wait
> to divorce him.
> DEFENDANT (SNEERING): Six hundred times!
> PLAINTIFF: Yes, yes, excluding those against my son, those
> reviles and insults against him.... He even beat me in front
> of my father. He said to my father: "I just want to beat her! So
> what?!"
> DEFENDANT: Beating savagely.... What are you talking about? I did
> not beat you; we were fighting against each other (对打).... All these
> years, what did you do for me? Have you ever done my laundry?
> What kind of food did you cook?

When the issue of domestic violence is raised in litigation, the response of men is often denial—exactly what this defendant did. Sneering at the suggestion of "six hundred times," he implies that his wife was exaggerating. For him, "beating savagely" was a mischaracterization. He testified that they were "fighting against each other," suggesting a neutral squabble between a couple rather than a one-sided battering. The justification of his behavior was cultural, citing the stereotypical role of women in Chinese culture: the wife should serve the husband at home, and she should bear the responsibility for housework such as cooking and laundry. When she does something wrong, the logic goes, she deserves to be beaten.

Apparently unprepared for her husband's denial, refutation, and justification, the woman turned less confident and slightly panicked. She could not substantiate her claims by evidence. This might have been her first time in the courtroom, and she had no lawyer present. Turning to moral integrity, she exclaimed: "Telling the truth! I swear to God that what I said is true, I swear."

As the quarrel intensified, the judge, to maintain order, distracted them by posing other questions. In her early thirties, with eight years' experience in family court, the judge was smart, competent, and professional. Her questions were detailed and specific, aiming to bring forth evidence of domestic violence.

> JUDGE: You said on September 27 you ran away from home. What happened?
>
> PLAINTIFF: Yes. I was afraid to return home. On October 4, he rushed to the gate of our department store. I was terrified when I spotted him. Oh, so scared! I then ran to the corner of our stall. He dragged me from there! Then . . . right at our Cigarette and Liquor Stall, the CCTV should have recorded. Oh! He dragged me outside of the store! saying "You go home with me, after then I will *zhouzhe* [in Cantonese, meaning "torture"] you, *zhouzhe* you slowly!"
>
> JUDGE: So is there a surveillance camera? Do you have footage of that?

The judge was looking for a smoking gun. Footage of the beating, of course, constituted substantial evidence of domestic evidence.

PLAINTIFF: Yes, I will see if we still keep it. Then I was dragged out, my colleagues tried to pull me back. Looking like a beast, he seemed ready to devour people. He said: "You go home!" He said he would tie me up. He wanted to pull me back and tie me up. He held my hands so hard that my hands changed color and turned swollen. He will *zhouzhe* me slowly. How can I go home with him? Do I dare to take a taxi with him and go home? As he pulled me to the other side of the street, one of my coworkers came over and tried to take my hands: "You should not twist her hands like this! You could break her hands. I already heard the noise of breaking bones!" He then threw a big rock against the road, breaking the rock. The coworker was so scared that she released my hands.

In this trial, the wife sought divorce based on domestic violence. With harrowing details and emotions emerging from her testimony, the allegations seemed authentic. But this was a laywoman's conception. The court needed evidence. No sooner had the plaintiff finished her emotional charge than the judge grilled the man as to how the beating occurred and what the wife's reactions were. The man, obviously unfamiliar with the law and the legal process, was caught off guard. He admitted that he had once choked the wife and their son. The judge later told me that, from that single admission, she already had enough evidence to find domestic violence. That saved the need to find whether there was footage of the beating.

After the hearing, the trial moved to the mediation phase, a compulsory stage for divorce cases under Chinese law. The man did not oppose the divorce. Since their child was already an adult, there was no need to determine child custody. The only issue left was the division of the couple's apartment. An agreement was swiftly reached through a bidding process. Bidding is one of several options provided by the Supreme People's Court (SPC) to determine the value of conjugal property: whoever offers the highest price, upon paying half of the price to the other party, obtains ownership. (For detailed explanations on this option and its gendered implications, see chapter 6.) The man received ownership of the conjugal property because he had outbid the woman. Within two hours, the divorce case was closed through mediation.

Gendered Outcomes

This represents one of more than 1.5 million divorce cases handled by Chinese courts every year. A major category of civil trials in China, divorce cases made up almost 20 percent of all civil cases in 2019 (SPC 2020). In many areas, designated family courts have been set up to handle the growing caseloads in this area of the law, most of which are petitions for divorce. In several aspects, the Saleswoman's Case is typical. A decision to divorce is easy to obtain as long as both parties agree. Domestic violence is prevalent. Official statistics showed that 14.86 percent of divorce litigation was triggered by domestic violence in 2016, constituting the second most cited reason for divorce petitions (SPC 2017). The conjugal property, usually a co-owned apartment, is divided through a bidding process. Judges usually do not identify moral culpability and rarely conduct out-of-court investigations. Under mediation, the process is efficient. A majority of parties are not represented by lawyers, especially in rural and suburban areas. About 70 percent of plaintiffs are women.

The woman who initiated this divorce petition was granted a divorce and was thankful. She did not have to return to the home, a fearful, unsafe space. No longer did she have to stay with a man who scared and threatened her. Harassment during work or her commute was over. The marriage dissolved, the dispute ended, and life moved on.

The woman's relief was misplaced, however. Because the judge granted her divorce and obtained evidence of domestic violence, the woman could have secured more compensation for damages resulting from domestic violence and for the marital assets. The litigation outcome itself was gendered.

First, the issue of domestic violence was sidelined by the mediation process. The wife had not been compensated, and not a word on domestic violence was recorded in the settlement. Second, when bidding is used to divide assets, women often receive the short end. The bidding process is listed as one of several legal options for dividing matrimonial assets, and most judges encourage the parties to adopt it. They suggest that it is more efficient and cheaper. When parties are talked into adopting this method, in most cases the bidding process ends within a few minutes without any further costs. However, the outcome is often that the man, usually the one with more cash on hand, is able to outbid the woman and secure ownership of the apartment. As will be detailed later, that ownership comes with tangible and intangible benefits and gains an advantage compared with the other party. This process, which is seemingly gender-neutral, favors the financially powerful party. Oftentimes the woman, upon receiving half of the bid price, moves to a small rental apartment and remains there for the rest of her life.

These gendered effects are not the most pronounced among women going through divorce litigation. In this case, the man did not withhold consent to the divorce simply to torture the woman or to extract additional financial benefits. Child custody was also not an issue. The woman did not need to sacrifice other rights to secure child custody, a common demand for mothers. Furthermore, the case occurred in the Pearl River Delta, a pioneer in economic and legal developments. The judge, professional and competent, was sensitive to the gender issue. If this case is unrepresentative of China's overall situation, then the gendered effects are likely worse in other parts of the country. Take domestic violence as one example. Despite its prevalence, domestic violence, let alone compensation, is rarely recognized by the courts (Palmer 2017). Empirical research (Chen and Duan 2012) based on all family cases filed in one district court in Chongqing, in western China, suggests that of 458 cases involving claims of domestic violence, in only three (0.66 percent) were the victims compensated for it. Among all domestic violence evidence presented in the cases handled by the intermediate courts in Beijing, in only 17.3 percent was such evidence admitted (Gao 2016).

The gendered outcomes are also conspicuous in regard to property division. According to an examination of 171 divorce lawsuits collected from Sichuan Province, more often than not "rural women walked away from divorce litigation with no farmland, no housing, and no financial compensation, let alone alimony. By contrast, their husbands were far more likely to retain *de facto* or *de jure* control over family and conjugal property" (Li and Friedman 2016: 161).

Existing Explanations

There is no doubt that the outcomes disadvantage women, but what explains gendered effects? The existing literature identifies three reasons:

incomplete protections in the existing law, disparities between the litigation capabilities of men and women, and patriarchal culture outside and inside courtrooms.

Incomplete Protections in the Legislation

Gendered outcomes result from incomplete protections in the legislation. Over history, legislation was inadequate in conferring protection, or protections were too narrow or ill-defined. The concept of domestic violence did not even appear in Chinese laws until 2001. As early as 2000, Zhao complained about the lack of legislation on domestic violence. Palmer (2005) characterized the legal treatment of domestic violence as a "long march." Chen and Duan (2012) contend that the law should lighten the burden of proof for domestic violence victims to make it easier to corroborate claims. Ogletree and Alwis (2004) call for a more concrete definition of domestic violence and a legal recognition of marital rape. Renowned women's rights advocates and practitioners such as Guo Jianmei and Liu Ying also believed that "existing laws do not adequately protect women abused by their partners" (Fincher 2014: 144). This "incomplete or inadequate legislation" argument remains influential, even after the Anti-Domestic Violence Law (ADV Law) was put into effect in 2016. Han (2017) criticizes the ADV Law for failing to criminalize domestic violence, and its endorsement of mediation may, in fact, lead to inadequate compensation for domestic violence victims. Palmer, while acknowledging the ADV Law as "a substantial step forward" (2017: 309), maintains that it lacks detail and precision in several key terms and mechanisms (2017: 309–10).

Promoting the notion that women were "half of the sky," Beijing hosted the UN Fourth World Conference on Women in 1995, presenting a pioneering image for building a more egalitarian society. The principle of gender equality is enshrined in the Chinese Constitution. Moreover, the Women's and Children's Rights Protection Law provides women facing divorce a range of protections. As a response to gender problems in a market-oriented country, the 2001 amendment to the Marriage Law codifies procedures to recognize "fault." It penalizes the party who conceals joint property in an attempt to prevent the fair division of property in a divorce; furthermore, it allows the wronged spouse the right to request compensation from a spouse who has engaged in bigamy, illegal cohabitation, domestic violence, or desertion (Art. 46). While these articles are gender-neutral in their wording, they are clearly motivated by the goal of protecting women. The ADV Law, despite its problems, is an official recognition that domestic violence is a serious issue and is a form of deviant conduct that can no longer be characterized as a private matter. It also provides a mechanism for obtaining a Personal Safety Protection Order, preventing potentially abusive family members from getting close to the victims. According to Runge (2015: 31), "These achievements would have been unthinkable a few years ago and represent significant progress." The question is: To what extent have the promises in these laws materialized?

A Disparity in Resources

Women are also disadvantaged because of their limited capability to mobilize resources during litigation. Socioeconomic disparities between the two genders exist in China. Gender discrimination abounds in employment, wage, age, and education, to name just a few areas of concern (Bauer et al. 1992). They all result in income disparity between genders. Fincher (2014: 5) contends that "Chinese women have largely missed out on what is arguably the biggest accumulation of residential real-estate wealth in history." Li and Friedman (2016: 159) state: "For women too old, ill, or isolated to amass enough money, mobilizing state law to resolve marital disputes was often beyond their reach." When divorcing women approached legal professionals for help, Li (2015) finds gendered patterns within the legal profession to filtering out women because they are not profitable clients. Any bargaining inside the courtroom further disadvantages women. Men, with more economic capability, are able to hire lawyers (or better lawyers). In the more evidence-based judicial processes, a new emphasis on burden of proof disadvantages most women, because "women have fewer economic resources than men" to make their stories heard (Woo 2003: 132). Husbands may be hiding assets, there is the danger of being left homeless, and pressure builds to give up custody and property in the hopes of obtaining a simpler process.

But this explanation—both true and persuasive—remains incomplete as to gendered outcomes. In Galanter's seminal paper "Why the Haves Come Out Ahead?" (1974), he assumed that a court is neutral. In China, this assumption is far from true. Chinese judges are subject to various extralegal influences (He and Su 2013). Like their counterparts in Israel (Dotan 1999) and the Philippines (Haynie 1994), they could have stood up for the poor and the downtrodden. In labor disputes involving migrant workers, Chinese judges have favored the "have-nots" (Halegua 2008; Su and He 2010). Why cannot they just tilt the balance toward women in divorce litigation? If the reality is that they seem to reinforce the economic disparity when given discretion, there must be other reasons than a disparity in resources for the gendered outcomes.

China's Patriarchal Culture

Another influential view blames patriarchal cultures outside and inside the courts. Outside the courtroom, China's society largely remains a patriarchal society (Honig and Hershatter 1988). Many Chinese still share a patrilineal belief that regards women as an instrument to bypass their men's bloodline; naturally children belong to the men's side. The patrilocal tradition commands women to stay in men's communities after marriage. Palmer (2017) believes that patriarchal socialism still characterizes many parts of China today. According to him (2017: 287), patriarchal socialism "was created in large part by the Chinese Communist Party's willingness to sacrifice socialist goals of gender equality and women's release from family patriarchal authority structures in exchange for the political support that would be generated by tolerating rather than attacking traditional family values." He also believes that females' lack of independent movement, a point related to social awareness of the gender issue, constitutes a major barrier to fighting domestic violence (2017). The prevalence of domestic violence and marital rape derives from the widely accepted norms about masculinity, according to a *China Daily* report (Fincher 2014: 147). When it comes to the partition of matrimonial property during divorce, patriarchal culture takes its toll on women. Li and Friedman (2016: 163) state: "In the countryside, longstanding patrilineal values and property regimes, coupled with norms of patrilocal residence after marriage, diminish the quality of legal advice women receive from legal workers and the value of settlements offered by judges and court-based mediators. In most cases, these outcomes reaffirm married women's outsider status in their conjugal communities and their weak claims to conjugal property still defined in patrilineal terms, irrespective of the letter of the law."

Inside the courtroom, scholars contend, judges lack the gender consciousness necessary to protect women's interests and fail to realize how serious this problem is. The patriarchal culture has caused biased norms to become internalized. The male's view is so dominant that judges do not even realize they are biased. Subscribing to this view, Ogletree and Alwis attribute the weak judicial protection to Chinese judges being "insensitive" and "poorly educated" on the gender issue (2004: 285). This view is echoed by Palmer (2017: 287), who states that "resistance to more enlightened understanding of the issue of domestic violence even in the post-Mao reform period was also fortified by unsympathetic and conservative attitudes within the judiciary." Li and Friedman (2016: 158) state: "Their [rural women's] marital grievances often fall on deaf ears; their efforts to correct conjugal wrongs are regularly dismissed; and at the time of the divorce, their endeavors to actualize property rights are frequently blocked or even derailed by a fragmented state whose divorce actors espouse uneven *commitment* to gender equality" (emphasis added).

Patriarchal culture is surely contributing to the gendered outcomes in divorce litigation, especially in rural China where the culture's impact is more pronounced. But if patriarchal culture was a major reason for the gendered outcomes in divorce litigation in the early stage of the reform, why hasn't its role declined significantly today? The Chinese state has continued to promote the idea of gender equality in its rhetoric and laws (Runge 2015). The norm of gender equality, along with globalization, has gained wide acceptance. The remarkable impact of the #MeToo movement is just one example. Woo (2003) argues that an increasing use of the formal legal process has altered women's sense of entitlement and equality (see also Lazarus-Black 2001). The judges, even in the hinterlands, are crystal-clear that domestic violence is wrong and must be penalized. Many training programs on gender awareness, according to Runge (2015: 39–41), have been very effective. After all, a law solely devoted to fighting domestic violence has been promulgated. Some judges have managed to prove domestic violence, the most difficult evidentiary obstacle in the hearing (He and Ng 2013a). If they subscribe to the patriarchal notion that women deserve to be beaten, then they do not even need to collect the evidence at all, let alone grant a divorce. If Ogletree and Alwis (2004) are right in that one of many barriers to enforce women's legal rights includes the problems inherent in the judiciary, then they would have not limited their focus on internalized judicial biases. There must be other reasons explaining gendered decision-making.

Institutional Constraints

The three explanations identified above, while not wrong, are insufficient. This book contends that institutional constraints play a crucial role in generating gendered outcomes. The importance of institutional safeguards in the judiciary is long noted (Cohen 1991: 187, 192, 193; Epstein 1990: 827, 838; Posner 1993; Sisk et al. 1998: 1498). As Ng and He (2017a) point out, the Chinese courts are embedded with constraints. Extralegal factors permeate the decision-making process. The judiciary is also a bureaucratic institution controlling the behavior of judges. As a result, divorce adjudication is driven by the bureaucratic incentives of the judiciary and its political concern. The judges are responding to two sets of interrelated institutional constraints: efficiency concerns and stability concerns (Kinkel and Hurst 2015).

Concern over "efficiency" means that judges are supposed to handle cases efficiently, that is, in a timely manner. The Civil Procedural Law stipulates that cases tried according to the Ordinary Procedure (普通程序) are to be completed within six months; those conducted using the Simplified Procedure (简易程序) have only three months to finish. Some senior officials managing their courts even shorten the limits to ninety or twenty days (Ordinary versus Simplified Procedures) to allow themselves more room to maneuver (Ng and He 2017a: 57). The so-called case closure rate—an indication of the effectiveness and efficiency of court operations—appears in every court's annual work report. By December of each year, many courts stop taking new cases so that they can increase the case closure rate for that year.

Concern over "stability" means that any court decision has to be accepted by the litigating parties and by society at large—that is, it cannot otherwise foment social instability (Minzner 2009; Liebman 2011; Trevaskes et al. 2014). This is controlled by appeal rates, remand rates after appeal, petition rates, and the number of "malicious incidents," including social protests and unnatural deaths. The judiciary trumpets a slogan whereby the decision is "to achieve the combination of both legal and social effects." While the legal effects suggest the observations of legal principles and rules, social effects imply that society accepts the decision peacefully. It would be ideal if the two were consistent and mutually reinforcing. But when they conflict, legal principles and rules have to make way for social effects where the law becomes compromised.

The best example to illustrate these two concerns is the revival of mediation. Since the early 2000s, the mediation rate has become an indicator of courts' performance, though such a requirement has been abandoned by some courts during some periods depending on the political environment, caseload pressures, and the preferences of court leaders (Fu and Cullen 2011; Ng and He 2017a; Li, Kochen and Van Rooij 2018; Fu and Palmer 2016). Mediation, by definition, means both parties voluntarily settle the issues and thus accept the courts' decisions. The litigants should not appeal or petition against a decision. In this way it addresses the stability concern. For some categories of cases mediation could also be efficient. It saves the time of the judge to divide property, for example. Arguably, it also addresses the caseload concern.

Judges often choose the most efficient, yet safest, way to handle issues in divorce litigation. They have to make sure that cases are finished before their deadline and are adjudicated without incident. They seek a balanced decision acceptable to both parties without provoking extreme reactions. This behavior pattern, I argue, results in gendered outcomes.[1]

First, many laws protecting women's interests are not fully implemented. These laws are created to reverse social, cultural, and economic biases against women. They are not necessarily gender-neutral; they may favor women or offer them a hand. Their implementation is crucial for rectifying gender biases and eventually achieving gender equality. The existing literature acknowledges the difficulties in obtaining evidence for victims in domestic evidence. While these studies point out the problems, they do not realize that the judges' concerns are one important driving force. Several laws fail to realize their potential in improving gender equality because judges are reluctant to do more. Should they become more active in this process, the outcome would be less tilted against women's interests.

Second, judges' behavior patterns privilege men in litigation outcomes because of their superior economic capabilities. Out of efficiency concerns, judges often press the weaker party to accept a deal proposed by the stronger party so as to facilitate the process. Out of stability concerns, judges often allow an economically advantaged man to gain the upper hand in highly contested cases. Men with more cash are allowed to buy out women determined not to be divorced. By contrast, women, with less economic capability, do not enjoy the same luxury when their husbands are equally steadfast against divorce. Women remain bound by the shackles of marriage, even though they are desperate for their removal (He 2017).

Finally, judges do not alleviate cultural biases against women—in fact, they perpetuate them. With such an approach, they accept the patriarchal culture and reinforce gender inequality, turning a blind eye toward cultural bias. Because of their concerns for efficiency and stability, they are reluctant to render custody of children to women, even if the law and evidence command it. This is not because judges are unaware that women's rights are infringed upon. They just do not want to infuriate or even confront the men. For purposes of disposing of the cases efficiently without lingering effects, it would be unnecessary to do so.

It is thus inadequate to say that the burdens on women during divorce litigation stem only from the incomplete coverage of women's rights or from vague definitions of key terms in the legislation. It is also not enough to blame the judges' lack of gender consciousness or inequalities and biases outside the court. Beyond these usual suspects, one fundamental reason is that judges, catering to institutional concerns, consciously and inadvertently, make decisions detrimental to women. Driven by these concerns, they allow the forces of inequality in the social, economic, cultural, and political areas to infiltrate their decisions. Put simply, institutional reasons prevent judges from offering a level playing field to women. Equality can be invoked and fulfilled only when the courts have acted (MacKinnon 1989). Thus, the institutional failure to enforce the laws has become a major obstacle to gender justice. In other words, even without the problems in legislative coverage, economic advantages to men, and patriarchal biases against women, one would still see the disadvantaged treatments of women resulting from the institutional imperatives of efficiency and stability.

This is not to suggest that China's litigation process is gendered by its very *nature*. The system contains little inherent bias against women. My argument is that the litigation process, because of the efficiency and stability concerns, favors the powerful over the powerless. In the divorce setting, this usually means that women are disadvantaged. Gender is not a separate dimension, independent of power inequalities: most men are more powerful than their wives and therefore benefit from the process. Judges are sensitive or even overreactive to the possible obstacles created by more powerful parties, and they are insensitive to the plight of the powerless. Domestic violence can be committed by women, and the judges' approach would be the same for women who committed domestic violence, but statistics shows that men commit more than 90 percent of domestic violence cases (SPC 2014). Powerful women would get the same "preferred" treatment from the court as do powerful men. Wealthy women could obtain the conjugal property by outbidding their spouses; strong women could also emotionally or physically abuse weak husbands. As O'Barr and Atkins (1998) argue, women's language should be better understood as powerless language, because powerless men also speak women's language. The problem is that few women are more powerful than their male partners.

In a sense, we witness a haves–versus–have-nots situation with a Chinese twist (He and Su 2013). In the United States, the "haves" come out ahead because they are the more resourceful party and can game a rules-based system. In China, the "haves" (mostly husbands) game the system of contested divorces, not so much the rules—hence the Chinese characteristics—but the fact that everything is subject to bargaining. When judges work to address stability and caseload concerns, men often come out ahead, as concerns of gender equality and women's well-being are left by the wayside when judges treat the various key components of divorce as exchangeable parts or, worse, bargaining chips.

Divorce Litigation in China

Divorce is common in China today. According to the Ministry of Civil Affairs (2017), a total of 4.16 million couples applied for divorce in 2016. That translates to a crude divorce rate of 3 percent. This rate doubled in the decade between 2006 to 2016, from 1.5 to 3 percent (Zhou 2018). The decade-long climb in divorce rates places China above most of European countries and close distance to the United States, which had a divorce rate of 3.2 percent in 2016 (Wang and Ng 2020 forthcoming). China's persistent increases in divorce rates are a testimony to remarkable social change (Chen and Shi 2013; Wang and Zhou 2010). National Public Radio reported that about 40 percent of marriages in Beijing ended in divorce (Lim 2010).

In China, only contested divorces go through court proceedings. When a divorcing couple works out the terms on their own, they can quickly obtain a divorce certificate at the government Department of Civil Affairs. But most divorce cases that reach the courts are contested, either on the issue of divorce itself or related issues such as property settlement and child custody. Of the 4.16 million couples who divorced in 2016, civil affairs departments handled 3.5 million, or about 83 percent of all divorces (Ministry of Civil Affairs 2017). The SPC (2018) reported that in 2017, the total number of contested divorces rose to more than 1.4 million cases.[2]

Contested cases—the focus of this book—are perhaps the most important for exploring gender issues in divorce law and practice. After all, bargaining outside the court depends heavily on the decisions made inside the court (Kornhauser and Mnookin 1979). As the stage in which the laws are interpreted and implemented, it is the baseline for bargaining outside the courtroom. Although it is important to examine other stages of the dispute pyramid suggested by Felstiner et al. (1980–1981), it is no less important to explore how judges make final decisions. As works based on other jurisdictions have demonstrated, whether judges make gendered decisions is crucial for understanding the relationship among law, gender, and power (Martin et al. 2002; Resnik 1996; Nagel and Weitzman 1971, 1972; Best et al. 2011; Kulik et al. 1996; LaFree and Rack 1996; Goodman et al. 1991; Burstein 1989). The litigation process will lay bare the issues related to divorce and the realization of women's legal rights.

Exploring the interplay between divorce litigation and gendered outcomes, this book addresses the following questions: How do judges make decisions on divorce cases? When the laws are clear, how do they interpret the laws? When the laws are vague or missing, how do they deal with that situation? How do they conduct mediation? How do they deal with contested issues such as child custody and sexuality? Has the Anti-Domestic Violence Law improved the well-being of women? According to the law, spouses can claim both material and mental damages for blameworthy marital conduct (Supreme People's Court Interpretation 1, Art. 28, 2001). But how should "fault" be identified in divorce lawsuits, what kind of evidence is needed to prove wrongdoing, how should damages be measured and compensated accordingly, and how can citizens hold police and prosecutors accountable when they fail to intervene in domestic violence? As to the division of conjugal property, how do judges and the courts jeopardize the interests of women? More generally, are court decisions on divorce cases gender-biased?

Such an undertaking tries to comprehend the behavior patterns of the judges through their interactions with the litigants and, when applicable, their relatives and legal representatives. This book tells a story of the judges who struggle to exercise power. They have to attend to the principles and rules, but they are faced by a group of people who are rearranging their lives through a procedure mandated by law. Most litigants are strangers to the world of law. Many come to the courts for help and hope for new lives. Many resist such changes. Many avoid the prescribed paths. They experience the legal battle with expectation, suspicion, mistrust, frustration, and even adversity. In this process, China's judges have found themselves to be in a situation similar to divorce lawyers, as documented by Sarat and Felstiner (1997) and Griffiths (1986). They have to deal with people who are emotionally agitated, in the midst of profound personal crisis, ambivalent about divorce, determined to hurt their spouse, and misguided about what they can reasonably expect from the divorce process. Judges need to worry about the emotional instability and unpredictability of litigants. In exercising power and discharging their duties, judges touch emotional turmoil and intimate secrets in the lives of real people. It is not easy for them to stay detached or hyperrational when making the decisions responsibly while also protecting themselves from becoming ensnared in the turmoil.

By focusing on how judges handle divorce cases and exploring the consequences, this book enriches a burgeoning field on judicial decision-making in China. The 2010s witnessed a surge of empirical studies on how Chinese courts handle various types of cases. This includes medical (Liebman 2013), media (Liebman 2005; He and Lin 2017), labor (Gallagher 2017; Su and He 2010; Chen and Xu 2012), environmental (Stern 2013; Van Rooij 2010; Wang 2013), corporate (Xi 2010; Howson 2010; Huang 2012), and criminal cases (Trevaskes 2007; Ng and He 2017a). Many have pointed out the role of politics and institutional constraints in this process (Kinkel and Hurst 2015; Ng and He 2017b; He 2012; Wang and Liu 2017). Specifically, Michelson (2018), based on adjudication documents available on the official sites of Chinese courts, has conducted a quantitative analysis on the role of domestic violence in the divorce decision-making process. Echoing many of my previous findings (He 2009a, 2017; He and Ng 2013a, 2013b), Michelson (2018: 70) contends: "By privileging competing institutional imperatives, including judicial efficiency, the preservation of marriages, and social stability maintenance, courts serve the needs of political priorities more than the needs of gender justice." Nonetheless, never before has a systematic treatment of divorce cases been conducted. Despite the fact that the gender problem is grave and Chinese courts handle an enormous number of divorce cases, the existing literature has rarely addressed the relationship between divorce law practice and gender inequality. Overall family laws in China have been one of the most complex yet least appreciated areas. Long regarded as a stepchild in Chinese jurisprudence, it is no more than a residue subsidiary of the mainstream civil law. But it is hard to understand Chinese courts without understanding how a major category of disputes are handled. If the phrase "embedded courts" (Ng and He 2017a) provides a general framework for the operation of Chinese courts, then this book is an in-depth analysis on a specific type of case. In this sense, this book helps form a more comprehensive yet more nuanced picture on the landscape of the operation of China's judiciary system.

This book describes how family laws operate in context of divorce proceedings. Following the scholarly tradition of law and society, I try to highlight the complex character of the immediate situation as distinct from the abstractions that generalization and the rules contemplate. The specific acts of Chinese judges, their character and background, the organizational constraints and policy tendencies of courts, and the nature of the litigants and their lawyers all contribute to actions and outcomes deeply responsive to the contexts. Legal doctrine is general and abstract, but my descriptions recognize more of the organizational and situational elements. In the cases depicted, I present particularities that abstract rules do not recognize or appreciate. The character of the plaintiff and defendant, the consequences of action at the time and in the place, the priority of organizational operation, and the many facets of individual cases may trump the realization of a just decision under the formal rules.

With the rise of the feminist jurisprudence movement, studies on the interaction between law and gender have mushroomed. This book, focusing on China from this perspective, provides a rich description on how these two fields intersect in China's political, economic, legal, and cultural contexts. It analyzes how courts have aggravated the plight of women: how domestic violence is ignored, how women's custody is dispensed, and how their property rights are sacrificed. Contributing to gender studies and the impact of society on the legal system, it eviscerates how social, cultural, and economic forces infiltrate the judicial decision-making process. It demonstrates that some of China's family laws have not been implemented by its own courts. This book reveals how courts' behavior is shaped by institutional constraints. It will also illustrate the extent to which the state has penetrated society in contemporary China. In this sense, my analysis on the practice of divorce law not only exemplifies China's civil justice but also evinces the broader relationship between the state, law, and society. It thus provides an aperture on how deeply the state has penetrated into what might be thought to be a "private" area of social life.

Fieldwork

By exposing the reasons behind gendered outcomes, rather than advocating equality rhetoric under the statutes, this book adopts a law and society approach. My inquiry centers on law in action rather than laws on the books. Our understanding of divorce law practice will be deepened not only by analyzing the legislatures and statutes but also observing the operation of the court systems: what the judges and litigants do and say. I first document the outcomes of litigation and operational patterns in the courts, then critically evaluate them and find the underlying reasons leading to such outcomes and patterns. I go further to locate the concepts, values, and assumptions embedded in these outcomes and patterns. That is why I pay special attention to the discourses used in the adjudication and mediation processes. They constitute law and power. What people do and say leads us to understand the social perceptions and institutional manifestations of law and legality. In addition, the implementation of legal rules will track and reflect the dominant conceptualizations of the major social and institutional changes. As with all laws, divorce law practices symbolically reflect more than what is considered to be legal policy. The approaches and norms evinced in this process also stand as eloquent statements about society's views on the nature of family, marriage, and parenthood. They are a mirror of enduring social change. This book is thus also a sociolegal history of China's rapidly changing society.

To conduct fieldwork investigations, I chose two basic-level courts, one in Guangdong and the other in Shaanxi. I chose basic-level courts because most divorce cases are handled there. The Guangdong Court is located in the heart of the Pearl River Delta, one of the most affluent regions of the country. The city's GDP per capita reached USD 22,000 in 2017. It has thus attracted a large number of migrant workers from the hinterlands. Of the 800,000 residents in the jurisdiction of the trial court in which our sample trials were heard, 300,000 were registered migrants. While the official language is Mandarin, a significant proportion of the population speaks Cantonese as their everyday language. The courts are widely regarded as a pioneer in judicial reforms pointing toward professionalism. This is an ideal place to empirically examine whether new reform measures such as the Personal Safety Protection Order are helpful in reducing domestic violence.

Compared to the Guangdong Court, the Shaanxi Court lies in the suburban part of its capital city, Xi'an, in western China. It is not at all the poorest region in the province, but it is not rich. By 2015 its GDP per capita was about USD 7,000, less than a third of that in the Pearl

River Delta area. While agriculture remains dominant, weaving and electricity are pillars in the local industry. But many companies are State-Owned Enterprises (SOEs) that have been pushed to the verge of collapse. Indeed, many male litigants that I encountered were laid off from these enterprises. The local language is mainly Mandarin with a thick northern accent. While the judicial reforms are a national agenda, many of the reform measures have not been implemented here. A lot of cases are still handled and concluded through mediation. The Shaanxi Court thus offers a contrast with the Guangdong Court and helps reveal the extent to which traditional culture and values take a toll on gender inequality. Numerous studies have indicated that the levels of economic and institutional development significantly affect the institutional responses of local courts in handling disputes (Balme 2010; Peerenboom and He 2009; He 2009a; Zhu 2007; Ng and He 2017b).

Obviously, these two places are also different in their levels of cultural development. In the Pearl River Delta, with convenient transportation and frequent interactions with Hong Kong, people are more exposed to norms and trends in the outside world. The influence of patrilineal and patrilocal biases against women is palpably weaker than in Shaanxi. The topic of sex—taboo in the Shaanxi area—was not uncommon in trials held in the Pearl River Delta. Together these two places help form representative cases that cut across a broad spectrum of socioeconomic, cultural, and regional differences.

My interest in divorce litigation began in the early 2000s, when I was researching contractual judgment enforcements (He 2009b) and women's property rights in South China (He 2007b). I was electrified when a judge, during a casual chat, mentioned that he rejected most of the first-time divorce petitions. The outcome was my first article on the topic of divorce cases (He 2009a). In the winter of 2013, my collaborator Kwai Hang Ng accompanied me to visit the Guangdong Court. Our goals were to examine languages and the court's operations. We sat in on various types of civil cases, including family, labor, tort, and contract cases. This resulted in several publications, including two articles on divorce cases (He and Ng 2013a; 2013b), which, after thorough revision and rewriting, are included in this book. My interests in divorce litigation and gender intensified after this trip. Taking advantage of the proximity of the Guangdong Court to Hong Kong, where I teach, I visited the court every year and stayed for one week or two for fieldwork investigations since 2013.

Obtaining access to Chinese courts is difficult and has recently become even more so (Clarke 2003, 2019). Through personal connections, I was introduced to the judges hearing the divorce cases on both courts. Before 2016, I was allowed to sit in the courtroom during the entire trial process, including pretrial mediation. After 2017, sitting in on the trial in the Guangdong Court needed the permission of the litigants because of the strict implementation of the national rule for trials involving privacy. Some litigants refused to let any relatives to sit in, not to mention a stranger like me. I ended up watching the video recordings of ten cases. In the Shaanxi Court, however, the rule on privacy was never seriously implemented, and nobody, including the lawyers, protested my presence during the trial and mediation process. I visited the Shaanxi Court in the summers of 2017 and 2018, each time for about a month. Over the years, I have observed more than fifty trials, and these observations constitute the first part of my data.

As an observer, I was present when litigants confronted the full range of issues that transpire during a divorce, from monetary disputes to allegations of infidelity. I was also present in the private caucus of a mediation session when the litigants confronted the judge with a death threat, as well as when they revealed their most private information such as rape and impotency. As an observer, I had an unusual vantage point inside the courtroom of an authoritarian regime, one virtually unprecedented in the field. From this perspective, I saw how the intended goals of the law are twisted and slighted, how the meaning of the law is constructed and contested, and how the ideologies of the judge and the litigants both clash and compromise. Rare and unfiltered tales behind the curtain of China's courts unfolded. Few outside researchers have enjoyed such access. As will be shown, my descriptions and qualitative analysis—by providing the contextualized mechanisms on the judicial decision-making pattern, the nuanced dynamics between the judges and litigants, and the psychological and behavioral reactions of the litigants—dovetail with the existing quantitative analysis (Michelson 2018, 2019). My data and analysis also go beyond the reach of most quantitative analyses. In scope, for example, they cover issue areas such as property division and male impotence. In depth, they reveal the psychological responses of the litigants to the approaches of the judges.

Civil trials in China proceed at a crisp pace; a trial typically takes only one court session, either in the morning or afternoon. Some of the trials I observed were as short as ten minutes (usually because the defendant did not show up), in which the judges just asked the plaintiff a few questions, but in most cases the hearing lasted one to two hours. Recording court proceedings is not permitted in China. During the fieldwork, I relied mostly on written notes. The short sessions made extensive note-taking a less exhausting exercise. Toward the end of my fieldwork, the judiciary of China kindly agreed to provide copies of the official court transcripts of a number of the trial sessions that I had attended. The transcripts had been prepared by court clerks who worked for the judges. The transcripts cited later are based on my own written notes and the official transcripts. While the transcripts are comprehensive, they are not detailed enough to allow me to pay attention to micro features such as lapses, overlaps, and silences or paralinguistic features such as stress and intonation in a detailed way. That being said, I consider the transcripts to be sufficient for the purpose of this analysis. Despite limitations, the data is valuable considering the very limited amount of sociolegal research on courtrooms in China. Names and other identifiers have been changed to protect the identities of litigants and counsels involved.

The second part of the data collection consists of interviews with the presiding judges and with other judges experienced in handling divorce petitions. I hoped to understand why judges asked certain questions and what evidence constituted the basis of the court's decisions. I asked their opinions on the performance of the parties, the weight they gave to certain evidence, and their rationale for making decisions. In particular, I asked whether the evidence on domestic violence collected at the court investigation stage is adequate. I also asked about what reform measures have been taken by the courts to prevent or reduce domestic violence and the extent to which they are effective.

Because judicial mediation has been a crucial stage in reinforcing social hierarchy and gender inequality, I also asked the judges why they mediate. The answers to this question help me understand how the broader institutional constraints affect divorce law practice and the relationship to gender inequality. They also allowed me to get a better understanding of how bureaucratic incentives compromise the pursuit of justice. A list of questions (not exhaustive) includes: Does mediation help female litigants? Does mediation undermine the rights of female litigants? Can it minimize social and family conflict? Needless to say, I also asked about their personal biographies to understand the link between their way of handling divorce cases and their sociological backgrounds: How long have they been a judge, specifically handling family issues? What did they do before becoming a judge? Have they received any formal legal education? As a group, they were candid about their opinions on the performances of the parties, the weight they gave to certain evidence, and their rationale for making decisions.

At the beginning of the fieldwork investigations, several judges that I interviewed did not see much gender inequality in the litigation process. They believed that gender inequality, if any, was negligible in litigation because the court had done a lot to minimize it. They defended their positions for good reason. They believed that they have followed the laws in most of the cases. Their decisions were not inconsistent with the requirements of the laws. What they did not realize, perhaps, was that they themselves are embedded in an institutional environment that pushed them to render decisions with gendered consequences. After I shared with them some examples I observed, to their own surprise they realized the rampant presence of institutional prejudice. Gradually they gained a clearer picture of my research. With numerous trips to the Guangdong Court and a relatively long stay in the Shaanxi Court, my friendships deepened with several judges who specialized in divorce litigation. Some provided me with examples and details that have contributed to gendered outcomes. They recalled cases from years back that might help my research. They also informed me of new materials related to the topic whenever they became available. My fieldwork investigation, originally alone, turned out to be a collective voyage.

To form a more comprehensive picture of court dynamics, I asked some litigants about their experiences and feelings on the court hearings. Following a tradition that examines the legal consciousness of ordinary people (Ewick and Silbey 1998; Sarat 1990; Merry 1990; Nielsen 2000; Gallagher 2006; Engel and Engel 2010), I also asked what the female litigants' perceptions of law and justice were. Specifically, through telephone interviews with litigants, I asked whether the protection order was effective in preventing domestic violence and what happened after the denial of a divorce.

My analysis is primarily drawn from twenty-nine cases, eight from Guangdong and twenty-one from Shaanxi, as shown in appendix 2. These cases occurred between 1991 and 2018, covering issues of divorce, domestic violence, child custody determination, property division, extramarital affairs, protection orders, male impotency, and rape. A majority of them were first-time petitions, but some of them were repeatedly brought, appealed, or still at the Adjudicatory Supervision Procedure (审判监督程序). While most of them were handled by the district-level court, some were processed by the intermediate-level court and one by the dispatched tribunal (派出法庭). The methods of ending the cases varied from mediation to withdrawal to adjudication. Consistent with national statistics, seventeen cases, or the majority, were filed by female plaintiffs, and in twenty-three cases the judge was female. Most of them were not represented by formal lawyers, though many had citizen representatives whose services were far from professional (Liu 2008).

Because my fieldwork sites were located in two regions with quite distinctive socioeconomic and demographic characteristics, I made further efforts to verify whether the judicial behavior and discourse patterns I identified from the two courts are a unique regional phenomenon or one that is more widely seen across the country. I interviewed by telephone judges experienced in divorce cases from the provinces of Jiangsu, Guangxi, Zhejiang, and Shaanxi. I also compared our findings with the literature on divorce courts in which the data were collected from northern parts of China (Chen 2007) and other regions of Guangdong (He 2009a; Li 2011; Wu 2007), Shanghai (Huang 2010), and Gansu (Wang 2007).

Roadmap

Setting the stage, chapter 1 documents the evolution of Chinese marriage law toward a no-fault rule on divorce. It then describes the institutional constraints affecting the behavior of rank-and-file judges. They are constrained by two concerns: efficiency and social stability. Together with the impacts on the judges, chapter 1 lays the groundwork for the interaction between laws with global norms and the courts' local institutional concerns.

Chapter 2 demonstrates the impact of the institutional constraints on Chinese judges' behavior. It shows that the overarching legal principle governing whether to grant divorce—"the breakdown of mutual affection"—has been replaced by routinized approaches. The judges deny divorce in most regular cases filed for the first time and grant divorce for subsequent petitioners. For highly contested cases that could threaten social stability, however, they rely on a new form of mediation aimed at closing the cases or pacifying potential threats to social stability. Each of these approaches is consistent with the incentives created by the performance assessment criteria imposed on judges.

In several ways, these approaches already disadvantage women. On whether to grant divorce or not, for example, in most cases the judges deny the first petition when the other party opposes it, despite abundant evidence for the breakdown of mutual affection. This seemingly gender-neutral process allows the continuation of domestic violence, in which most victims are women. Women feel themselves as a failure and men are emboldened. The delay also provides opportunity for men to hide, transfer, or squander the marital property, since men are often in a better position to control the property. For women, justice delayed is justice denied.

To illustrate how institutional constraints tie the hands of judges, chapter 3 offers an in-depth look at judges' pragmatic orientations by analyzing dialogues in actual trials. It reveals the pragmatic orientation of judges in handling divorce cases. Dominating divorce hearings is the quick-and-dirty, eager-to-find-the-middle-ground approach. Judges deploy an emergent "pragmatic discourse," one that is increasingly seen during the process of in-trial judicial mediation. Through deliberate and repeated deployment of this new pragmatic discourse, the judge transforms divorce court trials into a forum where specific official understandings of women's welfare take priority. In addition, chapter 3 uncovers the ways in which judicial mediation masks the assertion of power over litigants despite ideological claims otherwise. It contends that formally gender-neutral legal orders nonetheless reinforce gender hierarchies. Despite their effort to protect women's rights, judges often inadvertently reinforce and perpetuate patriarchal norms and values that render women passive recipients in their marital fates. The effort of this pragmatic approach is particularly damaging for women who are economically and socially vulnerable.

Echoing Chapter 2, Chapters 4 and 5 reveal how the stability and efficency concerns have prevented the laws intended to protect women from being materialized. Chapter 4 finds that courts offer little help to victims of domestic violence. The issue is sidestepped during the mediation session, even if the court is convinced that domestic violence exists. Evidence of domestic violence is often dismissed, and domestic violence is often ignored when a court delays its decision to grant divorce for obviously irreconcilable marriages. The Personal Safety Protection Order, a newly launched mechanism, is far from realizing its potential goals. As a result of institutional pressures, judges' inaction and indifference prevent full implementation of both the substantive and the procedural laws.

Focusing on child custody, chapter 5 illustrates how judges, operating under institutional constraints, thwart women's custody rights in contested cases. While the law claims to protect the best interests of children, in actuality the interests of women and children are often slighted. Child custody has become a bargaining chip for judges to soothe men who would otherwise reject divorce decisions. The laws and litigants' legal rights are not honored. This remains true even though some judges try to protect the interests of women and rescue children from hostile family environments.

Chapter 6 turns to the relationship between institutional constraints and litigants' resource disparities. It uses the division of conjugal property to illustrate how judges, operating under institutional constraints, have helped the "haves," mostly men, come out ahead. This chapter contends that, throughout proceedings, judges' concerns disadvantage women during the division of property. Longstanding patrilineal values and property regimes, coupled with norms of patrilocal residence after marriage, permeate the judicial decision-making process. They further exacerbate married women's inferior status in their conjugal communities and their weakened claims to matrimonial property, which are still defined in patrilineal terms.

Chapter 7 highlights how courts perpetuate cultural biases against women, a theme that has already emerged yet has not been explicitly explored in topics such as custody determination and property division. Focusing on women's hesitancy to raise sex-related issues, the chapter demonstrates how the judges, operating under institutional concerns, turn a blind eye toward their suffering. Judges rarely inform women of their rights; moreover, they avoid important issues even when they are aware of underlying facts. Occasionally, judges use an issue as a bargaining chip to facilitate closure of the case. Suffering from this sexual bias in court, women fail to make warranted claims and are awarded less property or compensation than they deserve. This chapter contends that, as a result of judges' inaction toward the traditional and cultural taboos of women articulating unfair treatment on sexual issues, women are denied fair outcomes.

Divorce litigation is at the core of many painful experiences. Decision-making in this context redefines many peoples' emotional and property relationships. Divorce litigation should have served to boost gender equality, as the law and official rhetoric promise. But it is far from achieving its intended goals. On the contrary, the divorce decision-making process has reinforced longstanding prejudices against women in many aspects of social life.

What is the fundamental cause? And what should be done? What lessons can be learned when global norms on gender equality clash with local practices? The epilogue answers these questions and discusses the implications of the findings. Underlying the inquiry is a broader concern for understanding the nature of the judicial system in an authoritarian state and its relationship to external contexts.

* * *

There is a systematic failure within the judicial system to fulfill its role in achieving gender equality in divorce cases. Gendered divorce practices systematically exist in almost every stage of the process, from the divorce itself to custody allocation, from the recognition of domestic violence to its compensation, from the ignorance about sexual problems to the reluctance in issuing protection orders. It reveals that the legal system is gendered, that it is a manifestation of power, and that it is detrimental to women.

If gender equality is to be achieved, the first step is to uncover the imbalance and unfairness resulting from the implementation of so-called gender-neutral principles and rules by the courts. Only when judges and other state agents act can such equality guarantees be invoked (MacKinnon 1989) and implemented. Such behavior patterns need to be uncovered before we evaluate divorce laws and the legal system. From the law and society perspective, laws are only the first step. It is time to evaluate how these laws can be effectively implemented in the courts. It is time to adjust the incentive mechanisms of the judges. It is time to see how the concrete realities faced by women can be rectified.

As this book goes to print, another round of judicial reforms has been under way. Developments surrounding judicial accountability, judicial integrity, and judicial professionalism are heatedly discussed (Clarke 2015). There is scholarly and public debate as to whether the judges' quota reform attempting to delink judicial salary from administrative rank, and raising the courts' budgets to the provincial level, will reinforce or undermine the bureaucratic and political nature of courts in China (Wang 2016, Lin 2016). According to some reform measures, judges seem to be given more room to make their own decisions. The courts seem to be more professional and rules-based. But how would the new reforms affect the way that judges handle divorce cases? What are the implications for gender equality going forward? While it is too early to make any comprehensive assessment, some signs already suggest that as the Party-state continues to influence the courts politically and ideologically, judges are still trapped in an institutional environment laced with tremendous pressures and uncertainties (He 2021 forthcoming). Judges become only more cautious, and thus the patterns documented by this book might become more entrenched. The challenge remains daunting: how to achieve gender equality outside and inside the courtroom.

1

Institutional Constraints

"Paid as lettuce farmers, we shoulder the liability of heroin trafficking."
—A common saying among Chinese judges.

"We are not pipeline workers. How can our performance be measured by production metrics?"
—A judicial informant.

The behaviors of Chinese judges are shaped by a complex interaction among institutions, politics, economics, and culture. Courts and judges are subject to multiple external constraints, which can limit when judges are able to use the law and when they have to do away with it (Ng and He 2017a). To use Bourdieu's term (1987), the Chinese legal "field" is limited in that a dispute cannot be handled solely by legal rules; other rules have roles as well. As far as divorce litigation is concerned, institutional and political concerns are the most immediate constraints in shaping judges' behavior. There are thus two components underlying Chinese judges' decision-making patterns for divorce cases: the legal orientation toward divorce, and the institutional environments in which they are embedded. This chapter will begin by contrasting the legal climates before and after the no-fault rule, a watershed in China's divorce law.

Before the No-fault Rule

Throughout the history of the People's Republic, the predominant legal criterion for divorce has been "whether the emotional relationship has truly broken down" (Ma 2002). As this criterion is elusive, the fine line demarking whether a divorce will be granted has shifted over time, owing to different political and social environments and the state's legal policies. Until the 1990s, it had been difficult to get divorced in China. An underlying reason for this was the state policy under the socialist marriage system, which decreed that divorce was to be avoided if at all possible (Tsui 2001; Parish and Whyte 1978: 194). The integrity of the family, and thus social harmony, was prioritized over freedom to divorce. This pattern was reinforced when the policy coincided with the state-centered industrialization plan and the Cultural Revolution (Tsui 2001: 106; Johnson 1983), which has been characterized as patriarchal socialism by Stacey (1983).

During that period, getting divorce was the equivalent of the Long March, as illustrated in *Waiting*, the popular novel by Ha Jin (1999). According to Parish and Whyte (1978: 193), "[O]fficial policy requires prolonged mediation, even when both parties agree to divorce. For a minor dispute, mediation is informal, involving neighbors, relatives, and friends. If the dispute becomes serious, more formal mediation begins. Because of a prolonged series of attempts at mediation at various levels, a divorce application might be delayed for months or years, even if the couple agreed on this matter." A divorcing couple had to go through a series of mediation hurdles within their communities, including work units and neighborhood or village committees, before they could even be heard by a court.

When pretrial mediation failed and court proceedings commenced, the court would usually attempt to restore an amicable relationship between the estranged spouses. As agents of the expansive state, judges assumed the responsibility of rectifying the "mistakes" committed by estranged husbands and wives (Huang 2010). To achieve this, judges frequently insisted on pretrial mediation in divorce cases. This "Ma Xiwu style of adjudication" (Zhang 1983; Cong 2016) is characterized by roving tribunals held on location in rural communities as a means to gather local information about a dispute. Judges would first conduct investigations into the causes of a collapsing relationship, and then attempt to "recover" the marriage through educating the couple. With all relevant parties present, the judge would criticize the couple. The various pressures mobilized by the courts often forced the divorce petitioners to make concessions and reach a so-called reconciliation (Huang 2010). Failure to reconcile would lead to further attempts at conciliation. Only if both of these judicial mediation methods failed would the court allow proceedings to be concluded by adjudication.

Nonetheless, many judges interpreted the "breakdown of mutual affection" in a restrictive fashion (Palmer 1989: 169). According to Huang (2010), before the 1990s most divorce petitions that reached the courts were mediated. Alternatively, spouses were pressured to reconcile before a final decision was made. This pattern was consistent with the trend in divorce cases. With the exception of the early 1950s (Diamant 2000), the divorce rate in China, until 2000, had been low (Tsui 2001; Wang 2001).

Toward the No-fault Rule

Such a legal arrangement became central to a series of unprecedented public debates in China that culminated in the 2000 amendment to the Marriage Law (Li and Ma 1999). The old law had been criticized for allowing too much state paternalism and too little individual freedom and choice (Alford and Shen 2004). Liberals argued that divorce could be desirable in some situations, freeing unhappy partners from unfortunate unions and sparing their children the prospect of growing up in acrimonious households (Li 1998; Pan 1999; Xu 1999). This freedom to divorce, coupled with the ideal of gender equality (rhetoric touted by the ruling Communist Party), soon gained a foothold. It promoted a new image of women as financially and emotionally independent. In a report titled "Legislation for Gender Equality," Xia Yinglan, chairwoman of the Family Law Research Association, suggested that "freedom of marriage" includes not only the "freedom to be married" but also the "freedom to divorce." She added: "Getting married happily and getting divorced rationally are both pursuit of happiness; both reflect the progress of our time" (Chinese Women's News 2009). As the ideas of marriage freedom and property rights took hold in the 1990s and 2000s, divorce law practices underwent radical change.

Divorce restrictions were relaxed in 1989 by the Guidelines promulgated by the SPC, which explicitly allowed divorce under fourteen situations, thereby initiating a period of liberty in matters of divorce (SPC 1989). This relaxation soon contributed to an increase in the divorce rate: some reports indicate that by the late 1990s, the rate had reached 20 percent in some areas (Palmer 2005). The fourteen Guidelines then suffered a backlash along many fronts: many criticized the law as too liberal, leading to unstable family relationships and rushed marriages (Yang and Qu 2001). Conservatives were worried that such a liberal approach would disadvantage women because men dominated the new market society (Su 1999). The Chinese government has been concerned that divorce has become a way for husbands to preserve their new wealth and transfer it to second families that may better satisfy their emotional needs and desires for a male heir. It did not want to make the process too easy or too convenient. They also did not want to turn divorce into a mechanism that made it possible for the economically stronger partner in a marriage to dispense with the weaker one.

In response, the Marriage Law, amended in 2000 and implemented one year later, reduced the fourteen Guidelines to five. The paramount article (Art. 32) governing divorce now reads:

> When contested divorce petitions are filed, the court shall first mediate; in the event that mediation fails to bring about a reconciliation and the emotional relationship has broken down, divorce shall be granted under the following situations: 1) bigamy or cohabitation with a third party; 2) domestic violence or maltreatment and desertion of family members; 3) incorrigible bad habits such as gambling and drug addiction; 4) separation for more than two years because of affection discord; 5) other situations leading to the breakdown of the emotional relationship.

This amendment, incorporated into the Civil Code (Art. 1079) in May 2020, once again left judges much discretion. Even the separation of two years stipulated by the fourth item, which seems most straightforward, could have numerous interpretations (Xu 2012). Furthermore, since it provides no detailed formal Interpretation for the "other situations" in the fifth item, the law in fact lists only four situations in which a divorce is to be granted. Many situations listed under the 1989 Guidelines have been dropped, such as "one party sentenced to prison" or "diseases preventing sexual intercourse or having children." Under the new law, whether these other situations have also led to the breakdown of the emotional relationship is subject to the judge's discretion. Even in the four listed situations, the seriousness of the problem is also to be determined by the judge. Other than domestic violence, for which the SPC provides a more detailed formal Interpretation, there are no definitive criteria for many key words and phrases such as "affection discord," "desertion," or "incorrigible bad habits."

The 2001 amendment was thus a compromise: it allowed for "freedom to divorce," but there was a price to pay if a party was "at fault." The purpose of the amendment was to protect the weaker party (usually the wife) from exploitation by the stronger party (usually the husband). Indeed, the 2001 amendment seems to have been intended to stabilize families. For the first time, the law explicitly included language that recognized the state's interest in marriage stability. It stipulated that "the husband and wife shall be faithful to and respect each other" and echoes the state's ideal of monogamous marriage. In some senses, however, the amended law is a throwback to a moralistic fault-based system (Woo 2003: 133).

Nonetheless, according to the amended law, people are now given freedom to decide the issues of divorce and marriage, so much so that persistent petitioning for divorce is now regarded as evidence of a ruptured emotional relationship and that, as a result, divorce will be granted (He 2009a). In addition, in 2003 the State Council eliminated the requirement that couples obtain employer or village cadre approval for divorce petitions (cf. Li and Friedman 2016: 154). Article 1079 of the Civil Code (2020) further states that, for petitions filed after one year of separation following the court's adjudicated denial, divorce shall be granted. The system can now be characterized as a de facto "no-fault" system (Davis 2010, 2011; Huang 2010: 204–8): spouses can divorce by choice. The old priority of preserving the conjugal bond has now been abandoned. While the law still punishes, among other things, the party at fault (such as an abusive husband) when dividing a couple's common assets, fault is no longer a necessary condition in the primary decision to grant a divorce.

The subsequent legal developments after the Marriage Law was amended, however, suggest a shift from attributing fault and compensation to empowering individuals to dissolve unhappy marriages and resolve property disputes. The state has become more confident in allowing marriage dissolutions. Li and Friedman (2016: 148) point out "fears of divorce as endangering both social stability and popular support for building a socialist nation have largely given way to efforts to empower citizens to dissolve unhappy marriages and to divide matrimonial properties." The marriage has been increasingly treated as a contract, as several judicial interpretations of the SPC endow husband and wife with greater autonomy to decide whether to end marriages and how to allocate marital assets. The shift is not surprising, as China has become more market-oriented and property rights have been emphasized. A constitutional amendment was introduced in 2004, confirming that lawful private property is inviolable. The Property Law passed in 2007 granted privately owned property the same degree of legal protection as state-owned property.

To some extent, these changes have offered women who want to end their marriage more freedom. "Today, Chinese women are initiating divorces and exercising their rights under the Marriage Law. In doing so, they speak a new, personal language of 'self-fulfillment' and express the view that divorce and marriage are private matters between two parties" (Woo 2003: 132). Woo suggests that the family laws have brought women "citizenship rights and equality." In any event, whether the change has favored women remains debatable, even as the freedom to divorce has permeated the popular discourse. People are more willing to, if not encouraged to, end unhappy marriages.

Assessing Judges' Performance

If the legal orientation on divorce is one leg underpinning Chinese judges' behavior patterns, another leg is institutional constraints. China does not have a specialized family court; family cases are usually processed in one of the civil divisions. Recently, several courts have launched specialized "family divisions"[1] with tailor-made procedures, such as cooling periods, psychological treatment, and mediation.[2] Nonetheless, family law judges are primarily subject to the same assessment criteria as judges in other divisions.

While the caseloads on family cases have increased steadily, the overall caseloads of courts have surged since 2000 (cf. He 2007a; Zuo 2018). In 2006, the courts received more than 5 million civil cases; in 2019, the number soared to 16 million. During the same period, however, the number of judges remained almost the same (around 200,000). The number decreased to 120,000 in 2017 after the courts finished the quota reform for designated judges (Supreme People's Court Information Center 2018). The problem of "too many cases, very few judges" has repeatedly appeared in SPC work reports since 2006.

Many judges are under high caseload pressure, especially in the more developed and coastal areas. In the Pearl River Delta court where I conducted my investigation, the designated Family and Adolescent Division has three judges specializing in family and divorce cases. On average, each handles 200 cases per year. Zheng et al. (2017: 190) highlight the problem:

> According to a judge in a basic-level court in Zhejiang, in the 1990s her court had about 80 judges and they handled fewer than 3,000 cases annually; by 2012, the total number of cases increased five-fold to approximately 15,000 per year, but the number of judges only increased to about 120 (Z1308). A judge in the first civil division of an intermediate court in Sichuan told us that the average number of cases that each judge in her division handled was more than 250 in 2012, with the highest as many as 340—nearly one case per day including weekends and holidays (S1304).

Handling a case means pretrial examination of the files, pretrial mediation if applicable, the hearing, mediation, and the writing of the judgment and the delivery of the adjudication documents (Ng and He 2017b: chapter 2). Unlike in Western jurisdictions, Chinese judges' responsibilities do not end with a judgment. They are also responsible for explaining and pacifying litigants who are unhappy with court decisions. It is also common for litigants to meet the judge several times before the hearing to express their personal views on the case. For some litigants who require special care, the judges have to arrange psychological services, either inside or outside the courts. Nobody knows exactly how much time a judge needs for this postjudgment work.

The skyrocketing caseloads and the need to resolve disputes and enhance legitimacy have compelled the courts to respond (Truex 2016). China's political-legal leaders believe an effective practice is to assess judges' performance by measures similar to controlling civil servants in other bureaucratic institutions (Minzner 2009, 2011). As many scholars have pointed out, Chinese courts are more or less bureaucratic institutions (He 1997; Ng and He 2017b: 64–67). Even after the judge's quota reform, Chinese judges are recruited, administered, and promoted similarly to functionaries in other bureaucratic institutions, with no life tenure and subject to various administrative penalties. They are not only officers of the court but also civil servants in the Party-state bureaucracy. In addition to their judicial ranks, all judges have administrative ranks akin to state bureaucrats in other government offices (Zheng et al. 2017). Liu (2012, 2014) regards the appointments of court presidents and vice presidents as a political process. While the local People's Congress, the upper-level court, and local government leaders all contribute to the decisions, the ultimate decision-making power lies with the Communist Party Committee (Liu 2012; Zuo 2015). The hierarchical system of judges and the relationship between the different levels of courts are indicative of this entrenched bureaucratic nature.

Sophisticated systems of cadre evaluation and judicial discipline have been established in recent years to institutionalize the bureaucratic control of judicial practices (Edin 2003; Kinkel 2015; Kinkel and Hurst 2015; Minzner 2009, 2011). Article 9 of the Judges Law states: "The appraisal of judges shall be conducted by the People's Courts." Article 22 continues: "The result of appraisal shall be taken as the basis for award, punishment, training, [or] dismissal of a judge, and for readjustment of his or her grade and salary."

In addition to the general requirements specified in the Judges Law (Amended 2001, Arts. 32–35), more detailed regulations—such as measures for holding adjudicating staff responsible for wrongfully deciding cases (Supreme People's Court 1998)—have been issued by various courts across China. A stipulation of responsibilities of the People's District Court in Guangzhou lists four measures for assessing the court staff (or judicial cadres): virtue, capability, diligence, and performance (Art. 3). While virtue and capability are measured by abstract terms such as participation in political and professional education, measurements of diligence and performance are quantified in detail. For example, Section 3 of Article 7, which concerns diligence, stipulates: "Four points for: no 'rude, cold, rigid, dodging' working style; congenial working attitude; no complaints from litigation parties or masses (no points for this item if there is any verified complaint, unless the complaint is unfounded or mistakenly filed)." Of the 100 possible points for overall assessment, performance constitutes 65 points. Furthermore, Section 1 of Article 8 reads: "[T]he staff of the adjudicating chambers and the enforcement bureau shall complete 90 and 85 percent, respectively, of the cases assigned by the petition filing division (37 points) (if the completion rate is lower than 90 or 85 percent for the adjudicating staff and enforcement staff, respectively, three points will be deducted for each percentage lower, until all 37 points are deducted)." Section 3 reads: "[T]he quality of adjudication and enforcement shall reach the basic requirement (20 points). For the following situations, points will be deducted accordingly: if more than five percent of the appealed cases are reversed completely for subjective reasons of the adjudicating staff, three points will be deducted; if more than three percent of the appealed cases are remanded for subjective reasons of the adjudicating staff, three points will be deducted; for each case completed beyond the statutory deadline, one point will be deducted; for each non-standardized adjudicating and enforcement document, or for a document with typos, one point will be deducted."

Starting in the early 1990s, and continuing into the twenty-first century, the main criteria for court performance have become the absolute number of cases completed or handled (结案数), the completion rate of received cases, the appeal rate, the remand rate for retrial, and the complaint rate (投诉率). This began when the SPC president Xiao Yang introduced systematic reforms toward adjudicated justice and "efficiency" and "justice" emerged as dominant themes within the judiciary (Supreme People's Court 1999, 2005). The number of completed cases and the completion rate are measurements of "efficiency" because they presumably indicate the overall number of disputes resolved by the courts, while the appeal, remand, and complaint rates are supposed to evaluate the quality of dispute resolution, or "justice."

Although the emphases have evolved over different eras and the practices of courts have varied across different regions, there are several core elements in the performance assessments. These patterns have been facilitated by increasingly sophisticated reporting of performance scores on formal, quantitative, and evaluation indices. In the 2011 "Guiding Opinion of the Supreme People's Court regarding the launching of case

TABLE 1.1: Selection of "hard target" indices in the Case Quality Assessment System (2008–present)

Case quality index type	Case quality system index name	Effect of higher scores on index
"Fairness"	Rate of first-instance cases in which judgment corrected on appeal (mistake) (*yi shen panjue anjian bei gaipan fahui zhongshen lü* (*cuowu*) 一审判决案件被改判发回重审率(错误))	Negative
	Rate of first-instance cases reversed and remanded (*shengxiao anjian bei gaipan fahui zhongshen lü* 生效案件被改判发回重审率)	Negative
	Rate of judgments corrected on cases in effect at first-instance level (*shengxiao anjian gaipan lü* 生效案件改判率)	Negative
"Efficiency"	Average cases cleared per judge per year (*fayuan nian ren jun jie'an shu* 法院年人均结案数)	Positive
	Rate of cases resolved within statutory (normal) time limits (*fading* (*zhengchang*) *shen xiannei jie'an lü* 法定(正常)审限内结案率)	Positive
	Rate of first-instance cases in which the simplified procedure is used (*yi shen jianyi chengxu shiyong lü* 一审简易程序适用率)	Positive
	Index of resolving cases in balanced time throughout a yearlong work cycle (*jie'an junheng du* 结案均衡度)	Positive
"Impact"	Rate of first-instance cases in which neither retrial nor appeal is sought (*yi shen fupan xisu lü* 一审服判息诉率)	Positive
	Rate of mediation (*tiaojie lü* 调解率)	Positive
	Rate of case withdrawal (*chesu lü* 撤诉率)	Positive
	Rate of citizen petitioning against court (*xinfang tousu lü* 信访投诉率)	Negative

Source: Jonathan Kinkel and William Hurst, "The Judicial Cadre Evaluation System in China: From Quantification to Intra-State Legibility," *China Quarterly* 224 (2015): 942.

quality assessment work," more than thirty indices quantitatively measure Chinese courts' "fairness" (公正), "efficiency" (效率), and "impact" (效果). According to this policy directive, courts must "establish a scientific and unified system of court evaluation." Kinkel and Hurst (2015) have listed the indexes, which are reproduced in table 1.

For example, according to indices on "rate of citizen petitioning against court," judges' performance is discounted, and judges are even punished, if litigants file a successful complaint against them. In 2002, the Supreme People's Court instructed all Chinese courts to focus on resolving complaints raised in petitions, ordering these complaints to be treated equally with court trials (Liebman 2011: 295). The SPC also instructed lower courts to tread carefully with petitions arising out of the litigation process, to persuade and guide petitioners, and to rectify those judgments in which they had erred. The SPC itself has as many as eighty judges working on petitions (Liebman 2011: 295). As a result, some courts have set "zero petition" targets.

In fact, the number of "malicious incidents" has become a major criterion in assessing judges' performance, for which they are held personally accountable (cf. Panyu Court 2004). If a malicious incident (usually referring to collective sit-ins, demonstrations, or unnatural deaths) results from court behavior, it will taint the political future of the court's directors, no matter the merits of the court's behavior (Sichuang Annals 2006: 85–87; Panyu Annals 2006; He 2007b). This is because, since the 1990s, social stability has become a defining social-political goal as protests and disputes over socially sensitive issues such as land, labor, and environmental protection are seen to threaten not only the success of China's economic agenda but also the nation's political life and the Party's future (Wang and Minzner 2015). How local courts and governments marshal the forces of law to resolve disputes and manage protests has thus emerged as a central political issue for China's authorities. As Trevaskes et al. (2014: 1) suggest:

> In official circles, social stability is understood as the political and social security that accompanies orderly, conflict-free social relations. Instability is manifest in what the Party deems unharmonious relations within communities and between individuals and the state, brought by crime, dispute, and protest.

In the regime's thinking, one of the most serious incidents affecting social stability is the loss of life (Cai 2008; Chen 2008; O'Brien and Li 2006). This is partly because a death may trigger collective action protesting the behavior of the government, as well as petitions for justice to upper-level governmental authorities. Protest is informed by a desire to hold officials responsible and encompasses a demand for economic compensation and even political concessions. According to a recent study, China is most concerned with social events that have the potential for escalation into mass incidents (King et al. 2013). To maintain social stability, a national policy stipulates that the number of malicious incidents and petitions forms the basis for assessing the performance of Chinese officials. In particular, an unexpected death may terminate a local official's political career. Not surprisingly, officials are desperate to avoid malicious incidents, especially those involving loss of life.

In the context of divorce cases, the problem has become so serious that the SPC (2017), stressing the need to safeguard the litigating parties' interests and personal safety, has stated that "family cases often involve emotion and personal interests, and some litigants are easily agitated. Divorce cases are laden with high risk. . . . The courts and tribunals at all levels shall analyse and detect the potential risk of the cases, take preventative measures, strengthen the safety of the courthouse, and prevent malicious incidents such as murder, injury, and suicide from occurring." The SPC 2012 Annual Work Report states that the courts should "take vigilant measures against those vengeful litigants and those uncontainable conflicts, to prevent them from being agitated, escalated into malicious incidents, or transformed into criminal offenses." These Guidelines from the SPC indicate the seriousness of the perceived problem.

Efficiency Without Lingering Effects

When these numbers and rates become the collective assessment criteria of the courts and the court directors, they are soon translated into evaluation criteria for individual judges. They are "deft, worldly administrators. They play the role of 'politician' for their courts" (Ng and He 2017b: 20). Much like other senior bureaucrats, they are motivated by power, income, prestige, security, convenience, loyalty, pride in excellent work, and a desire to serve the public (Downs 1967: 2, 81–91). Kinkel and Hurst (2015) maintain that court leaders' responsibility for the collective performance of their courts, and their concerns over their reputations within and among the judiciary, are of primary importance in shaping judges' thinking and behavior. This institutional environment generates incentives, or chilling effects, for judges. The evaluation of judges' performance has implications for their promotion and for competition among courts.

Under various cadre evaluations, judges are pressured to dispose of cases as quickly as possible. They first try to maximize the total number of cases they handle and the rate of case closure. "Disposing of cases assigned to them, whether it is by means of adjudication or mediation, is the most crucial duty of frontline judges" (Ng and He 2017b: 50).

Courts adjudicate divorce petitions according to either the Ordinary or Simplified Procedure. The choice of civil procedure determines the number of judges who try the case. A single judge presides over cases tried using the Simplified Civil Procedure, and a collegial panel led by a judge is required when the Ordinary Procedure is applied. Michelson (2018: 28) observes: "Courts carefully ration scarce judicial resources, and tend to devote collegial panels only to divorce petitions which, if granted, seem unlikely to lead to appeals, complaints, or 'extreme incidents,' and which are filed by plaintiffs whose claims seem credible and who seem deserving of divorce."

Efficiency also means that courts must dispose of cases in a timely fashion. China's Civil Procedure Law limits cases processed through Ordinary or Simplified Procedures to six and three months, respectively. Exceeding the limit entails grave consequences for the judges' performance reviews. Reducing delays is a primary goal of court management. This means that judges cannot delay the process, as common-law judges often do. Complicating matters, because senior officials managing courts want to leave themselves room to maneuver, they impose shorter limits for their own judges. Judges are given little latitude to extend deadlines. Sitting on unfinished cases without reason is sanctioned. In many courts, judges receive monthly notifications of cases that are newly assigned, in process (pending), and resolved (figures A.5 and 6). Some courts post these on their notice boards. Judges thus learn not only of their own performance but also that of their colleagues; peer pressure is built in to the system. This is what Kinkel and Hurst call "systemic praising and shaming." Nobody wants to be the one who goldbricks. One judge said: "The first thing I do when I get into my office is to turn on my computer and check out the cases waiting for me on that day" and "[j]ust looking at the case list on my computer sometimes gives me a headache. When the title of a case blinks yellow, it means its deadline is approaching. When it blinks red, it means I failed to close the case before the deadline set out by my court" (Ng and He 2017b: 56). Frontline judges feel that they work as proverbial cogs in a bureaucratic machine. At the court level, there are "league charts" ranking individual courts of the same rank within a region according to similar indicators applied to individual judges. That is also why, for fear that new cases will decrease courts' annual case closure rates, it is a common practice for courts to refuse new cases as December approaches.[3] Efficiency has thus become a primary concern, so much so that it sometimes trumps fairness (Pu, Li, Lin 2015).

However, they cannot focus on efficiency alone. Leaving no lingering effects is the second, yet no less important, part of their job description. They are to "conclude cases and put grievances behind" (*anjie shiliao* "案结事了") and do so "without unduly angering litigants or other actors" (Kinkel and Hurst 2015). Judges strive to lower appeal rates, reversal rates, remand rates, and complaint rates. The emphasis on each of these means judges have to take every measure to prevent complaints or malicious incidents. To reduce the likelihood of complaints against them, they naturally try to make decisions acceptable to both sides.

As Ng and He (2017b: 53–54) point out, the job of a Chinese judge does not end with the handing down of a judgment. Judges must be prepared for postjudgment work because they are also responsible for explaining and pacifying litigants who are unhappy with the decision. These disgruntled litigants may appeal decisions, exhausting legal resources. However, they can also express grievances through letters and petitions, or *xinfang* (信访) (He and Feng 2016; Feng and He 2018). They may even petition the court to review cases that have already been tried twice. These litigants, who "believe in letters and visits but do not believe in law," are a source of trepidation for many judges. However, the judges are asked to handle complaints from unhappy litigants who, for whatever reason, are dissatisfied with their case outcomes.

Many judges therefore have to spend considerable time interacting with unhappy litigants, explaining to them how legal regulations are applied, a practice usually called *shifa* (释法). This is done to dissuade them from appealing or petitioning to a higher authority. Some litigants are difficult to convince, either because they are "barely educated" or are troublemakers (Tan 2018). It is unclear whether the petitioners or the judges are in the more powerful position (Li, Liu, and O'Brien 2012; Tan 2018). Some judges joke that *dangshiren* (当事人), the Chinese term for "litigants," are human only at the moment (*dangshi* 当时) of the litigation process; they become inhuman after the litigation is over (事后不是人). A judge interviewed by Ng and He (2017b: 53–54) said:

> As a judge, you're responsible for the outcome of the case you handled. What is that responsibility? Well, it doesn't mean that if you follow the law, then the litigants will agree with you and say nothing. Some litigants still have a lot of things to say. They say you are wrong. And when you run into a difficult litigant, you can't say, "I can't deal with this litigant." It's your responsibility to find a way to resolve it.

Ironically, the judges have to please disgruntled litigants so they do not challenge court rulings.[4] This part of the job only becomes more difficult as the authorities require the judges and other bureaucrats to be more responsive to people's demands. Yet, the tactics of disgruntled litigants continue to evolve and escalate (Feng and He 2018; McAdam 1983). Some litigants mobilize others to protest (He 2014). Some visit the courtroom every day, blocking the court's entrance. Some sleep in the lobby of the courthouse. Some resort to violence, even murdering judges (Wang and Ng 2020 forthcoming). Consequently, courts across China have to install walk-through metal detectors and x-ray machines outside the courtrooms (figures A.7 and 9). Judges' offices also have to be walled off from the hearing area, preventing litigants from harassing judges in their offices.

Pressures on Judges

As with other civil servants, Chinese judges are subject to incentive structures. A high score will improve their chances of promotion or other career prospects. The pressures on the judges are enormous. According to Kinkel and Hurst (2015: 944), when a judge was asked "whether the court leaders post rankings to encourage everyone to work harder," the judge replied, "No, you can't really call it encouragement (*guli* 鼓励), it's really pressure (*yali* 压力), and we feel the pressure because it's embarrassing to be ranked lower."

Judges frequently complain that the institutional environment is utilized to assess judicial performance. The judges often describe themselves as "judicial *min'gong* (法官民工)." They use *min'gong*, a derogatory term to describe internal migrant workers, at the bottom of China's social ladder (Solinger 1999), to characterize their humble status in the bureaucratic machinery. A popular saying among Chinese judges goes: "In courts, women are used as men, and men are used as donkeys" (Zheng et al. 2017: 190). One of my judge informants complained: "We are not pipeline workers. How can our performance be measured by production metrics?" Many judges explained that by focusing on the speed of adjudication, the assessment mechanism distorts the reality of judging. Thus, many factors (including the technical or legal complexity of a case and/or scheduling difficulties) can influence the time needed to resolve a dispute. Therefore, Chinese judges perceive the tension inherent in applying numerical measures to complex phenomena and glossing over context in pursuit of comparability, classification, objectivity, and scientific assessment (Kinkel and Hurst 2015).

Unlike commercial and criminal cases, divorce cases involve meticulous procedures and various types of litigants; some are obstinate, some are uneducated, some are inarticulate, and some are too feeble to walk. One never knows which part of the process might go wrong. I have witnessed a judge meticulously ensuring that a litigant would mail her original marriage certificate back to the court address. Another judge offered to help a litigant in her sixties to apply for the social welfare for low-income citizens (低保) after she was divorced. Most judges are careful.

To make matters worse, the concern for stability has created enormous burdens for judges. Another popular saying among the judges, and society at large, is that "paid as lettuce farmers, we shoulder the liability of heroin trafficking." This suggests the imbalance between their poor treatment and the grave consequences should they make any mistakes. While only a tiny proportion of divorce cases turn into malicious incidents or petitions, a single such incident has major consequences for a judge. According to one judge: "[A] judge's career would be ruined if a death resulted from her case. With such a terrible social effect, she is regarded as incompetent for this job since she could not handle her litigants." Such an incident would be regarded as malfeasance on the part of the judge. In this sense—although these cases constitute only a tiny proportion of the millions of divorce cases handled by the courts each year—the judges have to pay disproportionally high costs in time and energy to handle them. To minimize "wrongfully decided cases" (错案) (Wang and Liu 2016), judges often seek guidance from higher-level courts. They also make ad hoc material concessions to litigants who pose credible threats of carrying out or inciting quintessentially "malicious" incidents (Su and He 2010; Li et al. 2012).

Concerns about personal safety loom large: judges often face threats or even physical attacks from angry or resentful litigants, especially after making controversial decisions (Zheng et al. 2017: 190). One judge indicated that she alerts her supervisor and fellow judges when it appears a case might become "explosive" so they can be ready to provide assistance. Judges have been known to make emergency telephone calls to police because of the possibility of imminent violence (Yang 2014). One judge said that "a divorce decision without careful deliberation may shift the conflicts to the court, which is too much for the judge to take" (Zhang 2018: 110). Another said that "some judges have been harassed, threatened, [and] humiliated by the litigants, which to some extent has forced the judges to be extremely cautious in handling divorce cases." Another judge persuaded a plaintiff to reconcile with, rather than to divorce, her husband: "He says he will kill you if you divorce him, and it seems he is serious. We cannot ensure your safety if we render a divorce decision. To tell you the truth, it is rather easy for us to render a divorce judgment. The reason why I bother to talk you into reconciliation is all for your good" (Wang 2013: 84). A Beijing judge in his mid-thirties said:

> Do I criticize a litigant? I have to assess who he or she is. For those who may accept my advice, I say more. For those litigants who are hooligans, I say nothing. They fight for divorce; there is no point to shifting the conflict to myself. For those who firmly oppose divorce, but the other party has filed for divorce several times, I work hard to reconcile. The point is to show that it is not the court which wants you to be divorced; it is the

wish of your wife. One of my colleagues was hit in the face by a litigant who got a divorce decision. The court detained the litigant. But at the end of the day, the judge was still being hit.

In her rich ethnography, Li (2021 forthcoming, chap. 4) describes the interaction between a Judge Lin and a "one eyed man,"—a divorce defendant who was "a petty thief and a nasty bully." When the man first learned of his wife's divorce petition, he said "I'll chop her entire [natal] family into pieces." He demanded 50,000 yuan (as this book goes to print, 1 yuan=0.14USD) in "breakup compensation" from his wife, a migrant worker with a menial job. This amount was almost ten times what any villager could earn, even in a good farming year. After the judge rendered a denial for the first divorce petition, the wife filed another petition six months later. The man would not go anywhere without that "breakup compensation." Li continues:

> When this demand could not be satisfied right away, he began stalking and harassing the judge and other court personnel. "He followed me everywhere," "he called me repeatedly, even at night," and "he sounded as though he would take my life if I didn't handle his case 'properly,'" Judge Lin recalled. Alarmed and frightened, Judge Lin started varying his commute between home and his workplace. He also tweaked his work schedule so as to make his whereabouts less predictable. That his tribunal was housed in the same building as the township police station—it would take a couple of minutes to walk from his office to the police chief's—did not give the judge peace of mind.

Although judges try to prevent malicious incidents through this approach, such incidents still occur. Ma Caiyun, a Beijing judge who granted divorce for a petition, was stabbed to death by the divorced husband ten years after the decision had been made (*Wenweipo* 2016). In May 2005, a woman in Gansu Province who had been the victim of serious domestic violence from her husband committed suicide after her divorce petition was rejected for the fourth time (*Lanzhou Morning News* 2005). Similar cases abound (All-China Women's Federation 2010; *The Paper* 2016). A judge-turned-lawyer told me in 2019: "Throughout two decades when I was judge, rarely have I heard that a judge was killed by the litigants because of criminal, commercial, or administrative cases. The judges on family cases are particularly vulnerable."

During the enforcement stage of a divorce case, a court in Wuyuan in Jiangxi Province deployed court sheriffs to the home of the parties. This was to prevent any malicious incidents from occurring when the wife moved out along with the property that the court had awarded her (Wuyuan Court 2012). Even though such tactics have proven effective in maintaining order, the need to resort to them takes its toll on the judges involved.

Furthermore, many judges inevitably become emotionally involved in the lives of the litigants. In order to settle a case, a judge must gain the trust of both parties. The result is that many judges receive daily calls from litigants, many of whom will ask for advice on even the most trivial matters. One judge stated that "at 11 p.m., I still receive text messages from my litigants." She continued:

> I am really not capable of handling this case [in which she had been so involved]. I am too familiar with the two sides and I am mired. I cannot judge whether they should be divorced or not because I have stepped into the ambit of their private lives. I can see the heartfelt desire of the plaintiff to leave the man, but I can also hear the outcry of the man to defend his marriage. Both requests are equally understandable and reasonable. I want to satisfy both, but I am not able to. My whole body and mind are submerged in the case.

In one case, the husband had threatened to cut off his wife's feet. The case had been discussed by the adjudication committee twice and had lasted nearly three years. Because the two sides originally could not stay in the same room, the judges in charge had struggled to arrange meetings. After interviewing each party numerous times, the judges interviewed several family members in order to better understand how they could assist the parties.[5] These efforts were not helpful. The wife sobbed each time she met the judge and repeatedly stated that she could no longer stay with her husband. He in turn threatened to kill both her and their child if they divorced. The judge in the case described the impact upon herself:

> I suffered insomnia because of this case. When the sobbing face of the wife loomed large, the threatening words of the husband emerged. One

day, the plaintiff in another case was killed by her husband. When I heard the news, my head exploded. I thought it was my case. I am tired, I am exhausted, I don't want to be a frontline judge anymore. I would rather be transferred to the administrative or logistics branch. I do not want to handle any cases. I just cannot do it anymore. I cannot afford to take it anymore because if I continue to do this, my life expectancy will be shortened.

The judge's description underscores the emotional and physical exhaustion caused by managing divorce cases. What she fears is not divorce per se but the potential fallouts that some bitter divorces may lead to. She believes that she would not be able to process ten cases per year if each of them was as complicated as this one. However, this realization would create another source of stress because a significant part of her income is determined by her performance, as measured by the number of cases she closes. Judges also find themselves forced to pick up cases that prove too difficult for less experienced members of the judiciary. One judge wanted to quit her job because of the difficulty of managing complex and emotional cases.

Conclusions

All of the above examples are illustrative of Chinese judges' workload and social and mental status. They are under tremendous pressure because of institutional constraints. Ultimately, they are the victims of institutional pressure. Of all these concerns, the efficiency and stability concerns seem the most immediate and dreadful. The mode of accountability is individually based. Yet, the inducements and sanctions must align with the pursuit of individual self-interest and organizational goals. Judges who fall short of deadlines or consistently fail to pacify litigants are subject to criticism and discipline, which has an adverse impact on their careers. As a result, they care more about their cases than about the collective good of the court as an institution or even the legislative intent of the law. As will be shown in subsequent chapters, these assessment criteria and the judges' concerns have enormous impacts on judicial behavior.

While the regime's fears that divorce itself endangers social stability and popular support for building a socialist regime have declined (Li and

Friedman 2016), it is less confident in the dispute resolution process for contested divorces. Family and marriage cases are one of the largest types of first-instance cases in Chinese courts. These seemingly mundane cases have frequently led to unexpected incidents. A divorce decision usually reshapes emotional and property relationships. For the parties, it will be an emotionally charged turning point in their lives. At stake are their life achievements: children, families, and property. For some, the maintenance of marriage and family is all-consuming; for others, the thought of another minute with the other party under the same roof is suffocating and unbearable. Realizing the importance of stability concerns for courts, some litigants strategically behave confrontationally and irrationally and become agitated and violent in order to gain an advantage. Extreme reactions include suicide attempts, harassment, and the threat of physical harm to the other party and their relatives and even to their own children. Frustrated litigants who blame the presiding judge may also afflict personal injuries on them. It is not surprising, therefore, that judges report abysmally low levels of work satisfaction (Hu 2015).

Due to the imbalance between income and work pressure, many judges leave the profession for a more lucrative career as a lawyer or for more powerful organizations (Kinkel 2015; Zheng et al. 2017). Even though they are better paid than some civil servants, many judges decide to leave the judiciary (Chin 2014; Finder 2016), and many courts in the developed areas have difficulty recruiting new judges (Chen and Xiao 2017).

Although some judges tend to remain in the judicial system for their entire careers, they are especially susceptible to mechanisms of control and motivation, as specifically facilitated by an increasingly quantified and visible reporting system. Some of them find this intolerable. The situation has not improved despite the implementation of a quota system. Under the reformed system, judges enjoy more decision-making power (Zhang and Ginsburg 2019), but they also have to shoulder more responsibilities (He 2021 forthcoming). The Supervision Commission of the Party is also intervening in the system more directly than before. Judges' insecurities have thus intensified. Judges and other officials privately complain that it is difficult for the officials to survive (官不聊生), a term usually used to depict the miserable lives of the downtrodden.

2

Routinized Approaches

How have the institutional constraints documented in chapter 1 affected judges' decision-making in divorce cases? The requirement for efficiency without lingering effects can be self-contradictory. In numerous circumstances, efficiency can be achieved only if other values, including fairness, are weakened. In that case, the grievance is not over and resentment persists. How have judges dealt with these contradictory requirements? How often and under what circumstances are the plaintiffs still denied divorce? Does mediation provide a solution as many have argued (Fu and Palmer 2016)? How widespread is mediation? How does the current mode of mediation differ from previous practices? What are the impacts on female litigants? This chapter contends that judges classify cases into different categories. They either deny divorce in adjudication or persuade litigants to withdraw cases that do not seem to carry a risk of causing lingering effects. However, they set aside much time for those difficult cases. There is a routinization of divorce law practice: denying first-time divorce petitions, but granting divorce on the second or subsequent attempts (He 2009a). Michelson (2019: 327) phrases this approach as "twofer." Mediation continues to be used, sometimes to address efficiency concerns and at other times to address stability concerns. Under both circumstances in which mediation is used, it differs from the traditional "Ma Xiwu style" of adjudication (Zhang 1983; Cong 2016) (characterized by roving tribunals convened on location in rural communities as a means to gather local information about a dispute) in both form and substance. All these practices, nonetheless, have generated gendered outcomes.

In divorce litigation, the foremost issue is whether or not to grant a divorce. If a divorce is not granted, there is usually no need to dwell on property or custody divisions. Thus, I begin with the divorce decision itself. As mentioned, the principle governing whether or not to grant divorce is "the complete breakdown of mutual affections." This is an elusive principle, allowing judges broad discretion. In addition to the vague wording of divorce criteria, judges are also given discretion through mandatory mediation procedures in the amended law, namely, that all divorce petitions must first be mediated by a judge. In handling divorce cases, judges are still legally required to help the couple reconcile, and even if the mediation efforts prove futile the judge may or may not grant a divorce. As a result of these compulsory mediation procedures, a contested divorce petition may lead to one of four possible court decisions: mediated reconciliation (调解和好), mediated divorce (调解离婚), adjudicated divorce (判决离婚), or adjudicated no divorce (判决不离). This flexible legal principle provides a fertile ground for extralegal considerations.

Indeed, mediation continues to be used and is even preferred by some. The revival of mediation is consistent with the institutional expectations of the courts. Since Zhou Yongkang (周永康) was in power, the courts have required their judges to settle, through mediation, a certain percentage of the cases they handle. The 2011 Case Quality Assessment System has made the mediation ratio a key index in court evaluations in an attempt to increase mediation (Li et al. 2016; Kinkel and Hurst 2015). Within the courts, this has been translated into individual personnel policy, and mediation rates have become important evaluative standards for the courts and their presidents as well as for rank-and-file judges (Minzner 2011). There is also competition among the courts to achieve higher overall mediation rates. Some courts even claim a zero adjudication goal, meaning that all cases are settled through mediation (Peng 2011). This trend was reversed in 2013 by a series of SPC Opinions and Guidelines on the proper use of mediation that caution against the practice of "overusing mediation and underusing adjudication" (重调轻判). Adjusting to the new political environment, the courts have endeavored "to let the people feel justice in each case" (see figure A.14). Like other components of the state bureaucracy, courts are sensitive as to which way the political winds blow (Moustafa 2014: 289).

Pressure from senior court administrators aside, some judges prefer mediation over adjudication because enforcement becomes less of a concern when the parties agree to settle. This is because there is no risk of a decision being overturned on appeal and also because judges are

TABLE 2.1: How civil cases are resolved in the Chinese courts (2002–2018)

	Cases closed*	Adjudicated	Withdrew	Mediated
2002	4,381,704	43.46%	19.95%	30.35%
2003	4,403,322	42.50%	20.67%	29.97%
2004	4,289,970	40.76%	21.60%	31.11%
2005	4,360,184	39.73%	22.14%	32.10%
2006	4,382,407	39.80%	22.52%	32.54%
2007	4,682,737	38.54%	22.75%	33.43%
2008	5,381,185	36.43%	23.67%	35.18%
2009	5,797,160	33.81%	25.77%	36.21%
2010	6,112,695	30.99%	26.49%	38.80%
2011	6,558,621	28.83%	26.62%	40.64%
2012	7,206,331	27.46%	26.45%	41.70%
2013	7,510,584	30.84%	25.13%	37.92%
2014	8,010,342	36.47%	23.67%	33.37%
2015	9,575,152	41.18%	22.71%	28.77%
2016	10,763,889	43.76%	22.96%	25.90%
2017	11,651,363	44.39%	24.00%	24.76%
2018	12,434,826	44.49%	25.82%	25.20%

Sources: *China Law Yearbooks* (2003–2019). Beijing: China Law Yearbooks Press.
* The number of cases closed from 2002 to 2010 excludes intellectual property and maritime cases.

spared the task of writing a judgment. Some judges also believe that it is unlikely that a mediated outcome will result in incidents that threaten social stability. Of course, many judges also believe that both parties are better off with a settlement (Ng and He 2014; Xiong 2015; Fu and Palmer 2016).

Each of these considerations compels judges to adopt a heavy-handed approach toward litigants during in-court mediation sessions. Despite the ebbs and flows of the political environment and policy changes in the courts, pretrial and posttrial mediations remain common, especially for courts in rural areas where efficiency concerns are less relevant. In China, the percentage of civil cases resolved through mediation increased from 30 percent to 39 percent in the first decade of the 2000s. While it has subsided since Zhou Qiang (周强) became president of the SPC, it was 26 percent as of 2016.[1]

The Decline of Traditional Mediation

Mediated reconciliation used to be the *modus operandi* of divorce law practice. This had been the case since the founding of the People's Republic. It would typically play out as follows. The presiding judge first conducts several on-site investigations to determine the reason(s) for the divorce. Then, in a ceremonial setting in which all relevant parties are present, the judge employs ideological indoctrination emphasizing family and social stability to criticize or educate the couple. The familial, community, and official pressure marshaled through the courts, along with material inducement, are difficult for the divorce petitioners to resist. More often than not, they have to confess their "mistakes" and "naiveties" and reach the "reconciliation" arranged by the court with the other party (Huang 2005).

Some scholars believe this picture has continued, even with revisions to the laws and other changes, both inside and outside the judiciary. Professor Huang asserts, for example, that "much of the old resistance to unilateral divorce persisted, even in the 'liberal' 1990s, and mediated reconciliations, though certainly reduced, still accounted for a large number of cases, with almost as many adjudicated denials in 2000 (89,000) as in 1989 (108,000)" (2005: 170) and that "in the twenty-first century, ex parte divorce remains difficult to obtain in China, and the preform legacy of mediating reconciliation remains an important feature of Chinese civil justice" (2005: 171).

Mediation continues to play a role today and consumes much of the judges' energy and time, especially in areas where the caseloads are not heavy (Ng and He 2017a: 48–51). However, the traditional mode of mediation described above has declined (see table 2.2). Although the picture illustrated above may be accurate for the prereform period or the early stages following reform, it has not persisted into the 2000s. Indeed, all the examples Huang (2005) uses are from the prereform period. But the treatment of divorce cases after the reform has shifted from the pre-reform style of justice in which on-site investigations had been required. However, it was time-consuming and thus became impractical as caseloads grew during the 1990s; Huang dismisses these points as exaggerated (2005: 170). Huang also uses more recent official statistics indicating a large number of mediated reconciliations to support this point, but as I detail below, this large number does not necessarily suggest the persistence of the prereform style of civil justice. Instead, it is a product of the new baseline in adjudicated denial. In other words, the meaning of mediated reconciliation has changed even though it still wears its original label. A closer examination of the numbers of contested divorce petitions, together with fieldwork investigation of case files, court hearings, and interviews with judges, shows that adjudicated denial has replaced mediated reconciliation as the dominant mode of handling contested first-time divorce petitions. Furthermore, adjudicated divorce has become routine for second-time petitions.

My examination of the court files of another basic-level court in Guangdong Province found that the most significant component of the case dossiers was the hearing record. This pattern was more obvious in "no-divorce" cases than in cases with divorce decisions (table 2.2). Although sometimes there was other evidence in the files, it was usually provided by the litigating parties instead of having been collected by the court itself. Sporadic investigation reports did exist, but more often than not it was the litigants who had provide investigation channels and facilities in an effort to influence case outcomes to their own benefit. Sometimes such investigation reports were provided by lawyers. Ng and He (2017a: 45) have called these investigations "occasional." We find that on-site investigations assume at most a complementary role and are usually conducted "at the request of litigants" (2017a: 45). Indeed, in those rarely conducted investigations, as far as the dossiers show, the purpose is not to pave the way for mediated reconciliation but to gather evidence to justify the judge's later decision, which, as will be shown, is usually adjudicated denial.

There are many reasons (some ideological, some practical) why judges today do not want to initiate their own out-of-court investigations. Ideologically, China's courts are shifting to a judicial philosophy of *dangshiren zhuyi* (当事人主义), meaning "litigant's choice." Courts have passed off the responsibility of proving a case to the litigants. There are many practical reasons why judges want to avoid out-of-court investigations: the ever increasing caseloads, limited human and financial resources, and pressure to boost efficiency by closing cases within short time frames. Judges now engage in a limited form of cross-examination

TABLE 2.2: How family cases are resolved in the Chinese courts (2002–2018)

	Cases closed	Adjudicated	Withdrew	Mediated
2002	1,277,516	37.97%	17.58%	43.09%
2003	1,266,593	37.58%	17.54%	43.58%
2004	1,160,346	36.75%	18.24%	43.66%
2005	1,132,458	35.17%	18.41%	45.29%
2006	1,159,437	34.37%	18.53%	46.04%
2007	1,215,776	33.41%	19.42%	46.13%
2008	1,320,636	31.51%	20.94%	46.45%
2009	1,380,762	28.93%	22.21%	47.73%
2010	1,428,340	27.11%	22.85%	48.93%
2011	1,609,801	25.85%	25.30%	47.72%
2012	1,647,464	25.02%	25.08%	48.80%
2013	1,611,903	27.36%	23.67%	47.80%
2014	1,618,904	30.56%	23.41%	44.77%
2015	1,733,299	33.89%	23.85%	40.77%
2016	1,752,052	35.57%	23.99%	38.52%
2017	1,830,023	35.58%	23.67%	36.97%
2018	1,814,441	36.14%	23.82%	38.17%

Sources: *China Law Yearbooks* (2003–2019). Beijing: China Law Yearbooks Press.

aimed at obtaining oral testimony that can be used to justify a decision. This kind of judge-initiated questioning has thus become an inexpensive substitute for the previously labor-intensive court investigation. In other words, the court investigation stage offers an important opportunity to collect evidence to form the basis of adjudicative decisions if a settlement cannot be reached. The evidence on which their potential adjudicative decisions are based must be strong enough to safeguard the judges from any potential liabilities for wrongfully decided cases (He and Ng 2013a).

For those rare cases in which on-site investigations took place, the investigation reports were brief or even summary, and many court interviewees provided no valuable information on the underlying causes for the divorce. As indicated in the case files, some staff on the neighborhood committees, especially those in urban areas, had not even heard of the divorce petitions when asked by relevant judges. What they could provide, at best, was a general impression of the couple (for example, their romance, children, income, and personalities). Indeed, it is not surprising that neighborhood committee staffs—often retired cadres— knew little of the family disputes inside each individual apartment. It is hard to imagine that through such a process the court could determine the underlying reasons for a divorce, which is crucial for a successful mediated reconciliation.

Yet this is not to suggest that during this process judges never accidentally uncover the real reasons behind a divorce petition. The point is that, as far as the files can demonstrate, they generally do not seek out these reasons on purpose. They also make no effort to salvage marriages from divorce. Even if they bump into some clues, they rarely conduct follow-up investigations to pinpoint the underlying reasons. Although they might occasionally persuade the couple to work on their marriage, in none of the dossiers I examined were there any ceremonial settings in which pressure could have been marshaled toward mediated reconciliation. This contrasts with the prereform picture painted by Huang in which the file was dominated by lengthy investigation reports (2005).

As far as could be told from the dossiers, most cases adhered to the procedures stipulated in the Civil Procedural Law—that is, adjudicating the cases using evidence provided by the parties rather than getting to the bottom of the matter by collecting evidence. The hearing records do indicate there is a procedure of judicial mediation in the adjudication process as required by the Marriage Law. However, in reality this new type of judicial mediation is unlike the old, prereform style. The goal of the prereform style had been to reconcile the marriage, and the means of reaching that goal was to determine the underlying reasons for divorce through an in-depth investigation in order to reconcile the couple through education and material inducements. However, as will be shown below, the goal of this new type of judicial mediation is simply to conform to the procedural requirements of the law and to handle cases in a way that is beneficial and convenient to judges and courts. This new type of judicial mediation has nonetheless generated a large number of mediated reconciliations: a result with the same label but different content.

It is difficult to understand how this kind of judicial mediation is conducted by merely examining court hearing records. Indeed, most

TABLE 2.3: Outcomes of divorce cases at Court P, Guangdong Province
(2003–2006)

Year	Mediated divorce	Adjudicated divorce	Mediated reconciliation	Adjudicated denial
2003	406	225	48	95
2004	280	236	36	84
2005	215	217	39	97
2006	199	231	25	105

Source: Author's fieldwork investigation, 2007.

hearing records only contain a few words indicating whether or not
the couple has accepted the mediation. From the hearings I personally
observed, the trend toward nominal mediation has become only more
obvious, especially in the more developed coastal areas and in cities.
The following is what transpired in a hearing that the presiding judge
regarded as representative.

In the Sexual Disease Case, the facts were straightforward: the husband had filed for divorce after one year of marriage, claiming that his
wife often left for work in other cities without even informing him of
her contact information. There were also personal grudges and quarrels
between the husband and wife and between the wife and the husband's
family members. While the facts suggested that the marriage problems
might not have been serious, the court hearing told a different story.
Each side had been accompanied by eight to ten relatives who had
traveled roughly fifty miles by hiring a minivan all the way from their
hometown to the courthouse. The courtroom was so crowded by these
relatives that a family member had to sit with the plaintiff on the designated plaintiff's chair. For questions raised by the judge, both the plaintiff husband and the defendant wife occasionally sought advice from
their respective relatives seated behind them. Obviously, both families
were invested in the marriage. Not until the end of the hearing did the
plaintiff speak the truth, about which he might have felt embarrassed
or been hesitant to indicate in the petition letter: his wife did not want
to have sex with him, claiming she had diseases that had prevented her
from engaging in sexual intercourse. All of sudden, the courtroom grew
quiet, and time stood still.

Had this hearing occurred in the prereform period, one would have expected the judge to suspend the hearing process. Presumably the judge would have sought to verify the claimed disease. After locating the real reason for divorce, the judge was supposed to criticize, persuade, and educate the couple in an effort to rescue the marriage.

No such thing happened in this case. It seems that the judge did not entertain any debate on this crucial issue, nor did she ask any follow-up questions. Instead, she raised questions about the couple's marital property. After both sides were given a final opportunity to add whatever they felt necessary, the judge said: "The court discussion is now over. Now we move to the court mediation stage. Could the defendant and your family members leave the courtroom, please?"

With only the plaintiff and his relatives present, the judge said: "As I mentioned to you [the plaintiff] before the court hearing process, you guys got married hastily and little affection has since been established. In addition, the defendant clearly indicates that she does not want a divorce. For this kind of situation, it is very unlikely that the court will grant divorce. I would suggest that you reconcile with the defendant or voluntarily withdraw the petition."

The plaintiff immediately responded, "I don't want a reconciliation; there is virtually no affection between us."

The judge replied: "Then I would suggest a [voluntary] withdrawal; if you insist upon a divorce and keep the process running, the result would very likely be adjudicated denial. If you withdraw, you can avoid direct confrontation with the defendant and her family. You guys are husband and wife, and in the meantime she still wants to keep the marriage intact. An adjudicated denial would create more conflict between you guys and the two families. Today all your family members have come; maybe all your fellow villagers will come the next time. There is no need to escalate the conflict."

The plaintiff's elder brother then asked: "What is the difference between voluntary withdrawal and adjudicated denial in terms of legal consequences?"

"It is the same," the judge answered. "Both voluntary withdrawal and adjudicated denial will give you guys more time to work on the relationship. The law allows you to file another divorce petition in six months.

By then, the state of this six-month observation period will be regarded as evidence for considering whether a divorce should be granted." The judge continued: "If the couple still have problems, then the court is very likely to grant a divorce. No marriage can be based on coercion, right? But marriage is something very serious: the court cannot hastily grant a divorce whenever a party files a divorce petition. If you agree to withdraw now, I can inform the defendant that after the court has made an effort, you guys still want to live together."

After discussion between family members, the plaintiff's elder sister said: "Let's withdraw first."

The plaintiff followed: "I withdraw."

Unlike the prereform style of legal practice, the judge in this case was not concerned with the underlying reason for divorce. She had no interest in verifying the alleged disease, nor did she want to spend her time reconciling the two parties. After the hearing, I asked her why she had not worked in that direction. She responded: "We do not have enough resources to check everything. And questions like that basically fall into the area of the couple's privacy. Most importantly, further inquiries into the question are not necessary: all I need to know is that the couple have problems in communicating with each other, and that is good enough." Moreover: "The seriousness of the problem can be detected from the court hearing, especially for experienced judges like me. As long as we know that the conflict between the couple and their respective families is not serious to the extent that they cannot live under the same roof, it is enough for me to handle the petition."

Here is the pattern for regular divorce cases: rejecting petitions for first-timers but allowing divorce in later petitions (He 2009a). This pattern has been confirmed by later studies (He and Ng 2013c; Luo 2016; Michelson 2018, 2019). This practice has become so entrenched that a judge-turned-lawyer said: "Usually we do not take the cases for first-time divorce petitions; nor do the potential divorcees hire us: with the outcome predetermined, what is the point of having a lawyer?" Some lawyers bluntly told their clients that at least two petitions are needed to get the divorce.

The common rhetoric of judges in denying divorces includes: "[T]he family is the cell of social stability; the party who made mistakes shall be given one more chance; the child is so young; and it is difficult for a man to find a spouse." This pattern of justifications has been widely used despite the fact that, in my sample, about 90 percent of applicants for divorce, after being denied on the first petition, cannot reconcile with their spouses and eventually come back to court for divorce. Evidence from empirical reports, the examination of case files, the observation of court hearings, and interviews with judges and lawyers each indicate that adjudicated denial has replaced mediated reconciliation as the court's modus operandi for contested first-time divorce petitions. This trend contrasts with the traditional picture of judges conducting aggressive mediation.

One might wonder: Why, although the percentages have been declining, are there still a large number of mediated reconciliations? One reason might be that judges benefit from mediation: no need for enforcement, no risk of appeal, and no need to undertake the task of writing judgments. Yet the above evidence and the examination of case files suggest another plausible explanation: a shift in the *modus operandi*. When adjudicated denial replaces mediated reconciliation in contested first-time divorce petitions, mediated reconciliations are still generated nevertheless. For contested divorce petitions in which a reconciliation seems impossible, mandatory mediation has become more procedural than substantive. The judges follow the standard procedures of civil litigation and inform the litigation parties of the new baseline—no divorce will be granted—to see if this will coax them into accepting a mediation decision as opposed to a real mediation settlement. Although judges will not make an all-out effort to seek mediation, they have little reason not to pursue it when the opportunity arises, especially with all the benefits that mediation entails.

As the above description of the hearing process illustrates, the judge conveyed the court's baseline to the plaintiff—adjudicated denial—and suggested either reconciliation or voluntary withdrawal. She also made an effort to inform the plaintiff of the advantages of voluntary withdrawal, including avoiding direct confrontation with the other party, and assured him that this choice would not affect his chances of getting a divorce six months later. Even though she was certain that this marriage was over, as she could tell from the direct confrontation between the two sides in the court hearing, she guided the plaintiff to choose voluntary withdrawal. It might be unfair to say that the judge manipulated the process; after all, she also made it clear that the plaintiff could make his own choice. However, as a judge, her suggestion and explanation of the law held sway over the plaintiff's final decision. Although the court mediation process has become less coercive and normative, the judge in this case was not neutral. Had she acted differently, the final result of the case could have been different. Although the plaintiff had chosen voluntary withdrawal, it is hard to say that the choice had come from the bottom of his heart. What he really had wanted was a divorce, as he had clarified in the petition letter and the mediation process; only when the divorce became unobtainable did he accept voluntary withdrawal—and only because it brought him one step closer to divorce. The decision had been made in the shadow of adjudicated denial and had been influenced by the judge (Kornhauser and Mnookin 1979).

Although in this example the result was voluntary withdrawal, one could imagine a so-called mediated reconciliation occurring under similar circumstances: it all depends on how the judge advises the plaintiff. Under the shadow of adjudicated denial, it is likely that many petitioners are persuaded to accept mediated reconciliations. This new baseline explains why so many mediated reconciliations still appear in the national statistics. Indeed, while mediated reconciliations are still included in the official statistics and documents, the meaning of the term has changed. In short, the large number of mediated reconciliations does not necessarily suggest the persistence of the prereform style of civil justice. What needs to be explored are the changes that have occurred beneath this label, how these changes have occurred, and the reasons behind them.

Many factors have contributed to this baseline change. First, the changing social environment has made the prereform practice less feasible. Community pressure, a supporting pillar of the prereform style of divorce mediation, has become difficult to marshal. While many family members might be involved, the village, the neighborhood committees, and the work units where the divorcing couple live and work know little about these people's family affairs. In a time when population mobility has increased and privacy has become more valued, especially in urban and developed areas, these institutions have lost much of their surveillance function. It is also common knowledge that the supervisors of companies, even under solicitation from the courts, are reluctant to lend a hand in criticizing their staff members for not correctly handling marital affairs or for infidelity. After all, marriage has become a private issue within the family. Work units might step in, but only when they are solicited by the couple themselves. The courts might be able to secure the support of family members in selling a mediation deal, but they have little leverage in marshaling community pressure. This is also a reason why many recent reports on divorce cases have found it difficult to conduct the traditional type of mediation (Ma 2002a; Zheng 2006).

Second, with the retreat of the state from society, the courts also lack sufficient moral authority and material resources to persuade or cajole divorcing couples to accept mediation arrangements. Ideological and moral indoctrination, effective during the prereform period, has lost much of its appeal in a time when money and happiness dictate. Other branches of government might be willing to cooperate with the courts with regard to significant issues such as those affecting social stability (Su and He 2010), but they are unlikely to support the courts on these politically trivial issues. Without the cooperation of other government branches, the courts, with limited financial resources, offer little material inducement to litigating parties. Moreover, since the early 1990s, and especially after the judge's quota reform, many courts, especially in developed areas, have been overwhelmed by mounting caseloads (He 2007a; Zhu 2007; He 2021 forthcoming). Thus, it is difficult to conduct on-site investigations, which consume both time and energy. For courts not under heavy caseload pressure, often in rural areas, it is more likely that prereform conventions have survived. Until recently, these rural courts were usually underfunded, and thus were incentivized to work on cases that could generate income (He 2007a). It was unlikely these courts wanted to pour resources into divorce cases which did not mitigate the courts' financial woes.

Routinized Treatments for Regular Cases

While the above two factors are important, I argue that the incentive mechanism within the judiciary is the most immediate and significant cause of the change. It will show that adjudicated denial for first-time divorce petitions is a calculated outcome by judges under current incentive mechanisms. The outcome of adjudicated denial fits with their own concerns, including workload and job performance. More specifically, adjudicated denial often becomes the baseline because it allows judges to close cases without getting into the messy division of matrimonial property and child custody. The changed baseline in divorce law practice has to be understood within the institutional context of Chinese courts.

Indeed, only in the context of these assessment criteria can one understand why judges refuse to grant divorce, even though they are certain a marriage has no future. What do judges have to say on this issue? Judge Song, who is in his early thirties, said:

> For most first-time divorce petitions, regardless of whether the emotional relationship has truly ruptured, we will not grant a divorce, unless the litigants themselves have already worked out everything. Why? If I grant a divorce, it is my duty to divide every penny of their matrimonial property and child custody, when applicable. Property division is an extremely messy issue. Sometimes you have to divide everything from an apartment to a teapot. These things are messy in nature, . . . whether or not there are legal guidelines. It is very likely that both parties would be unsatisfied no matter how we divided them or how much time we invested. Let me tell you this: to complete the process of an adjudicated divorce would consume five to ten times the time of an adjudicated denial. There is no point in getting into this process.

For the majority of contested petitions—regardless of whether the emotional relationship has obviously broken down—the real problem is division of property. Even if both parties reach a consensus that the marriage is over, fights over property or child custody may persist. From our perspective, granting a divorce simply offers them an opportunity to appeal. As might be predicted, the more complicated the couple's property relationship, the more likely courts will adjudicate against divorce.[2]

While granting few or no divorces for first-time divorce petitions increases efficiency, is this not too cursory a way of handling the cases? How do judges protect themselves against appeals or complaints? Judge

Wang, who joined the court directly from law school and has handled divorce cases for six years, was asked these questions. She replied:

> In addition to the efficiency consideration, whether the litigation parties can accept our decisions is a major concern. For first-time petitions, divorce is very difficult for the defendant to accept. Some litigation parties carry a bottle of agricultural poison to the court hearing. What if he (or she) commits suicide? What if he (or she) kills the other party or relevant family members? But when the relationship still does not work out after the first adjudicated denial and the couple comes back for divorce again, it is another story: the defendant will be psychologically more prepared by then.

Although Judge Wang's account reintroduces the social acceptance or consequences (Posner 1990) of court decisions, these two accounts are complementary in context. Because complaints usually occur when one party is dissatisfied with the court's decision, ensuring that the decision is acceptable for both sides can decrease the likelihood of complaints. Of course, granting adjudicated denial to first-time petition satisfies defendants. Yet even for the plaintiff, this is not a complete failure. The plaintiff can and will use this adjudicated denial as evidence for future divorce attempts, and the courts are likely to grant one when the couple reappear in court. When both parties approve of the decision, judges minimize the risk of complaints. In other words, adjudicated denial is the best strategy for judges under the pressures of "efficiency" and "justice"; they strike a balance between the litigating parties.

One may interpret Judge Wang's account as a pragmatic approach to dispute resolution in which judges employ local knowledge and legal analysis to balance the interests of the parties (Su 2000). However, judges' concerns in this process are important as well. While it is true that the judges balance various interests, they are also emphasizing their own interests, if not making them first priority. Even though they may consider the interests of the litigating parties, their overriding concerns are to avoid adverse consequences.

One may wonder whether plaintiffs would appeal adjudicated denials that do not consider the legal standard of "whether the emotional relationship is ruptured." The judges are usually safe on this point for two reasons. First, since judges are given discretion in interpreting the seriousness of a ruptured emotional relationship, it is almost impossible to say the adjudicated denial was wrongfully made, as long as no mandatory legal requirements are trumped. Moreover, adjudicated denial helps maintain the family and achieve social harmony. It conforms to the Chinese saying "maintaining a marriage is more desirable than building ten bridges." Denying a divorce petition thus serves the expectations of both state and society. Second, an entrenched legal principle of the Chinese legal system prevents most plaintiffs from appealing in this situation: all issues shall be offered an opportunity for appeal (*liangshen zhongshen* 两审终审). Consequently, even if the appeals court regards the trial court's denial of divorce as inappropriate or wrong, it cannot overrule the decision by directly granting a divorce. This is because when the trial court adjudicates against divorce, it does not determine the division of matrimonial property or award child custody. However, when the appeals court overrules the decision and grants a divorce, it does divide property and rules on child custody. No opportunity for appeal is available for such decisions because the appellate court's decision is final, according to current civil procedure. Therefore, when the trial court adjudicates against divorce, legally speaking, it is impossible for the appeals court to reverse the decision by directly granting a divorce. The appeals court can only remand this kind of case back to the original trial court. While a remand decision on appeal is not good for the judge responsible for the first trial, this process usually takes much longer than six months. Therefore, this route is not worth pursuing because the plaintiff can simply wait six months after the trial court's adjudicated denial and then file a second-time divorce petition. This almost guarantees a divorce. Put simply, all the plaintiff wants is a divorce. And the plaintiff has little incentive to fight the judge's determination. According to one of my informant judges, if a lawyer advises a defendant to appeal an adjudicated denial, the lawyer is considered to be either ignorant or greedy, hoping to extract more fees from the plaintiff.

With these considerations, it is understandable why judges' adjudicated denials are calculated outcomes. However, such outcomes would not occur if the courts stubbornly refused divorces in plaintiffs' repeated petitions. Although adjudicated denial might improve the judges' efficiency and performance, they cannot play this card forever. Otherwise the plaintiffs will, sooner or later, complain about the judges or appeal the denial decisions. This is why a second divorce petition is often allowed. While the current official reasoning for adjudicated divorce is that the emotional relationship cannot be established (or recovered) after the court's adjudication and education, a more fundamental reason is judges' fear of complaints and appeals. This is a crucial self-protective exit strategy. It is also why in the adjudicating process, as seen in the above court hearing, a judge often implicitly or explicitly informs the plaintiff that a divorce will be available upon the second divorce petition. By letting plaintiffs know how to get what they want, judges avoid the risk of appeal. In other words, they can manipulate the appeal or complaint rates to their own favor. In this sense, the law is not used merely as the basis of adjudication; it is also an instrument for judges' self-protection.

All these behaviors are understandable under the current institutional environment. Chinese judges lack sufficient protections: they have no life tenure, and their careers are affected by all the quantified measurements. When they are complained about or their decisions are appealed—especially when the event in question becomes known outside their courts—they make trouble for the court directors. After all, the directors have to spend much time and energy dealing with the complaint whether or not judges have made a mistake. Because "troublemakers" would leave a bad impression with or on the court higher-ups themselves, judges strive to prevent such incidents entirely. Furthermore, although Chinese judges are in the position to deal with many complicated social relationships, they lack the corresponding authority and legitimacy (Fu 2005; Ng and He 2014). Thus, they have to employ various self-protection skills. When American judges deliver judgments, everyone is listening: both the litigants and average people will accept the court's decision, even if they disagree with it (Tyler 1984). However, in Chinese society the litigating parties and the masses are always ready to challenge a court's decisions, not only through the normal appeal process within the judiciary system but also through other external mechanisms such as letters and petitions (He and Feng 2016; Feng and He 2018). While these other mechanisms might provide a way for upper-level government institutions and officials to collect information and constrain judicial corruption (He 2007a; Cai 2004; Minzner 2006), they also damage the authority of the court because their very existence indicates that the court is not the final arbiter (Peerenboom 2006). In light of these considerations, it is not surprising that various strategies—some lawful and some not—have been employed.

As a result, like mediated reconciliation, the content of adjudicated denial has also changed since the prereform period. During that period, adjudicated denial was a result of the no-divorce policy. Nowadays, adjudicated denial has been transformed into a strategy judges use to maximize their interests and protect themselves. These outcomes are the product of the institutional structure in which they are embedded.

The increased number of adjudicated denials for first-time divorce petitions in today's practice of justice therefore has little to do with continuing the prereform tradition, the restrictive orientation of the amended law on divorce, or the alleged penetration of the state into private life. Otherwise, the courts would not grant divorce even if the plaintiffs repeatedly petitioned. In this case, the current situation would be similar to that of the 1980s, when the courts "stubbornly" or "irrationally" adjudicated against divorce. The truth, however, is that, all else being equal, adjudication for divorce has become routine when the plaintiff reinitiates a divorce petition. Adjudication against divorce for first-time petitions and adjudication for divorce for second-time petitions serve the same function: to increase the judges' performance and reduce their risk of being penalized under the current incentive structures. This happens in spite of the standard in the law about "whether the emotional relationship is truly broken down."

Mediation for Stability-threatening Cases

The above discussion maps out the state of the regular cases, but for those cases in which one party opposes divorce with a death threat or a petition to the upper-level government, the courts are more cautious. They have to weigh whether a threat is realistic before making a decision. If a threat turns into reality, a dispute between family members could become an issue of social stability, a top national concern of Chinese authorities.

This section will demonstrate the role that social stability—the paramount political concern—plays in highly contested divorce proceedings, especially those with the potential to escalate into malicious incidents. In the Sobbing Doctor's Case (where I observed both the hearing and mediation sessions), a doctor in her mid-thirties had filed her second petition for divorce. She had moved up the ranks in her hospital. As the youngest child in her highly educated family, she seemed emotional and willful. When talking to the judges and during both the trial and the mediation process, she sobbed so much so that her eyes swelled. Determined to get a divorce, she said she would die without one. Her husband, originally discharged from the army and laid off from a State-Owned Enterprise, had been a successful businessman. He had finished only junior high school before joining the army. The husband was just as determined to prevent the divorce. Should a divorce decision be rendered, he said to the judge, both parties would have to die together.

The wife's first petition to divorce was considered to have been voluntarily withdrawn since she, for unknown reasons, had not appeared at the trial. Even since, she had moved to a rental apartment without the knowledge of her husband. She said that she had moved again once he had learned the location of the original apartment. She had also blacklisted his phone number and had been dodging their meetings. She said that she was afraid that he would hurt her. Even in the courthouse, she insisted on staying with the judges at all times, refusing to be left alone with her husband.

The trial was straightforward. The wife requested divorce on the basis of the incompatibility of personalities, supported by allegations of several quarrels that had occurred several years before. She said that he had cursed her in public and made a fuss at her work unit. Obviously, she had no evidence to prove this. He denied the allegations, and she started sobbing. He passed her tissues, but she refused to look at him during the trial, as if he did not exist. She did not want a penny of the conjugal property. She wanted child custody for their ten-year-old girl, who had been living with her grandparents ever since the wife's departure from the home, but did not want any child support. Because the husband opposed divorce vehemently, the trial ended within thirty minutes.

In the private mediation caucus with the plaintiff after the trial, the judge reminded her of the husband's changes over the two years of separation and suggested they meet to confront the problems. After all, they had not spoken for two years. She refused: "He is evil; I cannot be with him anymore." No room was left for negotiation. With the defendant, the judge suggested he let her go and find another woman. His position was firm as well. At one point, he said: "I will not appeal if you render me a divorce decision; I will then pursue her again, since she would be available." At another moment, he said, "I will cut off her feet if she divorces me, and then I will take care of her for the rest of her life, since then nobody would want her anymore." If the first statement had seemed reasonable, the second was outrageous. Given his military, business, and educational backgrounds, such an outcome was not impossible. After several rounds of mediation, he said to the judges: "Now that we are friends, you may see me in the criminal court should this civil one end with a divorce."

For the judges, the two parties appeared deadlocked. The wife might commit suicide if her petition was denied, and the husband's threats were realistic as well. After several interviews with both parties, the judges remained unsure how to resolve the matter.

This is one of those cases with the potential to escalate into a malicious incident. In such cases, social stability informs and shapes procedures and outcomes. Since the number of malicious incidents—the epitome of social instability—has become a dominant criterion assessing judges' performance, judges have become incentivized to keep the parties in check. As a result of this policy change, divorce law practice today departs from the prereform mode in which few divorces were allowed. Traditionally, judges preached socialist ideologies and sought to restore amicable relations between unhappy couples. By contrast, the current goal of mediation is to prevent malicious incidents. To achieve this outcome, judges employ tactics that transcend traditional approaches. They are now forced to assess the likelihood of the litigants causing social disorder. In particular, for cases threatening social stability, the legal criterion of "the breakdown of mutual affection" is marginalized. It is in part replaced by the political principle of "no malicious incidents."

Different from the routinized approach discussed earlier, for these cases the concerns over stability factor prominently. Judges invest copious time and energy into highly contested cases that threaten stability. The judge's first task is to determine whether the situation might escalate into a malicious incident. While the concern for social stability has never appeared explicitly in the Marriage Law, it nevertheless has pushed the Chinese courts into innovative responses. What has emerged is a mediation process that, on the surface, looks similar to its traditional form. However, the goals, procedures, and outcomes have shifted.

Shifting from Reason to Impact

The judges' first task during mediation is to interview the parties. Yet rather than simply determine the reasons behind the desire for divorce, judges today need to examine litigants' mental states. This is a means to assess their potential reactions if the court were to rule against them. Thus, instead of trying to understand the underlying cause of the deteriorating relationship, a judge will consider whether the litigants are mentally stable, whether they could peacefully accept a decision against their interests, and whether they have the potential to react explosively. This has become the measure of success in mediation. Only with a proper assessment of the parties' mental states can a judge propose a solution acceptable to both parties and thereby minimize the potential for malicious incidents.

In the Sobbing Doctor's Case, the judges held at least ten mediation sessions for each party. To gain the litigants' trust, these sessions were informal. The judges did not take notes and sometimes tried to find a place to meet that was more comfortable for the litigants. In conversations, they also shared their marriage experience to earn the trust of the litigating parties. The ultimate goal, however, was to assess the extent to which the parties could accept a court decision contrary to their wishes.

Below is one of the numerous conversations between a judge and the husband:

> HUSBAND: I am not going to be divorced. I have already passed my business on to my brothers. They will handle the business without me. The only thing I am expecting is the court decision. I will fight her the rest of my life.
>
> JUDGE: The plaintiff has been out of the home for two years. She is also very determined to get the divorce. You have seen this, right?

HUSBAND: My position not to be divorced is equally firm! I am deco-
rating a new apartment and will get her and the child back to live
there. I will live in the original place until she accepts me. For these
two years after she left, I have been under a lot of pressure from my
friends. I will never let her go until she comes back.

These words confirm the husband's firm position. The questions left
for the judges were: Will he do something outrageous once he gets a divorce decision? How likely will he carry out his threats? The judges were
no doubt concerned. This was a man with only a junior-high education.
As a discharged soldier, laid-off worker, and businessman, he might not
observe the same social rules as those in other upstanding professions.
He also had several pernicious habits such as gambling, fighting, and extramarital affairs. This profile indicated that he was an impudent person.
Ultimately, the judges were afraid to rule against him.

In the Alcohol Saleswoman's Case, the wife, an alcohol salesperson in
her late forties, had rushed to the court president's office as a result of
the court's delay in handling her petition. The judge had proceeded with
caution, interviewing the couple separately before scheduling a formal
trial. The wife was seeking a divorce on the grounds of incompatible
personalities and because of the fact that her husband did not assist with
their son. It was apparent from the interview, however, that the judge
was not convinced that her version was the full story. The real reason
for the petition, the judge believed, was that the wife had been involved
in a new relationship. This was never admitted by the wife, nor did the
judge attempt to verify the theory. Throughout the interviews, the wife
cried and threatened to commit suicide. From the wife's body language,
and from the way she interacted with others, it appeared that she was
determined, open-minded, and optimistic.

According to the judge, the husband's situation was different. In his
early fifties, he had never mentioned why his wife had been seeking a divorce, even though he was in the best position to know. According to the
judge, it seemed that the husband had something to hide. He struggled
to cope with the divorce process and avoided discussing details of the
marriage. The judge speculated that this might have been a result of his
eagerness to defend his dignity as a man. He might also have hoped that

his wife would change her mind. Moreover, he had maintained only a tenuous relationship with their son. He was having difficulty keeping a job and was in a financially precarious situation. In short, losing this marriage would mean a lot to him.

Despite the wife's threat to commit suicide, the judge believed she would accept a denial decision without a major fuss. It might be difficult for her to accept the divorce denial when first hearing the decision. She might make a fuss in the judge's office, or even in the court president's office, because she believed that the decision had destroyed her life. It had been the judge who had kept her in the horrible marriage. This might last for a couple of days or weeks, but it would not be the only frustrating outcome. She would likely feel that she had lost the battle with her husband, who could not bring her happiness without disturbing her life. This would eventually distract her from targeting the judge and the court. More important, she might eventually accept the decision for two reasons. First, from her lawyer's and the judge's advice, she understood that as long as she kept filing divorce petitions, she would eventually be granted a divorce. Even the judge had admitted that "there is no such thing as a marriage that can never be dissolved." The law sets no limit on the number of divorce petitions that one can file. Second, there was still hope in life because she had high expectations for her new relationship. She might be having a new relationship, but she never admitted this. This was because she could have been morally blamed and thus at a disadvantage in the litigation. Would she choose death before consuming her happiness? Doubtful.

However, the man had much to lose had a divorce decision been granted. He had already lost his job and had to support their son. A divorce would have taken away most of the hope that remained in his life. Such a decision would have also enforced the position of an "indecent" woman who likely had had an affair with another man. He would feel that he had been wronged. The main source of such mistreatment would have been the court and the judge, because he had always obeyed his wife's instructions and had been ready to follow her wishes as long as she was willing to go home with him. He might have committed suicide or hurt her, but more likely he would have targeted the court and the judge. Having difficulty understanding why the judge would have supported an immoral and blameworthy woman, he would believe that the judge had been unfair or had been bribed by his wife. He had lost his dignity, his family, and everything else as a man in the court. Psychologically, the husband was in a dangerous situation and posed a threat. Even though he had never uttered any threatening words, he may well have prepared a series of reprisals. He had intentionally hidden his real thoughts from the judge, and his life seemed abysmal. Given these assessments, the judge persuaded the wife to withdraw her petition. With another opportunity, the husband would realize that the court had "granted him face," helping him to overcome the animosity he felt toward his wife.

Delaying Decisions

If preaching does not work, the next tactic is to delay any decision. Traditionally, this has been common in divorce proceedings. As Palmer (1989: 169) notes: "*Prolonged* court mediation has served as an effective mechanism for blocking contested divorce applications, especially those in which the petitioner is a woman" (emphasis added). However, in today's practice, the purpose of denying a divorce is to handle the divorce peacefully and safely. In this process, the judges attempt to mediate, even though they know some marriages will collapse. The period allows both parties to negotiate and to further demonstrate their personalities and come clean on their marital problems. It allows the judges to assess the likelihood of violence if litigants eventually have to face a divorce decision. The first (or even the second) denial decisions offer hope, albeit slight hope, to the defendant that the marriage might still be saved. For those plaintiffs who have engaged in extramarital affairs, a denial conveys the message that the court supports the defendant. For other defendants, a denial suggests that the judges take their opposition seriously. The mediation efforts made by the judges also relieve the defendants: the judges have respected their opinions and have tried to rescue the marriage. It is now easier for them to understand that the continuation of the marriage is a decision that must be agreed upon by both husband and wife. The marriage cannot persist simply because one party wants it. Eventually they will accept this reality. Even if they still feel frustrated and wronged, they are unlikely to vent their hatred toward the judges. Preventing a recalcitrant defendant from blaming the judges is the priority.

Divorces are usually contested because the party being divorced does not accept the other party's desire to leave. However, in this situation, a cooling-off period (*lihun lengjingqi* 离婚冷静期) may be helpful. For example, the defendant's emotional suffering may become alleviated after the additional timeout and thus be able to move on eventually. By contrast, if the court grants a divorce immediately, over the protests of one party, it may aggravate a conflict. In the Shanghai Migrant Worker's Case, the wife, a migrant worker in Shanghai, sued for divorce for the first time in Shaanxi. The underlying cause had seemed to be that her husband was impotent (although the court never verified this). According to the wife, the couple fought over trivial issues almost every night, and the wife's genitals had been physically harmed. This appeared to be a straightforward case until the judge learned that the husband's family was impoverished, with a disabled brother and a mentally ill mother. With little deliberation, the judge ruled against the wife in her first petition. She explained her decision in her office to the wife's lawyer:

> No way will this marriage persist, but this time they cannot get a divorce. We must respect the husband's last dignity. Even though his request has little legal basis, at this moment we cannot wipe out the hope of his whole family. We have to maintain the form of this marriage. This is to give the husband's family some time to be psychologically prepared to lose this woman.

By contrast, the judge told me, any plaintiff expecting a divorce must leave with some hope for an acceptable outcome in the future. For the plaintiff, a delayed decision is acceptable because waiting another six months is not unimaginable. On the basis of this rationale, a divorce could be delayed by the court, even if several previous petitions had been filed.

In another case, in which the wife sought a divorce because her husband had beaten her and her family, the judge told me that the two families fought against each other during the first court hearing. During the second hearing, the husband was agitated and claimed that he would die at the judge's home should a divorce decision be rendered. Unsurprisingly, the court denied the divorce. Six months later, when the wife filed another petition for divorce, the husband beat the wife again. He was then taken into custody but was released three days later. His refusal to eat or drink while in detention frightened the responsible authorities. It was said (although never verified) that the wife had aborted their child without his consent. Once again, the judge was afraid to grant the divorce because of the unstable psychological state of the husband. When the wife's mother, through her connections, asked a veteran judge why there was still no divorce after the petition had been filed five times, the judge responded indirectly that "you had better find ways to compensate the other side and then try to get a settlement."

In a case from Guangdong, the wife had suffered from domestic violence at the hands of her husband for eighteen years, and they had been separated for six, yet the court dismissed her divorce request twice. A judge explained to me that this was because the presiding judge had been threatened by the husband. In another case, a battered woman from Jiangsu committed suicide after her divorce petition was rejected a third time. This was her final protest against both her husband and the court. As documented by He (2009a: 102), some judges "would never grant a divorce if the defendant is suicidal or homicidal, no matter how many times the plaintiff might file a divorce petition." This may be an exaggeration, but the point is that delaying a decision softens the animosity between the two parties and prepares the opposing party for the divorce when it eventually occurs. This is because, as one of my informants explained, "for one percent of recklessness, we will be held one hundred percent responsible." Another judge interviewed by Zhang (2018: 110) said: "Some litigants would threaten the courts, with a death threat . . . [and] the court is also afraid of any incidents. . . . Divorce cases are the most conflict-laden category of family cases, and due to various considerations, it is much easier to offer an adjudicated denial. Adjudicated divorce is difficult, with big risks." A judge with twenty years' experience in civil cases and with a master's degree explained:

> Handling this type of divorce case is not a test of a judge's ability to master the law or to apply the law. It is more of a test of a judge's holistic ability to solve problems. In this process, I did not consider whether "the mutual affection still exists," as provided in the law. My standard is to avoid

the malicious consequences that might result from a divorce decision. I would not approve a divorce petition even if "the mutual affection between the couple had already broken down."

This pattern has also been documented by Ng and He (2017a: 50). We found that when the parties fail to settle after repeated attempts, the judge's first option is to stall. However, stalling means that the judge cannot close the case by the mandated deadline. Meanwhile, the litigant is still pressuring the judge for an outcome. The second option is to render a ruling, but that might be disastrous for the judge because it may trigger malicious incidents.

Decisions for the Adjudication Committee

In addition to delay (i.e., stalling the proceedings to create a cooling-off period), reporting to the Adjudication Committee is another tactic often employed by judges in cases that might lead to malicious incidents. The purpose of adjudication committees is to decide difficult, significant, or sensitive cases. Their members are experienced bureaucrats who are alert to political concerns and the social impact of disputes (a subject on which junior judges may lack experience). Although defining the scope of "difficult, significant, or sensitive" cases is difficult to determine, it is rare for divorce cases to be placed on an adjudication committee's agenda. Historically, under the approach adopted through Maoist-style mediation, cases were reported to the committees primarily as a means to rescue marriages. For example, the committee might be in a better position to coordinate with the government and obtain resources for a family in need (Huang 2010). By contrast, in the current mode of mediation, a case is reported to the committee when malicious incidents are likely to occur. Submitting a case to the committee is the means by which the responsible judges ensure that the senior court officials take responsibility for making a decision, even though the committee may be no more qualified to do so. Once a case is decided upon by the committee, the responsibility for the decision no longer lies with any individual (He 2012). Instead, it can be argued that there is a collective responsibility for the court's decision. As He describes (2012: 693):

A wife filed a petition for divorce, but her husband contested it. The marriage had been extremely tense. The wife had left home and the husband had searched for her throughout the city. As a result of this broken relationship, he became mentally unstable. While the wife insisted on a divorce (死也要离), the husband threatened to kill his estranged wife and their child (离了就死). In addition, the two sets of in-laws and especially the wife's mother had been interfering in the couple's relationship. Although the law is clear on the issue—to grant a divorce or not depends on whether the emotional relationship between the two parties is disrupted—it is not helpful for solving the dilemma. The adjudicating judge decided for adjudicated denial for the first-time petition, but the wife filed the petition again six months later. While an adjudicated divorce would customarily have been granted in the second-time petition, the adjudicating judge was uncomfortable doing so. Under these circumstances, submitting the case to the adjudication committee was to be a feasible option, and so she did, suggesting another adjudicated denial. Needless to say, the committee upheld the suggested opinion. After all, nobody wanted to bear the blame if the husband carried out his murder threat.

At the end of the day, the committee could not provide any more useful suggestions. In the Sobbing Doctor's Case, the committee's final decision was that "[t]he collegial panel was in the best position to make the decision. Make sure no malicious incidents occur afterwards. Work shall be done so that the litigants are prepared for the decision and will accept it." The vice president in charge of the civil division said:

> I will endorse your decision no matter whether the collegial panel suggests divorce or not. I respect your opinion. You are most familiar with the case, and thus in the best position to have the say. The committee members all have their own views, but they never met the litigants. The committee's decision is not necessary the most accurate, especially on the issue of whether to divorce or not. The law on this issue is very general, and everyone has her own view.

In short, the committee delegated the thorny issue to the judges who were responsible for the case. The ultimate instruction? No malicious incidents.

Outcomes Predetermined by Procedure

Such routinized approaches are consistent with the court procedure adopted in divorce cases. As mentioned, China's civil procedures have two formats: Simplified and Ordinary. The Simplified Procedure is designated for cases with clear facts, straightforward rights and obligations, and few disputes. "Clear facts," according to the Judicial Interpretation of the Civil Procedure Law (Art. 256), means that both litigating parties present largely consistent versions of facts, each supported by evidence, that obviates the need for court investigations. "Straightforward rights and obligations" means that the liabilities the rights of the parties are clear. "Few disputes" means that neither party contests the rights or wrongs, the subject matter, or the liabilities. The two procedures are the same in terms of the trial process and the evidence threshold. The major differences are: The timeframes allowed are six months (for the Ordinary Procedure) versus three months (Simplified Procedure); and the Ordinary Procedure needs three people, with at least one judge, to form a collegial panel, whereas the Simplified Procedure is conducted by only a single judge.

Between the lines of these stipulations, the Simplified Procedure is the exception and not the rule: after all, only contested divorce disputes reach the courts, whereas the uncontested disputes are settled at the department of civil affairs. Due to efficiency and stability concerns, ironically, the Simplified Procedure becomes the rule, or the default choice. The responsible judge (承办法官) switches to the Ordinary Procedure only when she needs more time to handle the case, as documented by Ng and He (2017b: Chapter 2), or she needs the collegial panel, usually composed of three, to share the responsibility.

Under the recent heavy caseloads and the emphasis on efficiency, many courts have set assessment criteria for the rate of cases processed through the Simplified Procedure. When divorce cases are filed, except for seven scenarios prohibited by law (Art. 257 of the Judicial Interpretation of the Civil Procedure Law), the case filing division usually channels them into the Simplified Procedure. The three requirements—clear facts, straightforward rights and obligations, and few disputes—become almost irrelevant. This is consistent with the routinized denial for first-time petitions. The judge usually takes only a quick look at the files, conducts superficial mediation, and then sets a date for trial. Because denial is the norm, it does not necessitate further investigation of the facts; rendering a denial entails little risk.

If the judge, when handling the case under the Simplified Procedure, finds that the case is more complicated and that issuing a divorce denial to end the case is risky (i.e., the stability concern comes into play), she will switch to the Ordinary Procedure. With three people on the bench, whether judges or lay assessors, the liability is shared and thus diluted (He 2012). This happens often when the conflicts between the litigating parties are fully unfolded or escalated. A plaintiff may only apply for divorce; what she does not mention, however, may be that they have five (or more) properties to divide. The defendant may also present various counterclaims, making the trial more complicated. For courts under pressure to attain a higher rate of adjudication using the Simplified Procedure, the switch needs the approval of the adjudication management office (审判管理办公室) or even the vice president. The responsible judge has to provide clear facts to justify such a switch. For other courts, judges are entrusted to make the switch in their own discretion.

This process can be illustrated by the Case of Changed Procedure from Shaanxi in 2019. A peasant woman in her fifties had filed to divorce her husband for domestic violence for the first time (although she claimed that she had filed for a divorce more than a decade before). The most recent beating had occurred on the eve of the Spring Festival, and since then they had lived separately for five months. Married for thirty years, they had had two adult daughters. The couple's most valuable asset was their 400-square-meter house built ten years before. The house's value had spiked as the city has sprawled into the area. With a pending demolition, it was expected to generate significant monetary compensation.

The trial had been set to be adjudicated under the Simplified Procedure. The judge had also prepared to deny a divorce, given that this was a first-time petition and the messy issue of property division if a divorce was granted. The day before the trial date, however, the wife called the judge and insisted on a divorce. She said she could not live with the man anymore. Moreover, she had also hired a lawyer and would have four witnesses at the trial to testify about the alleged domestic violence.

The judge was alarmed: having four witnesses for a divorce case was unusual, and the woman could be a troublemaker. If domestic violence had actually occurred, as the wife claimed, then it could be inappropriate to deny her petition. Before the judge left her office, she arranged for two lay assessors to participate in the hearing the next morning and switched the trial from the Simplified Procedure to the Ordinary Procedure. Twenty days later, the judge received an ex post approval from her vice president.

The trial was confrontational. The man refused to be divorced: "People at this age do not get divorced." He did not deny domestic violence. Instead, he philosophized: "Why did I beat you? You danced with other men!" The plaintiff's witnesses included one of their daughters and other relatives, illustrating how ruptured the family relationship had become.

Two weeks after the trial, when the judge was still unsure what to do with this case, she received a call from the plaintiff's lawyer: the defendant had beaten her client again, breaking her nose and putting her in the hospital. She wanted to apply for a personal safety protection order. To make things worse, their younger daughter had injured the defendant-father with a kitchen knife during the fight.

What had been a routine divorce petition turned into a dramatic scene of domestic violence. With the new developments, a divorce decision seemed inevitable: there were no excuses for denying the divorce request, even though that meant the judge had to deal with the messy division of the house. Would she divide the house physically or wait for pending monetary compensation? If divided physically, how should the house be restructured for two entrances? The judge needed to make sure that the judgment would be enforceable (He 2009b, 2011), and she did not want to make the wife have access to her own house via a ladder! As the judge confided to me later, she had been so relieved that she had switched to the Ordinary Procedure. Otherwise, how could she have borne the responsibility for such a malicious incident? At the very least, she would have to retry the case, adding yet another case to her already tight docket schedule.

The choice between using the Simplified Procedure versus the Ordinary Procedure has much to do with efficiency and stability concerns. The outcomes are largely predetermined based on which procedure is adopted. The Simplified Procedure is a reliable predictor for denying the divorce petition. When a litigant files a lawsuit the second time, the judge, from the previous trial(s), has a better idea of the level of complexity and the seriousness of the cases. She will then choose the Ordinary Procedure if necessary. The rate of denial is thus much higher with the Simplified Procedure than with the Ordinary Procedure. Put differently: when a divorce case eventually gets tried using the Ordinary Procedure, the likelihood of getting a divorce petition granted increases. The case outcomes are for the most part determined before any trial. They can be determined by two signals: How many times has one filed the lawsuits? And under which procedure is the case being tried?

Gendered Impacts

Seemingly gender-neutral, these approaches nonetheless lead to gendered outcomes. In later chapters, I will demonstrate how stalling final decision-making—a widely adopted tactic for first-time petitions and for stability-threatening cases—influences women's property and personal rights. For now, I will focus only on how the institutional concerns of the judges affect the divorce decision itself—and how women can be disadvantaged as a result.

Let me first examine situations in which the husband initiates a divorce petition but the wife resists with a death threat. This type of case is usually contested because the man has either achieved higher socioeconomic status or is in a new extramarital relationship. Although the wife may be aware of the new circumstances, she may nevertheless oppose the divorce. Typically in these cases, the judge will attempt to persuade the wife to give in to the inevitable because she cannot ever be happy in a marriage if her husband no longer loves her. As for the man, the key is to persuade him—usually through moralizing rhetoric—to compensate the woman financially. The likelihood of the wife peacefully accepting the divorce decision correlates to the level of agreed compensation (more specifically, whether she will be able to maintain her accustomed standard of living). Of course, a necessary precondition to this mediated outcome is that the judge has demonstrated that the wife has exhausted all alternative strategies to preserve the marriage.

In one case, the wife, who was no longer employed, had contracted serious arthritis when giving birth to her daughter. She contested the divorce application brought by her husband, who now worked in another city and had been involved in another relationship. Although the wife and her relatives scolded the husband for his behavior, the husband's response silenced them at the hearing: "[A] divorce is unfair to her, but because of her disease, we have not had sex for five years. Is this fair to me? Not that I do not take care of her, but I have my own life." Nevertheless, the wife resisted the divorce, ostensibly because she wanted her daughter to be raised in a two-parent family.

Despite her objection, the court granted the divorce. The judge explained to the wife that the marriage was a burden for both of them. According to the judgment, the wife received all of the matrimonial assets and the husband was responsible for child support, an outcome that seems unjustifiable under the principles of no-fault divorce. Speaking to the husband in private, the judge attempted to justify her decision:

> When she married you, she was healthy and young. Now you abandon her simply because she is ill? You have to take care of her. Yes, she is ill, but she is also the mother of your daughter. Your life is full of hope because you will get married soon, but she will not. And if you mercilessly refuse to compensate her. How can your daughter respect you when she grows up?

The outcomes of this type of case may eventually be adjudicated divorce or agreement to divorce when the wife finally accepts the financial compensation or accepts the reality. Generally, it is easier for husbands to get what they want. This represents a gendered outcome.

The situation is different, however, when the husband resists divorce. Woman may not be on equal economic footing to compensate men, and thus this approach is less feasible. When a husband resists a divorce by threatening violence, the outcome is even worse: the court will likely deny the divorce petition. This type of case often occurs because the wife's social status has surpassed that of the husband. His objection to the divorce can be understood as an attempt to maintain his dignity as head of the family. The reasoning employed by men in this situation is exemplified by the following statement by a husband in one case: "I will die in front of the courthouse if you, judge, render a divorce decision.

After all, I do not have any hope. . . . Now that my life is destroyed and I do not want to live, I will make hers miserable for the rest of her life."

As a form of resistance, these threats are similar to suicidal protests (Lee and Kleinman 2003). In the political context of modern China, few judges or officials can afford to ignore them. The fear is that a man's emotional and psychological state may lead him to commit violence against a wife seeking independence through divorce.

In this scenario, divorce is often denied, even if one party has filed the petition multiple times. Because of the man's stubborn refusal, the court will force the wife to compromise, ostensibly so that his threats do not materialize. The rationalization is that she can always file another petition in six months and that eventually she will have a better life. She may also claim that she will die if the court rules against her, but if she was really determined to commit suicide, then she would have already had numerous ways to accomplish that. She does not need to die in the court. As long as she still seeks a divorce in court, she had hope in life. Viewed from this perspective, she is in a better position to deal with a denial. Besides, she can always file another petition in six months. However, an immediate divorce could have serious repercussions for the man. The denial of the divorce is thus intended to give the husband time to adjust to the new reality so that he will be better prepared when a divorce is eventually granted. In other words, the physical superiority of men and their capability to carry out threats to stability also give them an advantage in divorce cases. The judges' desire to dispose of cases efficiently and safely only reinforces this inequality.

Put simply, women face more barriers to obtaining a divorce than do men, even if the circumstances that have led them to court are similar. The difference can be explained by the court's need to protect the weaker party so as to avoid malicious consequences. When the Marriage Law was amended in 2001, it granted both husband and wife equal rights to obtain a divorce, a change intended to promote gender equality. The no-fault rule was the means to make this happen. However, concerns for social stability resulted in the perpetuation of gender inequality as it exists in Chinese society through divorce proceedings. While men are more likely to move on from the marriage and pursue new relationships, women find it difficult to extricate themselves from marriage because they are less able to act in a way that will be interpreted by the court as a "clear and present" threat to social stability.

Indeed, as far as gender inequality is concerned, this unfair predetermination is only the tip of the iceberg.[3] In the above cases, the resistance to divorce was open and known to all. Yet most women eventually consented to divorce when the husbands were willing to provide greater compensation. For most cases in which there is less resistance, this transaction flies under the radar. When outcomes are mediated or petitions voluntarily withdrawn, for example, the transactions are not known to outside investigators, since the outed party has already "agreed" that mutual affection has broken down. Men, with their superior financial condition, can obtain the consent of women by offering money and thus predetermine that mutual affection has indeed broken down. From the judges' perspective, a settlement is consistent with their goals: to dispose of cases in an efficient and safe way. Thus, they encourage and facilitate such transactions.

Conclusions

By examining how Chinese judges handle contentious divorce petitions, this chapter has demonstrated the impact of institutional constraints imposed on them. The criteria for assessing judges' performance— including when and how the cases should be disposed of and the occurrence of malicious incidents—shape judicial behavior. The first petition for divorce is often denied, and the chance of getting a divorce increases with more attempts. This approach makes perfect sense for judges given the institutional constraints they face: the denial on the first attempt helps judges clear their caseloads efficiently. It avoids the troublesome issues such as the partition of conjugal property and child custody. It also offers litigants cooling-off periods, and some of them may never come back to court. Even for those who do come back with another petition, judges can handle each one as a new case. It is not too late. The denial on the first attempt still leaves hopes for those who are determined to get a divorce: they can get it later. Thus a denial is the outcome that is least resisted, protested, and complained about. Extremely rarely would malicious incidents occur because of a denial. Judges' efficiency and stability concerns are addressed. "Under the pressures of performance evaluation, such as appeal rate and complaint rate, to deny a divorce on the first attempt can achieve their goals of efficiently closing cases and increasing the number of closed cases" (Liu 2012: 83).

This strategy only became more pronounced in 2018 when the SPC officially introduced "the cooling-off period for divorce."[4] Judges now can use this terminology to delay divorce proceedings. They can legally freeze a divorce case—once, twice, three times. By covering the genuine concerns in the name of cooling-off periods, judges can improve "the rate of first-instance cases in which neither retrial nor appeal is sought (*yishen fupan xisulü*—审服判息诉率) and rate of citizen petitioning against courts" (*xinfang tousulü* 信访投诉率) (Li 2021 forthcoming: Chapter 4).

As a result of these circumstances, the traditional mediated reconciliation has lost much of its meaning; instead, adjudicated denial has become routine for first-time petitions. Most of these cases are handled under the Simplified Procedure. They may be switched to the Ordinary Procedure when responsibility for handling the case becomes too great for a single judge, in which instance it moves to a three-person panel. Mediation, however, persists in cases that threaten stability. Similar in format, this type of mediation differs substantively from the traditional mode. The mediation process is beset with urgent emotional demands, complex and changing relationships, and unmet financial needs. It is not a process that emphasizes rules, expertise, disinterested decisions, or fairness and a commitment to justice. It is a process focusing on the relevance of individual character and personality, as well as pervasive arbitrariness and the search for advantage. The litigants' resistance complicates judges' task when it takes the form of a refusal to provide information or a refusal to cooperate in the judge's efforts to understand the litigants' social and emotional circumstances. Based on their experience and expertise, judges do engage some litigants and attempt to understand their crises—all the while avoiding entanglement in the central drama. Some judges are detached, callous, or antipathetic, but many cannot afford to behave so. Most are serious about the emotional instability of litigants. As a result, handling divorce cases is exhausting for most any judge, including those who are trained in both psychology and law. In response, they are forced to adopt the patterns described in this chapter.

These *modi operandi* in handling divorce litigation perpetuate gender inequality. Being rejected, discredited, or distrusted, women—similar to female divorce litigants in the United States—develop "a sense of powerlessness and futility," "personal worthlessness," and "self-doubt" (Epstein and Goodman 2018: 449). Furthermore, according to Li (2014: 87), "the 'breakdown of mutual affection' test is based simply on the number of times a divorce has been requested . . . which undermines women's freedom of divorce rights."

3

The Pragmatic Judge

To illustrate how institutional constraints hamstring judges, this chapter offers an in-depth description of the hearing process with a special focus on the mediation stage. Analyzing dialogues from actual trials, it will reveal the pragmatic orientation of judges when handling divorce cases (see also Cai and Qi 2019). Such an approach can be reflected by a newly emergent and pragmatic discourse dominating the mediation session within China's process for divorce litigation.

According to He et al. (2017), two styles of discourse may be identified in China's divorce courts: legalistic and mediatory. The distinction between these draws on Merry's (1990) classic categorizations of legal, moral, and therapeutic discourses. Merry's categorizations focus on the power underlying the discourses, that is, whether legal rights and facts (legal discourse), relationship and moral obligations (moral discourse), or attribution of fault (therapeutic discourse) form the discourse paradigms. While overlapped with Merry's emphasis on power, the legalistic style and the mediatory style are also distinguished by procedures and outcomes: the former emphasizes formal adjudication, whereas the latter facilitates reconciliatory outcomes. The legalistic style is characterized by the use of legal discourse, which, similar to Merry's legal discourse, refers to "a discourse of property, of rights, of the protection of the self and one's goods, of entitlement, of facts and truth" (112). The mediatory style entails nonlegal discourses, including mainly moral discourse, therapeutic discourse (113–14), and pragmatic discourse, aimed at achieving "a convenient legal solution." The mediatory style does not exclude legal discourse but uses it only as a supplement to the nonlegal discourses.

Pragmatic discourse is a form of mediatory discourse shaped by judges' preference for mediation. In the Maoist version, judges often engaged in "educating" the divorcing couple: put simply, they preached to the litigants. The goal was to persuade both parties to reconcile and thereby rescue the marriage. The discourses employed by judges were political and therapeutic. For instance, they would criticize parties who were lazy or who had engaged in extramarital affairs, accusing them of bourgeois ideas. In the current form of mediation, by contrast, the purpose of any preaching is to resolve disputes for more pragmatic reasons. While pragmatic discourse shares some similarities with therapeutic discourse in its nonlegalistic nature, these two approaches differ markedly. In pragmatic discourse, the judge seems to assume the role of social worker, but rather than fixing a broken relationship her ultimate goal is to resolve the immediate dispute. A judge does not address who is wrong and who is right, or which action is blameful and which is laudable. As will be shown, pragmatic discourse focuses on problem-solving as the main goal. Unlike her predecessors in the early period of reform (circa 1980s), the judge does not investigate the causes of a deteriorating relationship or reform the couple through ideological education (Huang 2005). Pragmatic discourse fundamentally redefines the court's "natural attitude" toward divorce as a social act, from taboo to inevitable reality.

The Case of Mrs. Li

How does this new pragmatic discourse negotiate gender equality and women's welfare? Through the dialogues between judge and plaintiff, one can see how the pragmatic discourse is creating a new social reality, thereby presenting and limiting options available to women facing divorce.

The main example draws from a trial brought before Judge Chen involving a contested divorce. In her early thirties, Judge Chen is part of a new generation of judges who are college-trained in law. The parties in this case are a migrant couple in their early forties, Mr. and Mrs. Li, originally from the mountainous areas of Guangdong. They have been married for eleven years and have a ten-year-old daughter. Mr. Li works for the postal service as a contract worker; Mrs. Li, who is uneducated, works as a janitor for a cleaning company. They are a typical working-class migrant couple who left their hometown to move to the city in search of a more financially rewarding life. Mr. Li earns around 1,800 yuan a month, Mrs. Li about 1,400 yuan. The couple had contributed a large amount of their income to repay the husband's family debt. Shortly after the debt was paid off, the husband asked for a divorce. He says he does not have emotional feelings for his wife. The husband also says that his wife does not get along with his parents. Mr. Li, in Chinese legal terms, is using "ruptured emotional relationship" as grounds for divorce.

As scholars have pointed out, the acceptance of "ruptured emotional relationship" as a legitimate reason for divorce in the current Chinese system, coupled with the lack of on-site investigations and witness cross-examination by judges, means that the system borders on a de facto no-fault policy (Huang 2010: 204–08; Davis 2010, 2011). Mrs. Li makes clear her objection to the proposed divorce to the judge. At the beginning of the trial, she asks the judge if the trial is merely a formality and that the court will approve her husband's application. Judge Chen assures that she has no preconceived idea about the outcome.

In court, the wife contends that the real reasons her husband wants a divorce is because the family debt is now paid off. She alleges that his economic well-being is better now and that he wants to abandon her. More important, her in-laws want a boy in the family; but that remains a pipe dream as long as she remains their son's wife because she is already too old to bear another child.

The contested nature of the petition notwithstanding, it is a simple divorce case that does not involve complex property redistribution and documentary evidence. Neither side is represented by lawyers. The judge listens to the arguments by the husband and the wife (mainly the wife) during the investigation phase, which lasts about an hour.

Judge Chen then moves on to the mediation stage. The judge has two options: either persuade the husband to drop his petition for divorce, or persuade the wife to agree to divorce. The judge chooses the latter, a choice indicative of the new realistic approach. She first asks Mr. Li whether he would consider reconciliation. When he refuses, Judge Chen shows little interest in trying to change his mind. She seems to have made up her mind that the husband cannot be persuaded to stay in the marriage. She quickly turns to Mrs. Li.

In a dialogue lasting approximately half an hour, Judge Chen tries to persuade Mrs. Li to agree to divorce. In the course of this long discussion, the judge attempts, through iterations of the pragmatic discourse, to undermine the wife's traditionalistic ethics and to steer her to see what she sees. The exchange between judge and litigant—questions, answers, parries, and rejoinders—exposes the elements of pragmatic discourse. Judge Chen and the two litigants all speak in Mandarin; the litigants, especially Mrs. Li, speak with a noticeable Cantonese accent.

As will be shown, even though the mediation talks proceed in the standard question-and-answer format, it does not carry with it a strict courtroom format. Many of the questions are rhetorical devices deployed by the judge to persuade the woman to give up her marriage. Similarly, the woman often does not directly answer the judge's questions. Often she offers what Goffman (1981) would describe as "response" to try to explain herself in light of the challenges implied in the questions.

TRANSCRIPT EXCERPT 1

[PLAINTIFF] I told her, if she agrees to divorce, I am willing to give her 10,000 yuan.

[JUDGE] You'll give her 10,000 yuan, right?

[PLAINTIFF] Yes, for the time she wasted on me.

[JUDGE] So if he gives you 10,000 yuan, would you agree to divorce?

[DEFENDANT] For 10,000 yuan of course I would not agree. He's completely . . .

[JUDGE] How much money would be a fair sum for you?

[DEFENDANT] I don't want money. It's our marriage. I think we can tolerate each other a bit more and we reconcile. That's what I want.

From the very beginning, the wife has expressed her unwillingness to bargain. This episode is illuminating for the purpose of understanding the implicit perspective from which the pragmatic discourse operates. In other cases involving couples who are willing to bargain, the judges' role is to facilitate the process, to nudge the parties toward a compromise, and sometimes to prevent the stronger party from taking advantage of the weaker party. But this episode is different: The pragmatic discourse reveals itself as a meta-discourse; facing a litigant who does not want to bargain, it has to justify first of all why it is good to bargain at all. In the process, it frames the wife's insistence on keeping her marriage as irrational and problematic. In Excerpt 1, the judge talks to Mr. Li. She wants him to offer his wife some compensation. The man readily agrees. He offers 10,000 yuan. But Mrs. Li says she does not want to bargain.

[JUDGE] Let me tell you now. You see, you two have been together for many years already. The marriage problem you have, you know it in your heart way better than I do. Can this marriage be continued? Right? . . . What should I say about him? You can't tie him down by your side! Let's just say the court rules against divorce this time, will he come back and live with you? This is what you really need to think about, right? I know as a traditional woman, you perhaps think that divorce is not good, it is not good for your child either. But this is the reality: He doesn't want to live with you anymore; he insists on a divorce.

[DEFENDANT] He . . .

[JUDGE] Your hope to maintain the integrity of your family; your hope is wonderful. But can it be fulfilled?

Judge Chen questions the sanity of the defendant's decision to insist on continuing her marriage. The writing, as it were, is on the wall. As the judge tells Mrs. Li: "You two have been together for many years already. The marriage problem you have, you know it in your heart way better than I do. Can this marriage be continued? Right?" The judge's way of describing the defendant's marriage is controlling in the sense that it leaves very little space for Mrs. Li to say that her marriage is fine. Her question is put to Mrs. Li in such a way that it already marks an affirmative answer as delusional: you know more than I do about your marriage, and even I can tell your marriage is failing.

Judge Chen moves on to establish another "fact" that structures the subsequent exchanges: in this day and age, a woman cannot keep a man from leaving an unhappy marriage. She appeals to the fact that marriage is a covenant between two free individuals: "What should I say about him? You can't tie him down by your side!" The judge's characterization of the husband as a free man determined to leave rather than as a flawed individual to be educated is evidence of the bigger shift: from the previous moralist discourse to the current pragmatic discourse. As mentioned, it adopts a firm noninterventionist position toward individual decisions whether to stay or leave a marriage.

The judge then poses another question that further suggests the futility of holding on to the marriage. "Let's just say the court rules against divorce this time, will he come back and live with you?" The question is rhetorical in the sense that it presumes a negative answer: the husband will not return. Still, the judge praises the defendant as a virtuous "traditional woman" (传统女性 or *chuantong nüxing*). This framing of Mrs. Li's identity as a *nüxing* is indicative of the gendered discourse that Judge Chen creates for the aggrieved wife. The term *nüxing* ("female sex") was historically used by cultural critics of China to counteract the Maoist label of women as *funü* (妇女), a concept that viewed women as desexualized socialist comrades (Barlow 1994). As used by Judge Chen, *nüxing* invokes both the traditional Chinese women as virtuous but also as passive, dependent, and emotionally laborious. Loyal as she is, Mrs. Li is, as a *nüxing*, blind to the stark facts she is facing (and that the judge is eager to point out). "He doesn't want to live with you anymore; he insists on a divorce." When the woman displays a hint of doubt, the judge follows that up quickly with another question that points to the pointlessness of playing the role of a virtuous wife: "Your hope to maintain the integrity of your family; your hope is wonderful. But can it be fulfilled?"

TRANSCRIPT EXCERPT 3

[DEFENDANT] When she [the daughter] was young, at one year old, I said if we divorced . . . back then he said it absolutely wouldn't happen.

[JUDGE] Ah, you see, each of us here handles hundreds of cases.

[DEFENDANT] He said it wouldn't happen, absolutely wouldn't happen. Now, you see, he just told me he wanted to divorce. I don't know.

[JUDGE] In fact, this thing called divorce, I think it is very normal. Every couple when they get married, they say they are not going to divorce; they say they will stay together forever. No one thinks about divorce when they marry. But in reality, every year there will still be hundreds of people sitting here, telling me they want to divorce. That's why I think it is very normal, right?

[DEFENDANT] But . . .

[JUDGE] I think, the more rational, or more effective way to deal with this problem is for you to propose some demands, and see if both sides can negotiate on them.

[DEFENDANT] What kind of demands? He has to give me money.

[JUDGE] Yes.

[DEFENDANT] But he has no money to give me.

[JUDGE] He now agrees to give 10,000 yuan.

[DEFENDANT] 10,000 yuan? I worked for his sake. Who is he treating now? He is not treating me like a wife. He's treating me like a messenger, like an entertainer. He is treating me like a stranger.

[JUDGE] But if there is no divorce, he won't give you 10,000 yuan. Will you then think he is treating you like a wife?

[DEFENDANT] He doesn't give me money but that's okay.

Mrs. Li tells Judge Chen that her husband had once promised never to leave her. The judge's response is unsentimental; promises are made to be broken. Once again, the pragmatic discourse is at work. It normalizes divorce. She does this by citing her own experience as a judge who hears hundreds of divorce petitions each year. It is instructive to notice that she uses the Chinese words *zheng chang* (正常), which means not just "common" but, more significantly, "normal." The normalization of divorce is a far cry from the old moralistic discourse's characterization of divorce as pathological. Rationality, not emotion, is what is required to deal with this "normal" life event. Thus, the judge asks Mrs. Li to deal with the situation in a rational manner—meaning to get what she can from her estranged husband before it is too late. In using the word "rational" to describe the option of seeking compensation and then moving on, the judge implies that Mrs. Li's clinging to her marriage—which would have been admired under the old system—is now considered "irrational."

The judge has already proposed and Mr. Li has also agreed to offer a one-time compensation to his wife. Now the judge asks the wife if she has a counteroffer. For the judge, monetary compensation seems to be the most realistic way of resolving the dispute. There are no legal mandates requiring Mr. Li to compensate his wife in this case because there has been no domestic violence and no extramarital affairs. The judge asks the husband if he is willing to use money to appease his distressed wife, to assuage her anger and frustration.

Mrs. Li seems to momentarily give in. She says her husband should give her money. The judge says Mr. Li has already agreed to pay 10,000 yuan. But Mrs. Li's subsequent reaction shows that she has a different moral interpretation of money. She sees the settlement money not so much as a means of compensation but as a moral token. That kind of money (10,000 yuan), she tells Judge Chen, is like treating her like a "messenger" or an "entertainer"—as anything but a wife.

Judge Chen refuses to moralize. She tells Mrs. Li that names mean little. If she chooses to remain a "nominal" wife, her husband will not even give her 10,000 yuan. She asks: "Will you then think he is treating you like a wife?" Mrs. Li sticks to her traditionalistic discourse: it is fine for her to receive no money if she can keep her marriage.

TRANSCRIPT EXCERPT 4

[JUDGE] If you think about it this way, doesn't it just make things worse for you? Right?

[DEFENDANT] No, it doesn't. My daughter goes to school; no one will say, "Oh no, you don't have a father. Did he divorce your mom?"

[JUDGE] So many people are divorced. Nowadays who will say this?

[DEFENDANT] No, that's not the case. . . .

[JUDGE] Besides, when you two divorce, you don't necessarily have to let your daughter's classmates and teachers know, right? Look, her father works in Guangzhou all year 'round. How can others tell? He will still visit his little child after divorce.

[DEFENDANT] How will people not know? Many will know. He said, I didn't give birth to a son. His family wants a son. He said I'm too old now. I'm not able to have a son. This is what he said.

[PLAINTIFF] Actually I said right at the beginning, they didn't say that. It's all your misunderstanding. . . .

[DEFENDANT] So I misunderstood again! Your father said that, when we were celebrating the New Year of 2009, when we went home on February 20, your father said that the daughter I bore, there were hundreds of thousands of them. . . .

[JUDGE] Have you considered the real reasons why you don't want to divorce? You think it is better not to divorce than to divorce, but what in fact is better if you don't divorce?

[DEFENDANT] This I don't know either.

[JUDGE] That's right.

[DEFENDANT] I think. . . .

Mrs. Li believes not divorcing is better for her daughter. At school, people will not accuse her daughter of not having a father. The judge once again tells the woman that divorce is very common. Besides, no one will know because her husband is constantly away from home and he will still see their child. It is in her rejoinder that the litigant reveals what she thinks is the true reason for her husband's insistence on divorce: his parents want a grandson. But she is too old to bear another child. Mr. Li denies the allegation. Mrs. Li remembers the date that her father-in-law said this to her. Judge Chen does not appear surprised. Among couples living in the rural China, the desire for extended families to have a son is all too common. However, the judge does not make any further inquiry on the subject. Instead, she immediately turns the question back to Mrs. Li. She does not deny the gender inequality Mrs. Li faces. She simply asks the pragmatic question: Is not divorcing a better option to deal with the problem? It is clear that, as a legal institution, the court no longer uses law to educate and to reform.

TRANSCRIPT EXCERPT 5

[JUDGE] I want to ask you a question. The key question is that do you think you two can still stay together as a couple? Can he treat you like a husband treats his wife?

[DEFENDANT] This [means] both sides have to be more tolerant.

[JUDGE] Why should you be more tolerant? Perhaps if you divorce, you can find someone who genuinely cherishes you.

[DEFENDANT] I don't think I will. We generally are deceived by others. This is not going to happen.

[JUDGE] Not necessarily. The situation you are in right now. Let me describe it in colloquial terms. Ain't no difference between having a hubby and not having a hubby. Right? Why do you want to keep this "nominal without substance" marriage? Why don't you . . . besides even if I rule. . . .

Judge Chen continues to ask questions: "[Do] you think you two can still stay together as a couple?" "Can he treat you like a husband treats his wife?" These questions are meant to expose the "irrationality" of Mrs. Li's moralistic view of her marriage. Under the pragmatic discourse, names and titles matter little. The presupposition that her marriage means little or nothing is interactively reinforced when the judge repeats these rhetorical questions.

When Mrs. Li says she and her husband can exercise more patience, Judge Chen again bluntly discourages her, then offers some consolation. Mrs. Li was uncharacteristically cynical in her response. She says a woman of her background will only be deceived again. Judge Chen tells Mrs. Li that she really has nothing to lose. The judge uses the words "nominal without substance" (有名无实 or *you ming wu shi*) to describe the defendant's marriage. She says, colloquially, "Ain't no difference between having a hubby (老公 *laogong*) and not having a hubby."

TRANSCRIPT EXCERPT 6

[DEFENDANT] This is not the same. You people have no experience of this yourselves and so you don't know. My thinking is different from you people. He will still be good. He has to; he has to try.

[JUDGE] But have you considered the other side of the picture? That is to say, because I am going to give a ruling this time, first of all I may allow the divorce, or I may not. Let's just say I decide against divorce this time. But then what if he comes back [in] half a year? What do you want me to do then?

[DEFENDANT] When he returns to petition again, I will ask him to pay his daughter child support once and for all. Right? I want, I want, my daughter [weeping]. I lived with him for ten-odd years. He said I didn't give him money for ten-odd years. You can . . . you can investigate [weeping]. . . .

[JUDGE] Where are you now?

Mrs. Li tells the judge that her thinking is different. It is important to point out that Mrs. Li uses the plural second-person pronoun *nimen* (你们) in Chinese, referring to not just the young judge but her even younger aide as a group. She said people like the judge do not have the kind of problems that she has. Mrs. Li is referring to the gap between herself—an uneducated middle-aged woman in a failing marriage—and Judge Chen, a young, educated, and affluent professional woman. The judge does not respond to Mrs. Li's thinly veiled challenge. She responds instead by referring to the institutional reality that, even if she rules against divorce this time, Mr. Li will simply file for divorce again later. Judge Chen now explains to Mrs. Li that the court will not and cannot force her husband to stay with her. Mrs. Li can reject the divorce this time, but eventually the divorce application will be accepted by the court, and Mrs. Li could be left with nothing at all because the law does not require one party to compensate the other.

At this point, Mrs. Li breaks down into tears and begins to recount, in a random, stream-of-consciousness way, the hardship she suffered for her husband during their years of marriage.

As defined by Merry (1990: 112), legal discourse is one of "property, of rights, of the protection of one's self and of goods, of entitlement, of facts and truths." But the conversations above are very much shaped by the judge's preference for mediation, an institutional preference that can be similarly found in family courts in the United States (Fineman 1988, 1991). During this process of mediation, the judge did not talk about rights and evidence. Pragmatic discourse is a cost-and-benefit analysis. What is the advantage of keeping the marriage? What is the point of prolonging it? So, if you think you are unfairly treated, how about if he compensates you?

In a sense, the judge does talk about the eventual legal outcome. But the "legal" analysis serves only as a background for strategizing. The facts that the husband can file for divorce six months later, and is more likely to be granted a divorce the next time, only add to the pressure on Mrs. Li to deal with the matter pragmatically. The judge is determined to persuade the wife to accept divorce and get the best deal while she can. If the reality is that "it is impossible to force somebody to live with you if he does not want to," then the law is not going to change the reality. It accepts it as its starting point. This again illustrates the stark difference separating pragmatic discourse from moralistic discourse.

If the reality was unavoidable, then the pressure brought to bear by the pragmatic discourse was pronounced. Mrs. Li must have been deliberating what resistance she could possibly muster. Had Mrs. Li known the law and could have afforded a lawyer, her arguments could have focused on the fact that their emotional relationship has not been ruptured. Indeed, there were many facts in the case that would have supported such an argument. At the court investigation phase, Mrs. Li stated that she and her husband visited each other and had an active sex life even though their work places were some distance apart. (Mrs. Li mentioned that she used a contraceptive ring at her husband's request.) Their affection toward each other had been lukewarm for many years, so why should the marriage be terminated on that day? If she had raised this argument, the judge probably would not have said that her approval of the husband's application was just a matter of time.

However, given her background and lack of representation, Mrs. Li was unable to come up with a legally legitimate argument. Facing the suggestions of the judge and the pragmatic discourse, her responses were poorly organized and full of discursive shifts (cf. Conley and O'Barr 1990; Hirsch 1998: 94). As the question-and-answer sequence progressed, Mrs. Li became more introspective. Pushed by Judge Chen's battery of rhetorical questions, she went through painful internal debates about her choice to continue the marriage. She also seemed to be most disturbed by her husband's allegation that she was not a good wife. She said that she did not deserve to be abandoned. The defendant told the judge that she had contributed to the family and recounted how she had taken care of the plaintiff's parents. In her mind, her husband's allegation that she was not a good wife was groundless, and as long as she conducted herself as a wife she would not be abandoned.

As mentioned, Mrs. Li believed that her husband's and his parents' craving for a son/grandson was the real reason for the petition. If this had come before a court during the Maoist period, the judge would have undertaken a thorough investigation. If Mrs. Li's claim was found to be true, the judge not only would have rejected the petition but also would have told the husband why he was in the wrong. After all, wanting to have a son was precisely the kind of feudal prejudices that the new China of the Communist Party had vowed to eradicate. A judge today will not judge unless he or she has to. "If he does not want to stay with you in a marriage, you cannot force him to do so" is the new noninterventionist motto of pragmatic discourse.

TRANSCRIPT EXCERPT 7

[DEFENDANT] I don't understand what you said. I'm not cultivated.

[JUDGE] I am explaining things to you now. I'm explaining things to you slowly.

[DEFENDANT] He is more cultivated. He can certainly win the argument. You think so too, Judge; you think he meant well.

[JUDGE] I don't think he meant well. I'm just trying to explain things to you, that is to say . . .

[DEFENDANT] You explain things to me, but I don't understand.

[JUDGE] So you should listen. You can only understand if you listen.

[DEFENDANT] How can I understand if I listen? You say divorce and it's divorce; you say go and date another man and then it's go and date another man. I am left with nothing.

[JUDGE] I am trying to . . .

[DEFENDANT] I am left empty-handed.

Not being able to argue with the judge on the likely legal outcome, Mrs. Li can only resort to a critical commentary on the nature of the law. The defendant, despite her lack of legal knowledge, knows the world enough to realize that the deck is stacked against her. She tells Judge Chen that the court is siding with her husband because he is better educated. In the original Chinese, she says her husband has more *wenhua*, meaning he is more cultured. She says the judge seems to think that her husband means well because he is more cultivated than she is. She laments that the law does not empathize with the weak; she laments that the law does not empathize with the poor; and she laments that the law, above all, does not empathize with "uncultured" members of society such as herself.

TRANSCRIPT EXCERPT 8

[JUDGE] Okay, it is difficult to achieve mediation now. You should go back and think long and hard. Okay, just think about what I just said to you.

[DEFENDANT] I don't understand what you said. You mentioned coming back for a second time. I hope we don't have to come back.

[JUDGE] I don't care if you understand or not. This is what the law stipulates. Today I have explained things to you so patiently; my goal is to help solve problems for both of you. When it comes time for me to rule, I don't have to discuss with you how I'm going to rule. I just base my ruling on the facts found and the law. This is a rather simple thing for me to do. I patiently said so much to you because I hoped that you could face up to your problem in a rational way and thereby solve the problem. The law is the same for everyone. The law applies the same rules to people who don't understand it. It won't offer special exemptions to those who don't understand the law. That's not how the law operates. You've got to understand this.

[DEFENDANT] I don't understand.

At this point, Judge Chen decided to give up trying to mediate. In her opinion, Mrs. Li was not helping matters at all. In Excerpt 8, the judge points out to Mrs. Li that the law treats all people the same way, whether they understand the law or not. She says that her ruling does not depend on the fact that the wife has been a good wife or has contributed to the family; rather, it is based on whether Mr. and Mrs. Li still want to live together as a couple and whether there are some other alternatives, such as monetary compensation, to relieve the pain involved in solving the problem. Mrs. Li's response to the judge's lecturing is terse: "I don't understand." The response itself displays Mrs. Li's resistance to the law and is double-voiced: its meaning is as much a professed lack of legal understanding on the part of Mrs. Li as it is a sense of disbelief in the current status of the law from this frustrated litigant.

Judge Chen and Mrs. Li were in fact arguing at cross purposes: the judge wanted her to receive maximum return for agreeing to a divorce, but Mrs. Li refused to consider divorce as an option. In Excerpt 9 (below), which is from the end of the mediation, Judge Chen reveals—in the most explicit and concrete terms—what she can probably get for Mrs. Li from her husband: her daughter, a settlement upward of 10,000 yuan, and perhaps a monthly allowance of around 500–800 yuan. But Mrs. Li is clearly in no mood to bargain. Her parting shot to the judge? "In my marriage, there is no hope, only disappointment." In Chinese, the pair of antonyms *shiwang* (disappointment) and *xiwang* (hope), rhyme, which aptly illustrates Mrs. Li's disillusionment with both her marriage and the legal system.

TRANSCRIPT EXCERPT 9

[JUDGE] When I said "mediation," I meant this: Based on what you two agree to, for example, if the two of you agree that your daughter belongs to you [Mrs. Li] and he gives you 500 or 800 yuan each month,

a sum which you can negotiate further, then we can write this down
in the agreement and it has legal power. Also, about that money—he
said that he will give you 10,000 yuan. Perhaps you think 10,000
yuan is too little and you want a bit more. We can write this down in
the court's agreement; this also will have legal effect. Understand?
[DEFENDANT] This only disappoints me; it gives me no hope.
[JUDGE] What did you say?
[DEFENDANT] In my marriage, there is no hope, only disappointment.

In her written judgment, Judge Chen, as she hinted, ruled against the
petition. She resorted to a technical argument. The plaintiff mentioned
in his petition that he and his wife had been separated since 2007, but
the judge wrote that he did not offer any evidence of that for the court to
consider. This implies that should Mr. Li offer more concrete evidence
of their broken marriage next time, he would stand a better chance of
success. Meanwhile, Judge Chen was making the process inconvenient
for Mr. Li. As mentioned, transaction costs for divorce applications in
China are high, but in her judgment, Judge Chen does not mention what
she told Mrs. Li: namely, that there is only so much that the court can do
to postpone the inevitable.

Gendered Outcomes

This kind of pragmatic discourse also prevails in other parts of China.
I informally interviewed by phone some experienced judges in divorce
cases I knew from several provinces including Jiangsu, Guangxi, Zhejiang, and Shaanxi. Because these judges were included based on our
personal connections, they did not make up a systematic sample. I also
did not observe the courtrooms in these provinces. But judges who
worked in the regions similarly suggested the existence of a pragmatic
attitude. They pointed out that "getting a good deal" for the weaker parties was an important goal, apparently because the reform to redefine
the role of the judiciary was applied by the central government from the
top down.

Pragmatic discourse entered the courts in part because of the re-
newed emphasis on mediation, as our case analysis has shown. The targeted mediation rate is now a formal criterion of judges' performance.

As mentioned, judges are understandably motivated to get litigants to agree to mediation. But the new noninterventionist policy and the concomitant reform in trial procedures make it all the more necessary for judges to resort to mediation. They simply do not have the resources to investigate all of the divorce petitions that land on the court docket. But this new game of mediation is different from the old idea of reconciliation. The reality is that judges today are more dispassionate. The ideological persuasion that had been effective until the 1980s is unheard of now (He 2009a). And neither does the moral discourse referred to by Mrs. Li in the case above work. Her husband is clearly aware of how the system works. When he files for divorce the second or third time, the court will eventually grant it. It is in this sense that, institutionally speaking, the marriage is hopeless for Judge Chen. She wants to get Mrs. Li something before it is too late. The pragmatic discourse is meant to be used by judges to extract, through bargaining, something of value for the weaker party. As we have seen, Judge Chen was not interested in assigning blame but was more concerned with getting Mrs. Li something more than nothing when her marriage inevitably ended.

It is therefore paradoxical to see that, in practice, pragmatic discourse can perpetuate gender inequality for some women in that it mocks their traditional beliefs of keeping husbands married against their will. The pragmatic discourse avoids mentioning the power struggles between husband and wife or taking the side of either one. Judges now presume that both spouses are ready and able to lead separate, independent lives after a divorce. Men and women are also assumed by the court to be equally responsible for the harm suffered by their children in the process and are asked to devote equal care to their children after the breakup.

As judges in China are eager to assume the role of alternative decision makers, they also contribute to the problems identified by Fineman (1991) in her critique of the rise of the discourse among social workers mediating divorce and child custody cases: They try not to judge, they do not lay blame or find fault, they look forward to the future, and they try to identify the best way forward for women and their children. By dispensing with the quest for fault, judges have also denied wives the moral high ground they formerly occupied during divorce litigation. Fineman also suggests that this pursuit of formal equality has sometimes overshadowed more instrumental concerns in divorce reforms.

For example, judges could ignore women's connection to children in an attempt to cast them as unencumbered, equally empowered market actors (1991: 175). As seen, a key reason for Mrs. Li's objection was what she firmly believed would happen to her daughter after the divorce.

Furthermore, in this form of pragmatic negotiation—not unlike what law and society scholars found in their studies of the United States—women are often less experienced in financial negotiations (cf. Conley and O'Barr 2005: 49). Mrs. Li, for example, was not at all prepared to talk about financial compensation under the assumption of "if divorced." She was still insistent on maintaining her status as a lawful wife and what she provided on behalf of her family. Had she been more alert to the money matters, she would have engaged herself in bargaining with her husband more proactively.

Pragmatic discourse is also constraining for spouses who are not ready to bargain. As Judge Chen stated: "In adjudication, you may not get any compensation." The pragmatic discourse is constraining in the sense that compromise is the only viable option. However unwilling, a litigant has to accept that a judge's mediation is the best remedy that the court can offer. In other words, it offers help in a coercive manner; a realistic and cooperative litigant will not leave empty-handed. Ironically, in trying to provide better remedies to the wife, the law paves the way for the reinforcement of patriarchy.

Even though the pragmatic discourse can be a reflection of the new social reality, its prominence as an institutional discourse also creates and reproduces this social reality. Specifically, the pragmatic discourse changes the way of talking and thinking about divorce. These new modes of talking and thinking are eventually, and subtly, inscribed in social action, sometimes with sad consequences for women. A wife who insists on preserving her marriage is destined to be a loser in this system, even when the presiding judge is sympathetic and well-meaning. Nonetheless, it is often in the interaction between judges and female litigants that hegemony and resistance are revealed.

Finally, a comparison with other societies clarifies the complex relationship between pragmatic discourse and gender inequality. Pragmatic discourse in China is a product of the growing economic disparity between men and women as well as the rapid retreat of the state from the family domain. Its entry has weakened traditional moral discourse.

While traditionalistic beliefs depict women inferior to men, they also offer some of the economically and socially most vulnerable women a thin layer of protection, often by obliging husbands to provide for their wives.

In her study of the practice of Islamic family law in Iran, Mir-Hosseini (2001) demonstrates that some of the most patriarchal elements of Sharia can in fact help socially disadvantageous women to achieve their marital goals. The lower-class women she studied in Iran fight marital battles armed with the traditional moral discourse of family relations. They are in a stronger position to drive a hard bargain. Some women, for example, use the threat of *mahr* in Islamic law (the amount a groom pays to the bride upon marriage, some of which can be delayed if the spouses agree) to resist their husbands' requests for divorce, and they are backed by the courts.

In China, at least in its urban areas, the former dominance of morality discourse has now been substantially undermined by the new pragmatic discourse to the extent that it can no longer offer that thin layer of protection. The problem with the dominance of traditional moral discourse in patriarchal societies is that it is hegemonic, in the sense that women, like it or not, must deal with this traditional discourse as the default.

For example, in her study of Swahili Muslim people in coastal Kenya, Hirsch (1998) shows how women there can sometimes navigate the discursive asymmetry between men's "pronouncing" (men can simply pronounce "divorce" to resolve marital problems) and women's "preserving" (women are expected to endure hardships in marriage). But even when they have developed a discourse of rights to fight for their welfare, that discourse, unlike the pragmatic discourse we discussed here, cannot be deployed by women as "just another" alternative. It is more of a last resort, a discourse that can be delicately deployed only after women there have "proved" to the court that all the other actions prescribed by available moral discourses of marital conflict—such as more love and commitment—could not possibly salvage the marriage (Hirsch 1998: 81–111).

This does not seem to be the case in China. If anything, the arrival of pragmatic discourse has removed traditionalistic moral discourse from the courtroom. Understood in this way, pragmatic discourse, promoted by the Chinese state might have unintentionally created some openings for other discourses to enter into the family domain. The problem with pragmatic discourse, as we identified, is similar to the problem Fineman (1991) found with the discourse of the social workers: it focuses exclusively on formal equality. Women are now "given" the right to divorce. But the interesting question to ask is this: Among the competing discourses (of which pragmatic discourse is one), can a new rights discourse that pays heed to substantive gender equality emerge in divorce-law practices?

Conclusions

By studying courtroom discourse, the above have illustrated a recurrent feature in divorce cases. While judges have always employed various discourses (He et al. 2017), pragmatic discourse is utilized to encourage litigants to adopt a calculating attitude, to be compensated, and to get out of bad marriages. Pragmatic discourse allows judges to pressure unwilling litigants by promoting the "new attitude" toward divorce as commonplace. Through the use of evaluative statements and rhetorical questions, judges often compare divorce favorably with the alternative of staying in a bad marriage. This is clear in the exchanges on issues of whether one shall be divorced or one shall go after financial compensation or child custody.

Dominating divorce hearings is the quick-and-dirty, eager-to-find-the-middle-ground approach. Through deliberate and repeated deployments of this new pragmatic discourse, judges turn divorce trials into a forum where specific official understandings of women's welfare take priority.

Pragmatic discourse is powerful. In most cases judges manage to "get to yes" and settle the case. But resistance is often encountered. Litigants often invoke moral discourse or assert their economic capabilities. Some may forgo the suggestions of the judges but pursue petitions and become a disgruntled troublemaker. In one of the classic articles on sociolegal studies, Kornhauser and Mnookin (1979) describe how private agreements in divorce and other cases are negotiated in light of known rules that are considered to be a form of bargaining endowment. The process is captured in their trenchant phrase "bargaining in the shadow of the law." The analysis of the mediation discourse between Chinese judges and litigants, however, suggests another type of bargaining: the play of power and the construction of meaning. When lawyers are bargaining with the other party, they are placed on more or less the same footing. In the Chinese courtroom, the judges, being the final arbiter of the cases, can invoke the law's shadow authoritatively. They construct meaning in the service of power. However, because divorce law is extremely flexible and because it expressly allows for a wide range of discretion in its application, the shadow that it casts over the mediation is partial and flickering. The judges try to talk litigants into a frame of mind appropriate to their pragmatic needs, which may be consistent with the judges' agendas to dispose of the case, but the litigants may wield resistance in both discourse and behavior. The possession of authority and legal knowledge does not itself ensure that the judges will succeed in their efforts. As shown, while goals are clear and agendas are set, explicit conflicts are common; closure about what is reasonable and realistic is hard to produce. Cases drift.

Through the perspective of pragmatic discourse, this chapter has shown how the courts perpetuate gender biases by offering "solutions"— particularly in divorce cases filed by men who want to satisfy their need for a male heir or a new romance. The judges we observed and interviewed genuinely believe that getting something for women who insist on salvaging failed marriages is the best that they can do. But precisely because of the judge-cum-mediator role that judges like Chen play, the pragmatic discourse used in China gives a whole new meaning to the expression "bargaining in the shadow of the law" (Kornhauser and Mnookin 1979). Despite the collective goodwill of judges, linguistic evidence indicates that this new discourse has become the pathway through which gender inequality is brought into being. The exchange between judges and litigants is a vivid case of "doing gender," in the sense that it is an active process reflecting the institutional shaping of gender relations (Cooke 2006). In demonstrating the power of the law in creating a new legitimate understanding of the breakdown of some social relationships, the study of courtroom discourse unveils the ideological dimension of the law.

It also shows the dramatic shift from the Maoist emphasis on reconciling marriage conflicts to the new belief that some marriages will inevitably dissolve and therefore the terms for ending a marriage must be negotiated. This shift has occurred because the courts, facing increasing caseloads and limited resources, have had to identify a convenient legal solution for a question that is sociological in nature, as seen in the cases analyzed. In some nongovernmental organizations or in programs run by the All-China Women's Federation, one may see a more therapeutic discourse rooted in the ideas of social work and human rights, but courtroom discourse is dominated by a pragmatic approach aimed not at repairing a broken relationship or instantiating a moral code but at finding a solution.

This genre of discourse is not completely different from the settlement language that other scholars have documented in the existing literature (Greatbatch and Dingwall 1989; Merry 1990; Trinder, Firth and Jenks 2010), but the pragmatic discourse identified in China is tied to Chinese courts' institutional contexts. While there is no denying that the use of settlement language in China is also driven by the practical demands for efficiency, there are many other factors favoring pragmatic discourse. As our analysis has demonstrated, it is a type of discourse derived from the institutional pressure on the courts to provide solutions in a society where traditional values and moral standards are losing ground. As such, it is as much a discourse that pushes for settlement as a meta-discourse that explicitly articulates why settlement is a better option for women. It thus uncovers the ways in which judicial mediation masks the assertion of power over litigants despite ideological claims otherwise. It argues that formally gender-neutral legal orders nonetheless reinforce gender hierarchies. Despite their effort to protect women's rights, judges often inadvertently reinforce and perpetuate patriarchal norms and values that render women as passive recipients of their marital fates. As seen in the analysis, the effort of this pragmatic approach is particularly damaging for women who are economically and socially most vulnerable.

4

Trivializing Domestic Violence

Living in physical security is the most basic human right of civilized society (*Custody of Vaughn* 1995; Schepard 2004: 85). Many Chinese women, however, have not secured this basic right. According to an official report, domestic violence exists in about one-third of Chinese families (*Xinhua News* 2009). An official survey reported that a quarter of Chinese women are victims of domestic abuse (Zhou 2016; CCTV 2017). A 2013 United Nations study finds that 50 percent of men in China had used physical or sexual violence against an intimate partner (citing Fincher 2014: 146). Although anyone can be a victim of domestic abuse, almost 90 percent of reported cases involve women experiencing abuse from their husbands (SPC Information Center 2018). Domestic violence also accounts for 60 percent of registered divorces (*China Daily* 2003). Indeed, one of the fastest growing, and most socially vulnerable, groups of civil litigants has been battered women seeking relief from spousal abuse. This is reflected in the prevalence of claims of domestic violence in divorce petitions. The SPC (2017) reports that 14.86 percent of divorce litigation is triggered by domestic violence, constituting the second-most cited reason for filing for divorce. Another SPC Report (2014) suggested almost 10 percent of intentional homicide occurred as a result of domestic violence. According to Wu (2007: 203), who reviewed 310 divorce cases from 1950 to 2004 from a county in southern China, in almost all of the cases the wives had alleged that they had been abused by their husbands.

However, domestic violence is rarely recognized by the courts, let alone compensated for its impacts (Palmer 2017). An empirical study (Chen and Duan 2012) based on all family cases filed in one district court in Chongqing, in western China, suggests that of all 458 cases involving claims of domestic violence, victims were only compensated in only three (0.66 percent) of them. Among all domestic violence evidence presented in cases handled by the intermediate courts in Beijing, only 17.3 percent were admitted (Gao 2016). Michelson (2019), based on 150,000 adjudication documents released by the Chinese courts, finds that a claim of domestic violence by plaintiffs does not increase their chance of obtaining a divorce.

Kim Lee, the former wife of Li Yang, the founder of Crazy English, speaks of the court approach as follows (Fincher 2014: 152):

> They would go to court and the husband would say, "She just fell off her bike" or "She bumped into a door." And the women would say, but I have here the police report. But the police report just says "family conflict"; it doesn't say domestic violence or that he beat her. Even when women have evidence in court, the judge just dismisses it.

Why were so few claims recognized or awarded compensation in divorce litigation? All these occurred despite progress in the development of China's laws against domestic violence. In this chapter, I will illustrate how the incentives to which the judges are subject have trumped the promises of the law. I will first document the evolution of domestic violence laws in China, showing remarkable progress in terms of legislative protections. Then, I focus on both mediation and adjudication, the two approaches judges take in dealing with domestic violence. The issue of domestic violence disappears during the mediation session, even if the judge is convinced that it exists; the situation is more favorable for cases that end in adjudicated decisions, but not by much. Evidence of domestic violence is often dismissed in the adjudicated decisions; even evidence of domestic violence established in the first trial is often reversed at the appellate level. In addition, the threat of domestic violence is often ignored when a court delays its decision to grant divorce for obviously irreconcilable marriages. The Personal Safety Protection Order, a newly launched mechanism, is far from realizing its potential. Overall, courts in China offer little help to victims of domestic violence.

Progress Under Domestic Violence Laws in China

A review of China's legal developments regarding domestic violence reveals that some progress has been made on this issue. Historically, battered women who take their cases to court have faced many difficulties. Law enforcement officers in China are not particularly concerned with domestic violence complaints (Liu 2001: 6–7; cited by Merry 2006: 149). They classify these complaints as "spousal quarrels" or "family trouble." In part because of the Confucian belief in social harmony and in part because of the Chinese reluctance to interfere in the "family matters" of others, there has been a general reluctance on the part of family members, friends, coworkers, and relatives to testify against violent husbands or to testify as witnesses in court (Xu 2006a, 2006b). "Even brothers and sisters of the abused woman may feel intervention [is] inappropriate" (Liu 2001: 6–7; cited by Merry 2006: 149). According to Fincher (2014: 141), there is a web of abuse in China, and the catchphrase "don't expose family ugliness" is commonly invoked to avoid addressing the issue.

Regardless, domestic violence has become an increasingly serious social problem in China, so much so that it has made it into the government's official agenda and public discourse. For example, in 2008 Sun Xiaomei, an NPC deputy and professor at the Chinese Women's College, said: "Domestic violence is a social phenomenon that crosses all social strata and is becoming more and more common. There is an urgent need for legislation" (Zhou 2016). In 2010, the state-backed All-China Women's Federation, announced that its branches nationwide had received 52,000 petitions from female victims of domestic violence (*China Daily* 2012). It further declared that "domestic violence poses a severe threat to women's rights in China" (*Xinhua News* 2009).

While gender equality has long been hailed by China as a fundamental social goal, the phrase "domestic violence" did not appear in Chinese law until 2001, when the Marriage Law was revised. In the SPC's 2001 Interpretation of the new Marriage Law, "domestic violence" was defined as behavior toward a member of the family that results in injurious consequences physically, emotionally, or in other ways by "beating, tying up, injuring, forcibly restricting one's personal freedom, or by other means" (Wang 2014: 182). Article 3 of the law prohibits domestic violence. Article 32 states that divorce shall be granted by the courts if domestic violence, or maltreatment and desertion of one family member by another, is found. Article 46 stipulates that the innocent party is entitled to compensation for damage in divorces resulting from domestic violence. The revised Marriage Law also provides a recourse, albeit a narrow one, to civil litigation for battered women.

The early 2000s saw an avalanche of legal provisions promoting gender equality. They have appeared in national laws, including the Law Protecting Women's Rights and Interests, the Law Protecting the Rights and Interests of Minors, the Law Protecting the Rights and Interests of the Aged, and the Law Protecting the Disabled. In addition, the promulgation of SPC's 2008 Guidelines for Hearing Marriage Cases Involving Domestic Violence represents a stride forward in the protection of women's interests and the fight against domestic violence in particular. The Guidelines incorporate many best internal experiences against domestic violence. For example, contrary to the general principle of burden of proof in civil justice, the burden shifts to men to prove their innocence as long as women claim that the men's behavior results in injuries (Art. 40). Although the Guidelines do not have legal force, they encourage courts to follow their reasoning (Preamble). Provincial legislation also mushroomed during this period. "By September 2008, 20 provinces, municipalities, and autonomous regions in China had adopted legal mechanisms to combat domestic violence. In addition, by October 2008, 23 provinces, municipalities, and autonomous regions had passed enforcement plans for the national Law on the Protection of Women's Rights and Interests, specifically addressing domestic violence" (Runge 2015: 35).

Two decades of intensive lobbying by women's rights groups and the All-China Women's Federation, which advocates for stronger legal protections for victims of domestic violence, culminated in the Anti-Domestic Violence Law, which was promulgated in 2015. This stand-alone domestic violence legislation is widely regarded as "a substantial step forward in the social and legal sense that it offers a firm official acceptance that domestic violence is a serious issue, and that domestic violence is a form of deviant conduct that may no longer be characterized in China as a private matter" (Palmer 2017: 310). Symbolically, it declares that "the state prohibits domestic violence in any form." It is also a major improvement to prior legislation such as the Law Protecting Women's Rights and Interests, which failed to provide tangible legal relief for victims. The ADV Law delivers a range of new legal protection measures. Chief among them is China's first statutory definition of domestic violence in national law. Article 2 states that "domestic violence" refers to "any physical and emotional abuse in the form of beating, bounding, maiming, restricting personal freedom, and frequent reviling, threatening between family members." This broad definition of domestic violence covers "psychological abuse" and "encompasses cohabitating non-family members" (Palmer 2017: 311).

Most noteworthy is the Personal Safety Protection Order for victims who "suffer or face the danger of domestic violence." According to this mechanism, Palmer (2017: 311) states that "public security organs (Art. 20) and medical bodies are required to produce evidence of abuse (Art. 7) upon the request of a court." "The court must make a prompt decision on an application (Art. 28) for protection against domestic abuse, although the application must have a clear respondent and contain specific details of the protection required." Also, courts require evidence that there has been, or that there will be, domestic violence (Art. 27). Protection orders can forbid the respondent from harassing, stalking, or contacting the applicant or force the respondent to move out of the applicant's neighborhood (Art. 27). State organizations and relevant bodies must help the court in enforcement (Art. 32). Penalties for noncompliance could be as high as 1,000-yuan fines, detention for 15 days, and even criminal charges (Art. 36). In 2015, the SPC, together with the Ministry of Public Security, the Ministry of Justice, and the Supreme Procuratorate, issued the Opinion on How to Handle Domestic Violence Crimes, a concerted effort to combat such crimes.

Doctrinally, these regulations represent steps toward protecting vulnerable women and children facing abuse. In response to the newfound attention to domestic violence, it now seems that China is taking legal steps to protect women from domestic violence. Despite several inadequacies and criticisms, such an achievement for a country engrained with the culture of gender hierarchy is remarkable, if not unprecedented: from no mention of domestic violence in 2000 to stand-alone domestic violence legislation in 2015. Two questions, however, remain: How do judges respond to issues related to domestic violence and To what extent are victims' rights protected?

Addressing Domestic Violence through Mediation

The trivialization of domestic violence is most conspicuous when a divorce case is ended through mediation. Despite much scholarly criticism on its role (Palmer 2017: 312–13; Han 2017; He and Ng 2013b), the 2015 ADV Law still allows mediation to end a divorce petition alleging domestic violence claims. Indeed, empirical evidence (Chen and Duan 2012: 31) suggests that in these cases the combined rates of mediation and voluntary withdrawal have been as high as 62 percent.

As mentioned above, mediation can mean voluntary withdrawal, mediated divorce, or mediated reconciliation. Voluntary withdrawal often means that petitioners are not granted a divorce the first time; if they insist on divorce, they have to submit a new petition, which is very often the case. The legal effect of voluntary withdrawal is the same as an adjudicated denial. For the judge, however, it means a mediated case. A mediated divorce, put simply, means the dissolution of divorce proceedings: both parties agree to a divorce and to related matters such as compensation, custody, and support. It is the same as an adjudicated divorce. However, mediated reconciliation suggests that both parties have reconciled and continue to live as a couple. In these cases, domestic violence is not an issue for the court. The remainder of this section contains a discussion of voluntary withdrawal and mediated divorce to demonstrate that, underneath the various dynamics, lies the same rationale from the judge.

Voluntary Withdrawal

If the case is voluntarily withdrawn, the issues of domestic violence often go unnoticed, as if they had never occurred. Since legally the couple remain a family, there is no need for monetary compensation. The judge may orally educate or persuade the perpetrators of harm to stop the violence, but that is it. No legal consequences are ensured.

In the Shanghai Migrant Worker's Case, a woman in her twenties sued for divorce for the first time, alleging that her mother-in-law had beaten her, and citing the incompatibility of the married couple's personalities. The twenty-seven-year-old husband, a chef earning 2,600 yuan per month, resisted. He had a deaf and unemployed elder brother and a mentally ill mother. Given his family situation, it would have been difficult for him, once divorced, to find another wife. Since his wife had left Shaanxi for Shanghai as a migrant worker two years before, the judge suspected that she might have had an affair, thus leaving her burdened family behind.

The real reason, as revealed by her lawyer, however, was that "the boy has that kind of disease [implying impotency], and could not have a normal sex life. As a young man, the way he had released his desires had been to scratch her genitals. The harm was so serious that at one point the girl could not walk. But the girl had been unable to speak up for herself." The judge was not convinced until the man requested that his wife return home with him. She became agitated: "We fight every night. Do you believe we can live together? I feel scared when I see you now!" The man's face froze in embarrassment.

Yet, the judge did nothing to pursue the issue of domestic violence. After all, domestic violence was not the girl's main concern. The petition letter did mention domestic violence from the mother-in-law, but what the wife really wanted was a divorce. For the judge, the goal was to find a solution to close the case. Any other distractions were to be avoided. With little deliberation, the judge explained her decision to the wife's lawyer:

> No way will this marriage persist, but this time she cannot get a divorce. We must respect the husband's last dignity. Even though his request has little legal basis, at this moment we cannot wipe out the hope of his whole family. We have to maintain the form of this marriage. This is to give the husband's family some time, to be psychologically prepared to lose this lady.

This case ended in voluntary withdrawal. Of course, it was not voluntary; it resulted from the judge's coercion. The judge seemed convinced of the presence of domestic violence, although she had not conducted any further investigation. She had already made a denial decision. Any investigation into domestic violence committed by either the mother-in-law or the husband, for whatever reasons, seemed unnecessary to the judge. Nothing was done to fix the problem: no protection order and no written reports were issued.[1] Upon hearing the judge's coercive suggestion, the wife and her lawyer cooperated, as do most litigants in rural areas.

If the issue of domestic violence is not addressed in cases withdrawn under pressure from a judge, it also goes unnoticed in cases that are genuinely withdrawn. In the Singapore Laborer's Case, the wife, out of pragmatic concerns mentioned by the judges, withdrew her case voluntarily. In their conversation, she detailed a beating that had occurred during the Spring Festival when her husband had returned from Singapore:

> The trigger was money. We always fight on this issue: I want him to remit the money directly to me instead of his father. On the date of the beating, he had returned home late in the evening after getting drunk. The children were asleep when he kicked the door. After I opened the door for him, he kicked all the boxes around him and stepped on the girls' toys while cursing at me. I asked him to lower his voice so as not to wake up our neighbors. He then threw a cup at me, which broke after I dodged it. The noise woke up my elder daughter. Staring at us from her room, she was trembling. He then vilified the girl, saying "I will kill you all," and tried to break down the girls' door. I blocked him with my body and this was the moment he started beating me. His fists were on my face and his hands pulled my hair. I did not fight back because I was trying to protect the children. The beating stopped only when he became exhausted and went to his room to sleep. That night I stayed in the children's room, crying with the two girls. The second day, I found my face swollen and both eyes [were] red with blood. I rested for three days before I was able to step out of my door.

According to the wife, the real reason for the beating was that she had not given birth to a boy. Whatever the causes, the judge was not interested in the alleged domestic violence. She did not pursue the death threat uttered by the husband that "I will kill you all"; nor did she investigate the swollen face or bruised eyes, as claimed by the woman. Her subsequent question was straightforward: "Are you able to afford to raise the two girls yourself after the divorce?" After sobbing and deliberating, the woman, who worked part-time as a supermarket cashier, decided to withdraw the case. Any narratives from the woman on domestic violence vanished. Not even a trace of this issue could be found in the case files.

The judge was skillful. She had guided the woman to consider her vulnerable economic capability, assuming that upon being divorced she would have to support herself and the two children alone. What the judge did not mention was that the court could have, according to the law, adjudicated a divorce for the couple. At the same time, it could have required the husband, who had a respectable income in Singapore, to provide child support. Had the woman been informed of this option, she might not have withdrawn the case. However, that suggestion would have been silly, since instead of eliminating a case it would have created a new one.

The only difference between these two types of "voluntary" withdrawal is the degree of resistance that the judge may encounter. In a reluctantly withdrawn case, the judge might be unable to persuade the litigant to accept the withdrawal decision. That was why, in the Shanghai Migrant Worker's Case, the judge first explained the decision to the woman's lawyer, who was a known player in divorce litigation and was in a better position to appreciate the judge's concerns. In a genuinely withdrawn case, there is little resistance. The woman in the Singapore Laborer's Case chose to withdraw the case after deliberating her financial capabilities. The judge's suggestion was impactful. Nonetheless, in cases ended through withdrawal, either voluntarily or reluctantly, the judge's approach toward domestic violence is the same: inaction, as if all claims fall on deaf ears. The judges' rationale is straightforward: as long as the litigating parties are willing to withdraw the case, this is the best outcome for the court, so why bother? Judges are supposed to find solutions to close cases, not to incite further disputes.

Mediated Divorce

In mediated divorces, the issue of domestic violence was also ignored or disappeared as an issue, even if the court had established its existence. In the 100 Yuan Case, the couple had been separated for several years and the husband was now living with another woman, and there was evidence that the husband had committed domestic violence and had engaged in extramarital affairs: the wife provided police reports and pictures of bruises. The two agreed to divorce; their disputes were mainly over how to divide their home (which had been in both of their names) and assign their responsibilities toward their son. The thirteen-year-old son had been living with his mother. As in many other divorce cases, the estranged husband and wife were fighting over various accusations throughout the court's investigation process. The atmosphere was tense and confrontational in the first hour of the trial. As if she had intended to prevent the confrontation from escalating, the judge quickly moved to mediation without formally announcing that the investigation and discussion stages were over. In fact, she did not formally ask the two parties if they would agree to participate in mediation, as most judges would typically ask at the end of the discussion. In this case, the judge started working on a settlement as soon as she knew that the two sides had no intention to remain in the failing marriage. After about thirty minutes of negotiations with the couple, the judge worked out a number indicating the sum of money the wife would receive after renouncing her half-interest in the property.

In addition to the disagreement over dividing the property, the couple also disagreed over the amount of child support to be paid. The plaintiff was willing to pay 500 yuan per month, but his wife (the defendant in this case) sought more. She asked for monthly child support payments of 800 yuan. The judge quickly decided her goal would be to get the two sides to settle on 600 yuan. To the judge's surprise, the plaintiff refused to raise his offer to make up the 100 yuan difference (approximately $15 per month). This put the judge in a predicament. She had already revealed to both parties a compromise figure that she determined to be acceptable, cutting the wife's request by 200 yuan. She had thought this could get the deal done, but the plaintiff's recalcitrance created an impasse.

In order to make a deal, as detailed in He and Ng (2013b), the judge marshaled all sorts of resources available to convince the man. She mentioned that the money would be used to support his son, not a stranger; she also mentioned that as his son was already thirteen years old and that the overall amount of support was not a big sum because the man was responsible for child support only until the age of eighteen; she even challenged the truthfulness of the man's salary, which according to the law had been used as the basis for calculating the amount of child support; and finally she preached to the man that it was his duty as a father to support his son. What was most revealing for our purposes was that the judge never mentioned domestic violence. Shouldn't the man have been held responsible for his abusive behavior, as stipulated by Article 46 of the amended Marriage Law? Could this not have been leveraged to coerce the man to agree to raise his child support payments by 100 yuan?

The above approach is not exceptional. In the Saleswoman's Case quoted at the beginning of this book, the judge successfully proved the existence of domestic violence during the hearing. However, at the mediation stage, when the judge managed to "mediate" the case between a confrontational couple full of mutual hatred, domestic violence was never mentioned (He and Ng 2013b). In another case documented by Wu (2007: 277–81), the wife repeatedly raised the issue of domestic violence and presented police reports indicating she had suffered minor injuries. The husband denied the link between the injuries and his behavior. The wife privately said to the judge during mediation: "I dared not disclose anything to anyone outside of the family. Sometimes I was all beat up and bruised. But when other people asked me how I got my bruises, I just said that it was because I fell. I dared not even tell the truth to my own parents." The judge responded: "If both sides can reach a settlement, we will ask you to sign the mediation agreement. If not, the court will adjudicate. We will try our best. The mediation ends here."

This conversation shows that the judge did not even broach the topic of domestic violence as raised by the wife. In mediation, as the term suggests, the two parties had tried to arrive at a voluntary resolution. The judge, who was now acting as a mediator, had removed the adjudicatory frame that looks for fault and denounces wrongful behavior. The judge, in order to achieve a mediated result, had been careful to maintain a less antagonistic atmosphere. Further allegations of domestic abuse would have invited more denials or refutations from the man and would have compromised her efforts to mediate. In other words, to get a mediation result, the judge had to exclude blame from her discourse.

The solution-oriented mind-set of judges is pronounced even when a crime is detected in divorce litigation. They do not report the criminal activities. Instead, they use the crime as a bargaining chip to facilitate a settlement. In the Attempted Rape Case, a lorry driver had sued for divorce a second time when he claimed his twenty-five-year-old wife had not returned home over a year. The husband had been left alone with their baby, who had been born with a disease that needed costly operations every other year. He also alleged that she was also lazy and did not do any housework. Both parties agreed to divorce but fought over custody (see chapter 5, on custody) and property. The wife insisted on 80,000 yuan land requisition compensation, which represented her share. The husband's family, however, agreed to compensate her only 10,000 yuan and insisted on child support from the wife should custody be awarded to him.

Unlike most divorcing wives, this woman was energetic. Short but stocky, she had a healthy tan on her round face. It was hard to believe that she was lazy, as the husband had claimed. Her chest vibrated as she talked. The wife later told the judge in private that her father-in-law had attempted to rape her twice and that this was why she had been so persistent in her requests. The fact that she had been wronged seemed clear from her facial expressions. The judge discussed this with the husband's legal representative. The husband's family immediately compromised and struck a settlement: the husband's family agreed to pay 40,000 yuan, and no ruling for child support was made.

Again, the judge's focus was on forcing a solution. Being raped by a family member, successful or not, is a heinous crime. At the very least, it is also regarded as domestic violence according to the ADV Law. However, the judge had no intention to verify this allegation. The father-in-law did not appear in court. From the fact that the family members always called the father-in-law for instructions, it was clear that he was a physically and mentally strong man. This is also why the initial mediation had been a stalemate. The allegation of an attempted rape, however, became a bargaining chip for the judge to coerce this man to budge.

Many couples are willing to endure judge-directed mediation, not so much because they want to stay together but because the judge pushes for it and there is still much to bargain over with their estranged spouse. The mediation session usually focuses on the division of child custody and marital property. However, in this process, it is almost inevitable that the issue on domestic violence is erased. As suggested by Han (2017), in court proceedings involving family disputes such as divorce (as well as in earlier judicial pilot projects on protection orders), judges have been known to be under pressure to "overlook and downplay" spousal abuse and instead push for judicial mediation. The pervasive use of mediation by the courts has been criticized as failing to assign blame and punish abusers, thereby leading to the continuation of long-term abuse against women in China.

The Judge's Rationale

The above analysis shows that in China, despite domestic violence being raised, discussed, and even established in the court investigation process, the issue is eventually forgotten, often disappearing during the mediation session. When domestic violence is examined during the investigation stage, the litigating parties are confrontational. It is common for parties to trade accusations, insults, and denials. If the judge still focuses on issues of domestic violence, it can undermine the reconciliatory tone required to facilitate a successful settlement. It is for this reason that sweeping domestic violence under the rug is a consequence of mediation.

Evolving from court investigation to court mediation thus involves a process Cobb (1997) has called "transformation." During the investigation stage, the rules are legalistic, focusing on rights and obligations, and based on the availability of evidence; but in the mediation stage, the rules are mediatory, focusing on needs. In mediation, the rules soon dominate and expand courts' authority and jurisdiction, crowding out concerns over legal rights and moral blaming. Cobb (1997: 413) points out: "The goal of mediation is to reach agreements, to meet the needs of individuals, not instantiate a moral code. In fact, mediation is designed to subsume moral differences by colonizing competing moralities: There is no 'right' way to live, except that morality which permits and enforces relativism." The rights-based focus prevailing in domestic violence investigations is now superseded by the needs-based focus of mediation.

Also, as demonstrated by Fineman (1988) in her analysis of custody mediation, the rights of parents collapse into the needs of the children through the discourse fostered by the "best interest" doctrine. Because the goal of mediation is to reach agreement, it has to meet the needs of the individuals, and therefore the overall discourse is pragmatic. Indeed, as Silbey and Sarat (1989) note, mediation legitimates itself as a practice by distinguishing between rights and needs: rights discourse is suitable for formal settings in which hierarchy and power are at issue; needs discourse is suitable for mediation where it is not power, but rather participation, that is at issue. The mediation session offers a setting for both disputants, as coparticipants with equal social and legal status, in the resolution of conflict. In this process, any violence, including domestic violence (especially if it is still subject to dispute because of a lack of evidence and vague legal stipulations), has to make room for relational and economic security. Thus, it has to be sidelined to the point of disappearing entirely from the proceedings.

Internationally, the mediation of family disputes where violence is present has long been controversial because of its perceived impact on victim safety (Greatbatch and Dingwall 1989). Common concerns include mediation's failure to account for the power disparity between victims and their abusers, as well as questions of coercion as a result of victims' fear and intimidation that are often present in abusive relationships. Western researchers have found that in community-based mediation sessions, domestic violence is often marginalized (Lerman 1984; Rifkin 1984; Sarat and Kearns 1991; Cobb 1997; Greatbatch and Dingwall 1989). By "marginalization," Greatbatch and Dingwall (1989: 187) mean that violence reports are "ignored or minimized," and events are framed as "relational as opposed to criminal." The situation is no better in court-based mediation programs. As Trinder et al.'s (2010) study of the English system found, family-justice professionals continue to marginalize allegations of domestic violence, sometimes even becoming punitive in cases where women insist on pursuing the issue.

If anything, the situation in China is more serious for two reasons. First, since it is the judge who mediates in China, she is entitled to adopt a more interventionist approach to sideline allegations of domestic violence. Compared to what is discussed as marginalization (Greatbatch and Dingwall 1989) or domestication (Cobb 1997), the erasure of domestic violence in China is more coercive; this is in part a result of the obvious power gap between the judge and the disputants. Judges are aggressive and proactive in setting a mediatory tone, compared to the subtler handling by mediators in community mediations. Second, from the perspective of the victims, the process is deceptive. This is because of the presence of judicial mediation within a framework of adjudication.

Victims who choose to settle their cases might think they have sought legal redress, but in fact they have unknowingly surrendered their legal rights in agreeing to a mediated deal. Moreover, in going through judicial mediation, they have already exhausted all their legal remedies and are left with no recourse. The Chinese government has finally come to realize the seriousness of domestic violence as a social issue. However, its judicial infrastructure, caught between the conflicting goals of achieving efficiency and protecting the socially vulnerable, is structurally incapable of addressing the issue in a systematic and comprehensive way.

Dismissing Evidence during Adjudication

A prevalent view for explaining the low recognition of and the low compensation for domestic violence is that the victims are unable to provide sufficient evidence (Gao 2016). However, according to Zhang (2018), 47 percent of victims do provide some form of evidence. As mentioned, only 17.3 percent of the submitted evidence is admitted (Gao 2016). Personal statements explaining the abuse suffered, the most commonly used form of evidence, have largely been ignored because they are one-sided and are frequently refuted by the other party. The next question, then, is: What criteria do the courts adopt in admitting evidence pertaining to domestic evidence?

In general, the burden of proof in civil cases rests with the claimants: he who makes the claims shall prove them (Art. 63 of the Civil Procedural Law). The standard is that as long as the claims are more likely than not, they shall be regarded as proven. On the issue of domestic violence, however, the SPC Guidelines on Hearing Marriage Cases Involving Domestic Violence (2008) provide that victims' statements are more trustworthy than defendants' statements (Art. 41). After the plaintiff provides evidence of injury and claims that it is a result of the defendant's actions, the burden of proof is shifted to the defendant (Art. 40).

The SPC Guidelines are promulgated by the Applied Legal Institute, a nonadjudicatory department under the SPC. Legally speaking, the Guidelines are not formal judicial Interpretations issued by the SPC: at most they are a directive from an organization subordinate to the

SPC. They are not law, and the judges are not obliged to follow them; some say that they are not even allowed to cite them explicitly in their judgements. According to the current rule of evidence, if a victim cannot provide strong evidence (e.g., a medical certificate of the injuries suffered and/or police reports), she is not considered to have satisfied the burden of proof required for convicting an alleged abusive husband. In these cases, most courts are left with no option but to disregard the existence of domestic violence (Huang 2010: 133–34). At any rate, this is an area in which the judges enjoy much discretion. The law does not specify to what kind of abuse rises to the level of domestic violence. Are all light injuries to be regarded as domestic violence? Is a single beating enough? If not, how many times is sufficient? For how long? None of these questions are specified by the law but instead are left to the discretion of judges. Furthermore, judges also enjoy discretion over whether to collect evidence themselves. The Civil Procedural Law states that the claimants are to provide evidence for claims, but judges can take their own initiative in collecting evidence when they deem it necessary. Regardless, nowadays courts rarely collect evidence outside of the courtroom (He 2009a; Huang 2010; Woo 2003).

Left with this discretion, how do judges adjudicate claims of domestic violence? The following episode (the Case of the Coerced Video) was taken from a trial in the Pearl River Delta, a pilot region for combating domestic violence. The wife claimed that the husband had beaten her on numerous occasions. She presented the police records, medical reports, and photos of her injuries. However, her husband, a college professor, was determined to fight every claim. With medical reports and photos of his own injuries, he claimed that it had been she who had beaten him. When asked by the judge to detail the incident, the woman said:

He complained that I shut the door too loud, and it could damage the door. Thus we had a quarrel. He then pointed his finger at my head, which had always been the precursor to beating. I dodged his hands and ran away to the living room. He chased me and beat me five times with his fists. Then, holding my hair, he hit my head against the ground. My forehead had been swollen, which I had shown to the judge when I applied for the protection order. I then held up a chair to repel him, until the community security guard arrived.

The man responded, "Yes! When I pointed my finger at her, she threw books at me. I ducked. She then threw at me whatever was available. I tried to stop her, and she picked up the chair."

When the judge asked him where the injuries on her head and forehead had come from, he first said that he did not know. He then said: "It was she who scratched me and injured me. I have a photo to prove it. I did not beat her. I may have injured her when I was defending myself."

In this conversation, despite the woman's detailed descriptions, the man framed himself as the victim. Avoiding the woman's point that "he chased me and beat me five times with his fist," he said "she used the books to beat me" and "she then threw at me whatever possible" and "she picked up the chair." He denied all the injuries claimed by the woman, even though he could not explain how the injuries to her forehead and head had occurred. He only suggested that he might have injured her in self-defense. Apparently, the judge had not elicited any confession from the husband. When asked about each of the plaintiff's injuries, he either said "I do not know" or "I did not see it." Obviously, this man was cunning and difficult. Moreover, he was sophisticated enough to have kept the medical reports of his own injures such as bruises and cuts on his forearms, chest, and fingers caused by biting and stabbing.

Nonetheless, the evidence presented by the wife was more compelling. The record suggests that the wife had called the police after being beaten by her husband, resulting in a swollen head. Her medical reports show that the skin on her right leg, left knee, and left elbow had turned green and purple, and there were injuries to soft tissue all over her body. There were also bruises on her left pinky and swelling on her head. The majority of her injuries were from hitting and beating. The husband's injuries were more likely to have resulted from the wife's attempts at self-defense.

Moreover, the judge had testimony favoring the woman. While she had not conducted a thorough investigation of the couple's neighbors or work units, as had the earlier generation of Chinese divorce judges, she did have five pieces of testimony from the litigants and their son. These addressed issues of child custody and domestic violence. The following is an excerpt from the judge's interview of their eleven-year-old son:

JUDGE: Has your mother been injured before?

SON: Yes. Normally, my father would push her on the ground and kick her. My mother's head was injured.

JUDGE: Do your parents beat you?

SON: Yes. Both of them.

JUDGE: How do they beat you?

SON: My mom usually beats my hands with chopsticks, and my father hits my face with his palm.

JUDGE: Are the beatings rough?

SON: My father hits me hard. He once hit my head against the wall.

JUDGE: How often does your father hit you like this?

SON: Not much. But in another instance, he hit my head against the ground.

The judge was professional: her questions covered whether there had been a beating, how it had occurred, the frequency, and who had been the most violent. Overall, the son's testimony suggested that that his father was more violent than his mother. He had "pushed her on the ground and kicked her." Following a similar pattern, he had also beaten his son, hitting his head against the wall and the ground, while the mother had only "used chopsticks to beat my hands."

Indeed, as shown in another testimony recorded two months later, when the husband had learned that the son preferred to stay with his mother, the husband had beaten the son and coerced him into shooting a video saying that he wanted to stay with his father.

It is true that the evidence favoring the woman was not overwhelming. The man had also recorded the injuries made in "self-defense," thus countervailing the effectiveness and validity of his wife's evidence. However, it is more likely that the husband had indeed committed domestic violence: physically he was strong; the woman's serious injuries were difficult to explain by self-defense; and the son's testimony also indicated that "my father hit me hard." The son's testimony was more compelling, since he was a neutral party; unless coerced or guided, he had little incentive to lie about the situation. According to the SPC Guidelines (2008), this kind of evidence is to be given "critical weight." Even according to the rules on the burden of proof for civil trials, this should have been enough to rule in the woman's favor.

Eventually, the judge courageously granted the divorce and awarded custody to the wife, even though this had been the first petition for divorce. She had been sympathetic to the wife and the son and had wanted to free them from the violent family environment as soon as possible. Yet, the judge did not acknowledge the presence of domestic violence. The judge told me her rationale:

> The reason for not acknowledging domestic violence, in short, is that the husband is such a troublemaker and difficult person. We often call this kind of litigant who warrants our special attention "the VIP." My thoughts were that a divorce and a custody decision for the wife would free the wife and the son from the violent environment. Without acknowledging domestic violence, I hoped that the husband, without wearing the hat of a violent abuser, would be less resistant to the decisions, and would let go of the wife and the child.

This episode reveals the balance that a judge often strikes. She had already granted two victories for the wife: divorce and custody. It was better to allow the man to have regained some face on the issue of domestic violence. She hoped that the man could accept such an outcome without appealing the decision. If he had lost all three battles, the husband, as sophisticated and violent as he was, would almost certainly have appealed the decision. It was a pragmatic compromise because the main concern for the wife was to leave the man and live a more peaceful life with her son. Had the judge recognized domestic violence and supported all the woman's requests, the man could have prolonged the proceedings with various procedural tactics, and the outcome may have been more miserable for the wife. Such a concern was not baseless. Indeed, as it turned out, the man was still unhappy about the custody decision, and he appealed. The appellate judge, as detailed later in chapter 5, reversed the trial court's decision and awarded him custody of the child. The genuine reason for the reversal was that the appellate judge did not want to offend the man. Despite their different decisions on child custody, both judges shared the same approach to the issue of domestic violence: the concern to pacify and soothe the man, because an acceptable decision for both parties trumps the legal criteria for domestic violence. Thus, the social effects supersede the legal effects, and the legal rules yield to the institutional constraints that judges face.

This trial, which occurred in a pilot area promoting measures against domestic violence, is not typical of common practices in Chinese courts. The situation in other areas of China, as far as the recognition of domestic violence goes, is even more tilted against women. A Shaanxi judge told me that she handles domestic violence only if it occurs during the court trial process or right after the trial. Incidents occurring before the trial would be regarded as one only factor in weighing whether the emotional relationship had disintegrated. Some judges would regard a dispute as if it had never happened once a petition was withdrawn by a plaintiff (Wang 2016: 52, citing Michelson 2018: 48). According to Zhang (2018), judges are reluctant to recognize the existence of domestic evidence, even when victims have provided substantial evidence. A judgment excerpt read:

> The court investigation finds: . . . on September 24, 2014, the plaintiff and the defendant were having a conflict. During the mutual pushing, the defendant hit the plaintiff once on the face, causing her face to swell and changing the colour on the right side. . . . The court held: in this case, the evidence provided by the plaintiff to the court can only prove there was one beating, and the beating did not lead to serious consequences. It is an example of a routine quarrel or occasional fighting between a couple, and thus will not be regarded as domestic violence.

Zhang (2018) commented that "the court dismissed the domestic violence claim because the beating had occurred only 'once,' even though the beating led to a swollen face with the color changed. Is this consequence not serious enough?" Zhang (2018) further found that in another case, the court had dismissed the harm (appraised as "light injury" by a judicial appraisal institution) as inadequate to establish domestic violence because, again, "it did not lead to serious consequences," even though the injuries would have fulfilled the standards for criminal liability. In another case, the judge even disregarded a "Domestic Violence Warning Letter" issued by the police in addition to the police report and also ruled that the evidence for domestic violence was insufficient

(Zhang 2018: 107–08). According to his study, most judges do not take the victims' statements seriously. Furthermore, in the 13 percent of cases involving domestic violence claims, judges paid little attention to other, more solid evidence provided by the victims.

Michelson (2018) documented poignant examples of the courts' refusal to recognize domestic violence. Take one example from Chun'an County, Zhejiang Province: in this case, the plaintiff claimed her husband frequently "beat her black and blue." In particular, she alleged that on May 28, 2014, her husband had beaten her ruthlessly (死命打), after which she called 110 for help (the equivalent of 911 in the United States) and the next day sought assistance from the All-China Women's Federation. She went on to claim that on July 8, 2014, the defendant almost choked her to death and that he released his hands from her throat only when she bit his hand. She submitted medical documentation as evidence to support her claims of domestic violence. The defendant challenged the evidence by arguing that it failed to prove he had caused the injury in question and that she was the one who had started it in the first place when she had rubbed food in his face, obscuring his vision (Michelson 2018: 46).

The court nonetheless ruled "no divorce" for this petition. While the record does not explicitly mention whether the court recognized domestic violence, it can be assumed that it did not because domestic violence is a statutory reason for divorce. "No divorce" implies "no domestic violence." The decision was made despite medical documentation of her claims, including that he "almost choked her to death," in addition to records from the police and the Women's Federation. It is not because the victims do not provide evidence; it is because the judges are reluctant to take into account the evidence. Similar to US judges, they tend to be "discounting women" (Epstein and Goodman 2018), though for different reasons.

A Rare "Success"

Among all the cases I encountered during my fieldwork, in only one was domestic violence recognized, at least at the trial stage. The rarity of this speaks to the courts' difficulty in recognizing the existence of domestic violence. Even in this case, I have to place quotation marks around "success" because the victim's victory was eventually reversed by the appellate court. While under certain circumstances a victim may have a chance to win the battle over domestic violence, such conditions are rare. This case demonstrates how courts fail to enforce laws protecting women's interests.

In the Fish Retailer's Case, the plaintiff, a thirty-eight-year-old woman, sued to divorce her husband, a fish retailer, mainly because "he beat her numerous times." Prior to this marriage, she had been married to a drug addict and had a son and daughter from that marriage. The daughter from the first marriage had been living with the plaintiff and the defendant, and there was another son from this second marriage. One of the focuses of the trial was domestic violence. The plaintiff stated:

> I was beaten since the month the child was born. He beat me with [an] iron. He said that I was a divorced woman nobody wanted with no place to go. He took me in because he was sympathetic. So he could beat me whenever he wanted . . . we quarreled over a trivial matter and he started beating me. He used a huge iron hose to whip my waist, and used a brick to hit my head.
>
> The defendant responded, "The plaintiff wanted to beat me and I was running away. So she chased me out in the street, but fell when she slipped on a banana peel." In addition, the defendant, in his written reply to the divorce petition, stated, "The plaintiff had a quick temper, and she hit me with a beer bottle. Before I almost lost consciousness, she used a knife to chase me. She was stopped by neighbors."

The plaintiff presented a medical report and their agreement prepared by the police: the defendant had moved out of their apartment on the condition that the plaintiff pay him 1,500 yuan. Under the suggestions of the police, she applied for a protection order in the court. Indeed, the couple had been separated for more than four years, during which time several attacks by the defendant had occurred.

The judge then delivered a judgment in the plaintiff's favor:

> The plaintiff claimed that the defendant committed domestic violence against her and she provided the medical report and the agreement prepared by the police. From the medical report: there was a 2 cm injury on

the back of the plaintiff's head, some skin on the scalp had been ruptured, a rib was broken, and there were several injuries to soft tissue on various parts of her body. These injuries could not have all been the result of her falling, as claimed by the defendant. Rather, they were consistent with her claims that the defendant had hit her waist with a big hose and had hit her head with a brick. The defendant claimed that he had been hit by the plaintiff, but he provided no evidence. The defendant was much larger, physically, than the plaintiff. It would have been unlikely for the plaintiff to have attacked the defendant. As an adult, the defendant should have realized the serious consequence of hitting somebody in the head. Using a brick to hit the plaintiff's head suggests that he was reckless in his violent behavior, and thus, this constitutes a significant personal threat. We thus uphold the presence of domestic violence.

With domestic violence established, the judge then awarded the divorce for the plaintiff, despite the fact that this had been the first petition. She also awarded custody of their fifteen-year-old son to the woman, as a domestically violent man was unsuitable for raising the child. Nonetheless, no monetary compensation was offered, obviously to balance the interests of the two litigating parties. The official reason was that neither had requested child support when the other party had been granted custody.

This is a rare case in which domestic violence was acknowledged and recorded in the judgment. Such success was achieved for two reasons. First, there was strong evidence for the victim: the medical reports, detailing the injuries, consistent with victim's statements; the agreement prepared by the police; and the protection order. Like most other men facing claims of domestic violence, the man denied all the claims. But his defense was not sophisticated. He had suggested that the plaintiff had stepped on a banana peel and hurt herself. This was inconsistent with the plaintiff's injuries on her waist and head, as shown in the medical reports. He also claimed that she had beaten him using instruments such as a beer bottle and a knife. However, he presented no evidence of the injuries or anything else that could have substantiated his claims. Second, the judge was willing to help the victim. The judge was young, gender-conscious, competent, and professional. She was sympathetic toward the woman, trying to rescue her from the violent husband. She cited the details of the medical reports as proof that the injuries had been the result of beatings and were unlikely to have been the result of a fall. She also provided a sharp analysis: physically the man was superior and it was unlikely that the woman could have attacked him. As He and Ng (2013b) have found, a judge's skills and willingness to collect evidence is crucial to protecting domestic abuse victims.

At the end of the day, even this rare "victory" for the plaintiff was short-lived. The defendant appealed. While the appeal court agreed with the facts found in the first trial, it took the safe route: adjudicated denial. "In this case the woman, for the first-time, had filed a divorce petition. Both parties had lived together for more than 10 years, and had nurtured a son, together with the daughter from the woman's previous marriage, thus having a certain level of emotional foundation. During the appeal process, the man objected to divorce and pleaded with the court to mediate for reconciliation. We thus acknowledged that the emotional relationship between the two parties had not completely broken down."

This appellate decision, denying the divorce, reversed the recognition of domestic violence found in the first trial. It indicated how entrenched the routine practices of divorce law are: denial for most first-time divorce petitions, even for cases in which serious domestic violence has been committed (He 2009a; Michelson 2018). For the appellate judge, this was straightforward: no divorce for the first petition. Why bother to explore the issue of domestic violence?

Given the reversal, would the trial judge change her approach in the future? Put differently, why should she rule in favor of women if the decision cannot be supported by the appellate court? The president of her district court told me that for this kind of reversal they were lenient on judges whose cases had been overturned by the upper-level courts. However, in most other courts in which an overturned case would discount the judge's performance, why would a judge take the risk? In my interview with her, she did not regret her decision. However, she was concerned whether this book, once published, could have a negative effect on the appellate judge. While I immediately assured her that any identifying information would be removed from my research, her concern spoke volumes about the pressures that judges face. If this case was unrepresentative of the national situation, in other regions the courts' protection of women's rights would be even weaker. The judges would be more concerned with self-protection and less willing to collect evidence of domestic violence or to confront violent abusers.

In many other cases, the victims are not as lucky. A male judge in Beijing said: "I know that the domestic violence mentioned by the woman was true. But she did not provide evidence. Without evidence I am unable to support her. Why does the judge have to collect evidence? First, I am really too busy to do that; Second, it is unfair. The law makes it clear that whoever makes a claim is to provide evidence." For this judge, fairness had become an excuse for inaction. What a female Beijing judge in her early thirties said may be more representative of judges: "As long as the evidence is not a slam dunk, I tend to reject divorce petitions filed the first time. After all, I have to take into account the opinion of the appellate court. The appellate court rarely reverses our decisions on divorce denial, even if the reason to grant a divorce is clear. Their attitude toward adjudicated divorce decisions, however, is different. When it is being appealed and the appellant makes a fuss, the appellate court, with relatively little experience dealing with those troublemakers, just reverses our decisions." For appellate judges, reversing a decision by the trial court may cause complaints from trial judges, but failing to soothe a troublemaking litigant may adversely affect their own career prospects and job security. In this sense, the failure of the courts to recognize domestic violence is systematic. A maverick judge is unable to change the overall situation.

Indeed, most judges avoid addressing domestic violence in their rulings. This reluctance stems from their own efficiency and stability concerns. In particular, the concerns for reversed appeal decisions factor significantly in not recognizing domestic violence. Subject to heavy scrutiny from upper-level courts, these judges do not want to issue any decisions that are not a slam dunk. The institutional environment drives most of the judges to ignore the existence of domestic violence. There are good reasons for judges to exercise caution in this area of law, with self-preservation perhaps the foremost psychological driver. China's lower-level trial courts have been, and still are, consistently plagued by a high appeal rate for their judgments. A junior judge can be subject to disciplinary measures or other punishments for adjudicatory mistakes.

For example, in 1999, about 50 percent of trial court judgments were appealed. Among these judgments, only about a quarter (26.6 percent) of them were sustained (Zhong and Yu 2004: 428).

Perpetuating Violence by Delaying Decisions

If mediated and adjudicated decisions result in violence, so does the process of handling the cases. As mentioned, one entrenched practice of courts in divorce cases is to deny first-time petitions despite the fact that a couple's mutual affection has broken down. Delaying decisions is also a common strategy of courts in any highly contested case, even if the parties are not first-time petitioners. According to several studies (Zhang 2018: 109; Michelson 2018; Wang 2013; Wang and Ng 2020 forthcoming), some courts refuse to grant divorces even though domestic violence has been admitted or established. The court's judgment simply ignores this issue and jumps straight to adjudicated denial; more discussions on the issue of domestic violence would inevitably delegitimize or even contradict the decision to deny the petition.

This delaying strategy, though ostensibly neutral, has gendered consequences for women who are threatened by or are victims of domestic violence. As long as a divorce is denied, the marriage remains intact. The courts, until the protection order became available, do little about claims of domestic violence. Some judges may offer superficial oral warnings or persuasion. For many others, there is no warning, no compensation, nothing. Bureaucratic antipathy looms. A denial decision seems to support the claims of the men who refuse to divorce. Men's hatred and retaliation toward women might be channeled through further domestic violence. Many brag to their wives: "You want to divorce me? Even the court cannot do much about me; it is on my side. What else can you do?" It is not surprising, then, that some men retaliate against women for initiating divorce petitions. However, women who seek divorce might themselves escalate a conflict so as to collect more evidence for the next petition. Others, feeling helpless, see themselves as failures, and self-harm and even suicide are the result (Fincher 2014: 159; Chen 2020). In some extreme cases, out of desperation, they murder their partners (Luo 2019; Palmer 2017: 290–93). While individual cases vary, there is a pattern: domestic violence persists, and in some cases it is aggravated. As the adage says: justice delayed is justice denied.

Horrifying consequences resulting from divorce denials have been widely documented from interviews, court files, and even court judgments posted on the internet. A second-time petition letter reads (He 2009a):

> Had divorce been granted last time, none of the following would have taken place: On December 28, 2000, the lover of the other party [the husband] came to my apartment when I was out. They locked my daughter outside the apartment while they were having an affair, despite the freezing temperature of the winter night and the fact that we are still married. When I accused him of doing this the next day at his work unit, he beat me with a wooden paddle. My neck, waist, and spine were seriously injured and I could not even stand up. Even after spending 20,000–30,000 yuan on various medical treatments, I remain nearly paralyzed. As a result, I have lost the ability to work. All I want now is a divorce.

An application for a Personal Safety Protection Order stated: "After the court rejected the first-time petition for divorce, the defendant was not remorseful. Instead, the situation got worse. He threatened me, cursed at me, and beat me. Even now, I still have scars on my body and head."

In the Overdosed Woman's Case, a Shaanxi applicant for a Personal Safety Protection Order said in a telephone interview: "I lost consciousness one day and was hospitalized. I suspected he had overdosed me with sleeping pills. He has schizophrenia and thus may have tried to have sex with me after I lost consciousness. But I had no evidence to support this and the court rejected my divorce petition." She continued: "I went back to my natal home, and he found me there. He said that as long as the court did not grant a divorce decision, I remained his wife, and I must go home with him. Otherwise, he would make a fuss at my natal home. One day, when he grabbed me forcefully, my mother blocked his way. He pushed my mom down."

This woman's experience shows that, once again, delaying court decisions can be disastrous. It places the victims in danger. The woman, unable to provide evidence of the sleeping pills, was denied her divorce petition. Staying with the occasionally violent husband meant that her life was at risk and she could be raped. The man became more confident and even bragged that he would hit his mother-in-law.

Another Shaanxi woman who had appealed the first denial decision told me: "I am afraid of going home since he beats me whenever he gets drunk. Now I am living in a rental, working temporarily, barely able to support myself. He refuses to divorce since he heard that once divorced, a large land compensation sum would belong to me. And the court denied my divorce petition." She explained further: "I appealed, but almost six months have passed, and I have heard nothing from the appellate court. I called the appellate judge, but the call was only answered by his clerk. The clerk said that I should just wait, since arranging the hearing would take time. The clerk became impatient after I called four times. He would just hang up on me on subsequent calls."

It was unclear why the judge had yet to schedule a hearing six months after the case had been appealed. For difficult litigants, the judge would simply stall the hearing and prolong a decision. That might have been why the judge would not even take the plaintiff's calls. As a result, she was still afraid to return home.

It is difficult to know the extent to which these incidents occur as a result of inappropriately adjudicated denials. However, in many cases, the judges know at first glance that a marriage cannot be reconciled solely by granting a six-month observation period. Nonetheless, they render an adjudicated denial as long as the evidence suggests that the couple can still live under the same roof. While a small percentage of this sort of judgment might rescue a collapsing marriage, in most situations such judgments only further deteriorate the already tense relationship between the couple, and the conflict between them is likely to escalate (Zheng 2006). After all, when the plaintiffs decide to bring a divorce petition, they must have already had many debates with the spouse. When they eventually overcome their hesitancy and decide to fight in court, there is little chance that the marriage can be salvaged. As fieldwork investigation shows, a plaintiff's confidence in the other party sinks further after getting an adjudicated denial (Zheng 2006).

The delaying approach is gendered. Since 90 percent of plaintiffs who make apparent abuse claims are women, they are disproportionally affected by this delayed strategy. Given that about 70 percent of plaintiffs are women, their claims are more likely to be delayed.

The Limited Impact of the Protection Order

Before the ADV Law went into effect, it was almost impossible to get a protection order in China. Fincher (2014: 154) wrote: "No Beijing court had ever issued a protection order." When Kim Lee, the beaten wife of Li Yang, the founder of Crazy English, the very successful language program, went to court for such an order, she faced a game like Ping Pong: the police asked her to go to the court for this, but the court asked her to go to the police for evidence (Fincher 2014: 154). On March 1, 2016, the Personal Safety Protection Order in the ADV Law went into effect. Has the situation been changed?

Ten interviewees who had obtained such orders from both the Shaanxi Court and the Pearl River Delta Court suggested that it was effective. Most of them had lived precarious lives—vulnerable, fragile, and helpless. Some were lucky enough to be able to return to their natal homes. Others were less fortunate. The men harassed them at their workplaces, and they lost jobs as a result. For all these victims, the protection order from the courts was a lifeline. One applicant said: "After the order was issued, he no long harassed my natal family members." Another said: "He was summoned by the court to have a talk. Since then, he has stopped intercepting me on my way to work. He also does not make a fuss at my workplace." And another: "He stopped sending me reviling and threatening texts, and we did not stay together." A Guangdong judge told me that a man under a protection order had refrained from going home. Apparently, he had misunderstood the meaning: the order only forbade him from getting close to the applicant, but he thought he was forbidden from returning to his own home. Such misunderstandings aside, the story reveals the power of the order. Judges were of the view that the order made a difference, even to those men who believed that they had every right to beat their wives and were recalcitrant to change their behavior.

Such positive feedback cannot override the bleak overall picture: both the statistics and my own field investigations suggest that both the number of petitions and the number of approved orders are ludicrously low.

The Work Report of the Supreme People's Court (2018) shows that for the preceding five years, all courts across the country issued only 2,154 such orders, in contrast to 8.5 million divorce cases processed. Given that China has more than 3,000 courts, this suggests that on average each court issued less than one order over the five years. Another report estimates that from March 2016 to June 2017, courts across the country issued only 1,284 of such orders (*Equality* 2017). Again, for sixteen months, each court, on average, issued only less than one order. Chen and Duan (2012: 34) have found that over three years a Chongqing district court issued only two protection orders. Jiang's recent research (2019) also confirms the rarity of the application. In all of the courts in which I conducted field investigations, issuing protection orders was a rare occurrence. The Pearl River Delta Court, a pilot court promoting the measure long before the promulgation of the ADV Law, issued only three applications each year, despite more than 500 divorce cases received. The Shaanxi Court, extolled as a model for the implementation of the mechanism, issued less than ten orders over two years.

Several reasons are suggested for such low numbers. The lack of awareness of the order among the general public, including the victims; judges' lack of knowledge of domestic violence; and concerns over the enforcement of the orders (Runge 2015: 39). The woman in the Fish Retailer's Case, for example, did not learn of this mechanism until the police intervened. In the Overdosed Woman's Case, she learned of the mechanism from her neighbor after her petition for divorce had been rejected and the man had followed her all the way to her natal home.

Such explanations are, at best, incomplete. Television is widely available, even in rural areas. Information on the mechanism can be found across various media, and antidomestic violence posters hang in many government buildings and offices. Training sessions for judges and lawyers have had a "profoundly positive impact"; public awareness has been increased significantly through demonstrations and high-profile cases (Runge 2015: 39–40).

One explanation missed in the existing literature is that the courts' incentive mechanisms work against the issuance of such orders: issuing them creates extra work for judges and thus undercuts their efficiency concerns. Issuing a protection order is not counted as a separate case; it is part of the divorce case. However, the workload for issuing and enforcing such an order is no less than that of handling of another divorce case without one. To approve such a request, the judges have to investigate, orally warn the alleged abusers, and make extra trips to deliver the order to all relevant parties. To determine whether or not to approve it, the judge has to assess the domestic violence evidence. According to one study, between 2008 and 2014, the pilot period of the mechanism, only about 29 percent of applications were successful (*People's Court Daily* 2014).

More troublesome is the enforcement process (Kan and Liu 2017; Li 2013; Yi and Li 2017). Compared to the enforcement of property issues, the enforcement of the Personal Safety Protection Order pertains to personal rights, which are fluid. The judge usually lacks the capacity to supervise such a process. Then, the judge has to seek help from the police and the street or village neighborhood committee. While the neighborhood committee has little problem receiving the order, police are more resistant: it seems that courts, contrary to their stereotypically inferior role among the three political-legal apparatuses, are giving orders to the police. At any rate, it is an extra task that the police are unwilling to undertake. Inaction on the part of the police on this issue has been well-documented (Kan and Liu 2017). A judge told me that according to relevant stipulations, the police and the neighborhood committee also are expected to provide feedback to the courts on the implementation of the order. Never once had she received any feedback from the police.

These issues have become headaches for judges. As a result, some applicants are dissuaded from filing the applications, or the judges simply refuse to grant an approval, citing inadequate evidence of domestic violence (Lu 2016; Zhuang 2014). Article 27 of the ADV Law stipulates that such an order is to be issued under two circumstances. One is when there is domestic violence. Some judges set a higher threshold on "whether there is evidence of domestic evidence" than they do in the litigation process. The other circumstance is "the realistic danger of domestic violence," which lacks a clear definition. Judges often take advantage of this vague definition and persuade applicants to withdraw their applications. Frequent responses to women's requests are as follows: "You have been with each other for so many years. Why can't you stay together for a few more months?" or "You are about to get divorced. Why do you still need such an order?" or "If he were such a scum, why do you choose to stay?" Once again, mediation is widely used at this stage (Jiang 2019). Indeed, many victims filing divorce petitions should have been told about this mechanism during the process, but the judge may not have informed them of the protection order. As the Overdosed Woman's Case revealed, she had learned of the mechanism through her neighbor in her natal home, not through the judge.

Put simply, the Personal Safety Protection Order is effective once it is granted. This mechanism would have been more widely used and granted earlier if not for judges' efficiency concerns. The performance assessment criteria and the judges' concerns nonetheless have taken a toll on the effectiveness of a well-intended mechanism. The reluctance of judges to issue such orders is one major reason behind their limited numbers.

Conclusions

It is hard to say that the judges have not complied with the law. After all, they do enjoy much discretion. For this reason, evidence of domestic violence is often dismissed. When they adopt mediation and allow the issue of domestic violence to be sidelined, their decisions are justified because mediation is allowed by the law and because the litigation parties, including the victim, have agreed to the deal. When they persuade potential victims to drop applications for protection orders, the victims, reluctantly or not, bow to such persuasion. Domestic violence is rarely relevant to decisions on whether to grant divorce, on custody battles, and on property division merely because judges have ruled that mutual affections have not been irreparably broken. Michelson (2018: 2) even asserts that "[c]ourts at best ignore and at worst abuse claims to justify denying women's divorce petitions."

My views are not as dire as those of Michelson. Nonetheless, it is fair to say that the judges have not made enough effort to protect the victims' interests. As a result, domestic violence is trivialized and the stated promises of the law are not fulfilled. They could take a tougher position. Why don't they? The answer lies on the other side of the question: Why should they? What incentives do they have for doing so? As mentioned, their goals are to close cases in a safe and, if possible, efficient manner. For many of them, domestic violence is only one piece of marginal evidence in determining whether a marriage should continue. If the victims present strong evidence, they may accept it. If not, judges rarely undertake special efforts to do so. Obtaining evidence of domestic violence may simply increase a judge's workload. The underutilized Personal Safety Protection Order is just one example. This means that only a gender-conscious, capable, and responsible judge would collect evidence on the existence of domestic evidence. The judge in the Fish Retailer's Case is the exception, not the rule. Some evidence is buried regardless—as long as the case can be ended peacefully and safely. When a divorce petition is denied, there is no need to look into the issues of domestic violence. When a divorce is granted, no matter the form of mediation or adjudication, the main issues are custody and property division. Why should the judge still focus on domestic violence? When both parties have accepted a divorce, why should they still hang on to the issue of domestic violence? Furthermore, many abusers are of bad temperament, mentally unstable, or physically violent. Confronting these people may divert their hatred from their wives to the judges. Why draw fire against oneself?

5

Sacrificing Women's Rights to Child Custody

In the past, petitioning couples in China predominantly focused on obtaining the divorce itself and on the division of marital property (Wu and Xia 2009). Child custody was sometimes regarded as a burden rather than as a privilege, since raising a child was difficult when financial resources were meager (cf. Zelizer 1994). With China's economic and social development, however, maintaining connections with children has become one of the most important sources of happiness (Chen and Rang 2009). With the dissolution of marriages, children are a source of crucial emotional attachment for their parents. It has been estimated that 54 percent of divorce cases in China involve the issue of child custody (Zhao and Ding 2016: 25). Hiding minors away from others during divorce proceedings has become commonplace. According to one report (Yan 2016), in more than 60 percent of cases involving child custody battles, children are removed or hidden from their original domiciles, making guardianship—and even visitation from the other party—impossible. These cases predominantly involve children younger than two years old. These parents try to create an impression that their children live solely with them (Zhang 2017: 48), which, according to the Supreme People's Court's Opinions on Adjudicating Issues on Child Custody (SPC 1993), constitutes a basis for child custody.

The Case of the Infant illustrates the prominent role of child custody in divorce litigation. The husband-plaintiff, his parents, and several close relatives stood along with an infant held by the paternal grandmother. They had traveled forty miles to attend the divorce trial, scheduled in the early morning.[1] Standing across the lobby of the courthouse were the wife-defendant and her relatives. The air was palpably confrontational. To see if there was any chance to mediate, the judge held a pretrial mediation with the plaintiff and his relatives. In the session, the judge said that usually the court would award child custody to the mother if the baby was less than two years old. Upon hearing this, the paternal grandfather, pulling the infant from his wife's chest, said: "We will withdraw the case and wait until the baby reaches two years old. No need to take such a risk now." His son, the plaintiff, immediately filed a motion to withdraw. The brewing altercation ended.

How do judges make child custody decisions? What factors are taken into account? One of the principles in China's Marriage Law is the protection of the interests of women and children. If the laws have been tilted toward women, and women are regarded as more suitable for child care, to what extent have these laws been implemented? Some empirical study already demonstrates that women in fact are disfavored in the fight over child custody (Chen and Zhang 2015; Li, Wang and Zheng 2016; Zhao and Ding 2016). Drawing on 144 cases in which child custody was at issue, Han (2014: 104–105) found that, when there was only one child, men more often than women gained custody; when the only child was a boy, men's chances to gain custody were even higher; and when there were more than two children, men had a better chance of gaining custody of the eldest child. Zhang (2017: 52) contends that some courts, for the sake of enforcement, awarded custody to whoever then controlled the children; when some women, for fear of violence, reluctantly gave up their custody rights, the courts failed to identify the genuine reason behind the apparent "consent." Li's (2015) ethnography also demonstrates how rural legal workers have suppressed the interests of divorcing women on the issue of child custody. She argues that legal workers, through their screening process, perpetuate gender inequality, even before the cases reach the courthouse. In the United States, mothers who allege domestic violence are more likely to lose custody than mothers who do not make such assertions (Meier and Dickson 2017). This is because judges believe that those mothers are fabricating evidence as a strategy to get custody. Bemiller (2008) also finds that corruption, denial of due process, and gender bias exist in the family court when battered mothers lose child custody.

If existing studies provide a macro picture of child custody divisions, here in this chapter I offer a micro-analysis of how Chinese judges, under institutional constraints, thwart women's rights to child custody in contested cases. I will show that when the issue is contested, the interests of both women and children are often slighted. When men are aggressive, the judge often sacrifices women's rights in order to reach a solution acceptable to the man. The courts simply do not fulfill the promises of the law; they fail to protect women's welfare or to resist the gender biases engrained in Chinese society. Child custody has become a bargaining chip for judges to soothe men who would otherwise be unwilling to accept a divorce. This remains true even though some trial judges try to protect the interests of women and rescue children from hostile family environments. These decisions are often reversed when appealed. Each of these cases demonstrates that the approach of China's judges is correlated with how their performance is assessed.

Child Custody Laws

Child custody has only a marginal role in China's family laws. On the issue of awarding child custody, the Marriage Law remains murky. It states that the relationship between parents and children will not be dissolved merely because of divorce. For children at a tender period, the mother has priority in determining child custody, and the party without custody must provide child support. The general principle is vague: the standard is "beneficial to the development of the child," similar to the international standard "the best interests of the child." A more detailed Opinion issued by the SPC in 1993 suggests that courts rule from the perspective of children's interests, that is, constructive to their health and well-being. The decision is supposed to consider factors such as the parents' capabilities of fulfilling child custody obligations. The laws stipulate what is beneficial to the development of a child: a stable, friendly, loving, and healthy living environment; the capability to take care of the child; educational opportunities; an environment safe from domestic violence; and whether one parent already has a child. If both parties can satisfy these conditions, the judges may determine which party can provide better tangible living conditions. Judges also consider the intangible: which party has lived longer with the child since the separation, who has devoted more time and care to the child, who the child prefers to spend time with, and so on. For children ten years and older, the court must consider the child's opinion when making decisions, if only for reference. Indeed, rarely is a child summoned to the court to indicate a preference. In most situations, written preferences are conveyed through the parent who seeks child custody and are thus biased. However, parents who have not fulfilled the obligations of nurturing the children or who have mistreated the children are not to receive child custody. This has been generally interpreted to cover domestic violence: that is, those who commit domestic violence have a lower chance of being granted child custody. The SPC Opinion (1993) also stipulates that parents can ask courts to alter the child custody, and in these cases child support arrangements have to be changed as well.

Since all of these elements are difficult to quantify, judges have tremendous discretion. To paraphrase Shakespeare: a thousand judges would have a thousand interpretations of what constitutes the best interests of the child. The facts in each divorce case vary. The judge can always find a specific reason to award child custody to a parent by following general guidelines. Judgments usually include certain facts such as whether one party has certain medical conditions or bad habits, the sex of the child, the parent's income level, and the parent's education. Overall, the laws favor mothers' interests and never privilege fathers with respect to child custody rights.

Mediation: Turning Biases into Bargaining Chips

When the laws are implemented by courts, a mediated outcome is usually preferred, especially in jurisdictions where caseloads are light (Xiong 2015; Ng and He 2017a). How do the judges persuade women to give up child custody? What tactics are employed? How are the women pressured? How do they respond and resist? As mentioned, the child custody laws are designed to reverse economic and cultural biases in order to provide women a level playing field. As will be shown, however, judges take advantage of these biases and parlay them into powerful weapons in order to achieve mediated outcomes.

Financial Disparities

Among all the tactics used, financial capacity is the most frequently mentioned. The law states that financial status is one element in determining child custody. At face value, the law appears fair to both genders. However, financial inequality between genders is an entrenched social reality; most women earn less than their male partners. This is unlikely to change in the foreseeable future (Davis 2010). This inequality is also factored in when the income level is low, because a slight difference makes a huge impact. In economics term, the marginal utility is high. As income levels rise, marginal utility declines, even when lower earners still make a good living. Thus, this tactic is more common in regions with lower levels of economic development.

In the Singapore Laborer's Case (see chapter 4), a woman, originally from a rural area, had been working as a part-time cashier in a supermarket and had sued for divorce, seeking child custody of both daughters. However, she could not provide a valid address for her male partner, who had been a laborer in Singapore. He had remitted money only to his father, who would then give the woman 2,000 yuan per month. The money was barely enough to cover living expenses. The underlying reason was that the man's family had been unhappy that the woman had not given birth to a boy. During pretrial mediation, the judge had quickly persuaded her to withdraw the case.

The judge asked: "Now that you are only working as a part-time cashier in a supermarket, can you support the two children if you divorce?" Upon hearing this, the plaintiff's inaudible sobbing became noticeable. She could not articulate any words, so instead she cried louder, her head buried in her arms. Conversation was suspended, and the room stood still. The judge had to give her time to regain her composure. As the sobbing continued, the hair on her forehead stuck to her face. Her fat body shaking and her lips twisted, she quivered: "I already knew that a divorce will not be easy . . . [sobbing] . . . I cannot support the two children if their family were to stop supporting us." The judge softened her tone: "Did you think about this before filing the divorce petition?" The plaintiff responded: "Yes, I did. But that night when he beat me and threatened to kill us, my elder daughter was trembling and the younger one was crying desperately, I decided to divorce him. Should we divorce, I would not be beaten by him; nor would the kids be so scared. But I only earn 800 yuan per month. None of us can survive without his support. The apartment we are living in belongs to his father. He would definitely kick us out." Following these sentences came another round of weeping. After a long period of silence, the judge suggested: "So you have decided not to divorce?" The plaintiff replied: "Yes I withdraw the petition. I will raise my children. I gave birth to them. I could never be relieved if I could not raise them myself. As long as we stay married, his father will give us the money and the kids can go to school. For this reason, I would rather tolerate him and suffer."

This case suggests the profound impact of poverty on the woman and the effect of the judge's tactics to thwart women's child custody rights. The woman's sobbing and silence revealed how desperate she was for a safe home away from the man. However, she could not afford it. Without the money provided by the man, via his father, the two kids could not receive proper education. An 800-yuan monthly income could barely maintain the lowest living conditions in the region. Throughout the process, the judge said little. She only pointed out the financial barriers that the woman would face if she were awarded child custody through divorce. This was enough for the woman to drop her lawsuit, and the judge achieved her goal. As analyzed in chapter 4, the judge did not mention that the court could have granted the woman a divorce and order the man to pay child support. The procedural problem (the woman could not provide a valid address for her husband) can be overcome by the public notice, a common step taken by courts in a time of high population mobility. The divorce decision would have rescued the woman and her two daughters from the hostile environment. However, it would have undermined the judge's priority: to dispose of cases as efficiently and as safely as possible. To enforce such a judgment against the husband—a man lives overseas and remits money back home only to his father—would be a hassle as well, given Chinese courts' limited capacity in enforcing their own judgments (He 2009b). Maintaining a marriage in which the man was still willing to support the mother and two daughters might have been the most pragmatic solution for the woman as well, given the social and legal environments. In any event, for the judge, encouraging the woman to file a petition and award a divorce was almost out of the question. Indeed, the judge told me later that she was doing an exceptional job interviewing and advising the woman. Such an interview might have made her feel a little better. Given that the plaintiff could not even provide a valid address for her husband, normal practice would have been outright dismissal of the petition.

Sometimes judges do not have to say the words themselves; they just take advantage of pressure by a woman's family members. In the Oil Refinery Worker's Case, the plaintiff, a thirty-year-old woman had sued to divorce her thirty-three-year-old husband, who worked for a state-owned oil refinery thirty miles away from their home. The couple had been geographically separated for the entire marriage. His salary was about 2,500 yuan. The plaintiff was from a rural area and did not have a stable job. During the divorce proceedings, she had found a job as a saleswoman for a real estate developer and was earning 1,100 yuan per month, to be raised to 1,700 after a three-month probationary period. They had an eight-year-old boy, who had been raised primarily by the plaintiff and her mother-in-law.

The judge, a middle-aged woman with more than twenty-five years of experience, was skillful. The plaintiff supported her request for child custody on several grounds: the man lived in an oil field thirty miles from home, and he could not take care of the child. Indeed, he was incapable of taking care of the child since he had never previously done so; the child had always been cared for by his mother. If child custody was awarded to the man, the mother-in-law would have inevitably turned the boy into another "sissy man" like her husband, who never seemed to grow up. That would be a dreadful outcome for her. Finally, as the only person in the family with a high-school diploma, she could help the boy with his homework throughout primary school. The woman also had a house in the countryside and compensation from land requisition.

The plaintiff was determined to get child custody. The judge also understood that the plaintiff's income and assets were sufficient to support the child. The plaintiff should have been in a better position than her male counterpart. Yet, she was hesitant to fight the whole extended family that was supporting the man. She worried that if she insisted on child custody, then she might encounter difficulty exiting from the marriage in the first place.

It turned out that the man's family also wanted the boy. In rural areas, a son is crucial to a man's lineage. The mother-in-law was strong-willed. She had been the rule-enforcer in their household. She had approved of the marriage to her son, a Stated-Owned Enterprise worker, to the plaintiff, a rural woman without urban household registration or a stable job, simply because, in her derogatory terms, they had wanted to "get a baby through her womb" (借个肚皮生个娃). With the traditional patrilineal ideology engrained in her mind, it was unlikely she would have easily given up child custody.

The trial was confrontational. Both parties traded obscenities and presented forceful arguments. During posttrial mediation, the judge decided to meet the plaintiff in private. She also allowed the wife's aunt and younger sister to participate in the mediation. Since both parties approved of the divorce, the issues remaining were custody of the child and property partition. To begin, the judge wanted to explore whether the trial's heated debates had changed the plaintiff's positions:

> JUDGE: Now that you know their stance, do you still insist on divorce, the house in the countryside, and child custody?

The short sentence conveyed the message: the plaintiff might not get the divorce if she waged a full-scale war against the defendant. In her tentative tone, the judge stressed that there were three disputed issues: "Do you still insist on a divorce, the house in the countryside, and child custody?" Her question hinted that it would be impossible to achieve all three. She also took advantage of the aftershock of the intense trial: "Now that you know their stance"—reminding the woman of the defendant's determination. These words made the plaintiff hesitant to fight. The plaintiff became less eager and assertive. Reluctantly, she signed with frustration: "I am determined to divorce. The house in the countryside was allocated to me, so I also want it. As to the child, I am afraid that they will not give up." No sooner had the plaintiff finished her sentence than her aunt whined: "The boy belongs to them. We do not want him! With a kid, how are you going to make a living?!" The plaintiff's sister also cut in: "That is right. Who will pick him up to and from school?" The plaintiff lowered her head and gazed into her cell phone in silence. The judge softened her tone: "This is her business, and she is the one to make the decision."

With her face red, her aunt shouted: "What does she know? Marrying herself to them for so many years, what has she got? Delivering a baby for them, her own house is to be partitioned! The law is so unfair!" To maintain order and to protect the court's sanctity, the judge interrupted: "The child is also hers. How can you say that she bore the child for them? The mother-in-law also took care of the child. And they also invested in the house after the marriage." The aunt calmed herself: "It was a boy. Within several years, she [the plaintiff] will not be able to control him. Now that it is costly to go to school, can she, a *dagongde* [migrant worker, 打工的], raise him? Once grown up, he needs to go to university and get married. Can she support all of these? The boy is nothing but a burden. Why would she want him?"

In this mediation session, although the plaintiff had been eager to obtain child custody, both the aunt and sister employed various tactics, which will be elaborated on later, to persuade the plaintiff to give up custody. The most persuasive was the plaintiff's inferior financial status: "He needs to go to university and get married" and "The boy is nothing but a burden." As a temporary saleswoman, she was only a *dagongde*, a condescending term describing migrant workers who leave the countryside to work in urban areas. As Li (2015: 164) has analyzed, this is status-based stereotyping. Labeling the woman a *dagongde* led to a sudden conclusion: she must have few resources and move around constantly and thus her boy would inevitably live an unanchored life. Then, the sister pushed the issue with more concrete implications: "Who will pick him up to and from school?" Both the aunt and the sister had placed the plaintiff into a category that invited stigmatization and discrimination (Bourdieu 1991).

Cultural Biases

Despite China's increasing openness to the outside world since the late 1970s, cultural biases toward divorced women with children remain engrained, especially in rural areas (Stacey 1983). Divorced women's marketability depreciates if they bring children from previous relationships into new ones (Li 2015: 164). Adding insult to injury, the children would become *tuoyouping* (拖油瓶), a derogatory term for those who follow divorced mothers into remarriages. It is difficult for women with children to get remarried. In the Oil Refinery Worker's Case, the plaintiff's sister had insisted: "Should you get the child, it will become a big issue in your next marriage. Who will want to marry a person with such a big boy? The whole purpose of divorce is to live a better life and be left alone from being bullied. With a child, you would be bullied forever. They want him, so let it go." The aunt pushed further: "You are not even as sensible as your younger sister. The point is as simple as this: with a boy, who will marry you?"

This echoes what had been said by the family members in the Attempted Rape Case. It was the second divorce petition filed by the man. While the woman had agreed on divorce, she insisted on custody of their two-year-old boy, who had a medical condition requiring periodic operations. The man had claimed that she was lazy, but the real disagreement was over financial compensation. The woman wanted 80,000 yuan from the land requisition compensation, as well as child support. She expected that the compensation would reach 100,000 yuan. With this amount of money, she could support herself and her son in the city without burdening her natal family. However, the man's family was willing to pay only 10,000 yuan. The wide gap was why the first-time petition had ended in denial.

Her grandfather, in his sixties, said to the judge: "A girl needs to be remarried after being divorced. With a sick child and especially a boy, who will marry her? Isn't it self-destructive?" When the woman argued that she could rent an apartment in city with her son with medical problems, her mother pleaded to the judge: "Nonsense! You see, judge comrade, she is so young and must be remarried. With a boy in the rural areas, there is no chance to be married again."

Divorced women also face patrilineal bias. One of the goals of the patriarchal system was to maintain an unbroken lineage that would reside on the ancestral property for all time (Stacey 1983: 32). In the Oil Refinery Worker's Case, when the aunt had bumped into the mother-in-law at the entrance of the courthouse, they traded vicious words. That was when the mother-in-law had said "we get the baby through your womb" to humiliate the plaintiff and her family members. Although the aunt had fought the mother-in-law, they both believed that a woman was nothing more than an instrument passing on the genes of the man's family. At the posttrial mediation, the aunt said: "You just delivered a baby for them," a sentence almost identical to what had been said by the mother-in-law. According to this cultural precept, a baby, not to mention a boy, should belong to the man's family. That was exactly why the aunt had later shouted: "The boy belongs to them. We do not want him." The sister concurred: "They want him, so let it go." This fits with what the defendant's father had said in the Attempted Rape Case: "We do not want it even if it were a girl! The kid belongs to their family. Why should we raise the kid for them?"

The bias is less pronounced when a girl is in dispute: it is easier for women to obtain child custody, but they have to raise the girl without child support or even a partition of the communal property. Chen et al. (2018: 116) documents this pattern: "In one divorce case closed by this court in 2011, both parties reached an agreement on property division and child support as follows: The wife was given custody of the 15-year-old daughter and would bear the responsibility of raising the child on her own. The community property (the marital house) was awarded to the man. Again, in a divorce case in 2012, both parties had reached a divorce agreement in judicial mediation: the marital house and all the family appliances were both awarded to the man; the woman was given custody of a 14-year-old daughter and assumed all responsibility for child-rearing." They urged the judges to rectify the practice (2018: 116): "Judges should be aware of rural women's weak status and consider it a factor in dividing community property, so as to provide financial protection for their post-divorce lives. However, as mentioned above, in the surveyed cases, many wives are assigned little property." This line is destined to go nowhere because the real reason for so doing, as demonstrated, is that the judges are using the bias to facilitate their own causes.

Third, once a woman is married, she is not supposed to return to her natal home. She can visit relatives but not stay for long. She is not even supposed visit the parents' family during the eve of the New Year. Doing so would mean that she had been unfit for the marriage market, and the parents would lose face because they had not cultivated a quality daughter. It would be a nightmare if the returning daughter came with children: she could not be remarried and would have to live with the parents forever.

In the Attempted Rape Case, when pressed by her natal family members to give up child custody, the woman had argued: "What's wrong with the boy? Why can't I live with him? I will live with him if remarriage is not possible." This would have been a reasonable argument if taken out of the context. In reality, it was unacceptable by local norms. Upon hearing this, her father was so enraged that he almost hit her in front of the judge. Luckily, his wife stopped him. He could not stop complaining: "This kid troubles me to death! How 'pretty' it looks living in the natal home with a child? Who will support you? And where should my face be placed?" Indeed, the woman also understood the cultural pressure. She said: "With the money from the land requisition, I will rent a home in the city with my boy. I will not go back to the village and stay with my mom." This cultural pressure was shared by the family members. Her grandfather, in his sixties, had travelled with her parents four hours from their hometown to attend the early-morning trial. They were serious about the issue! At the court, all of them objected to maintaining child custody and pressured the woman to lower the amount of financial compensation and settle as soon as possible. For them, to cut off all connections with the man's side was the best solution. Any link, including child custody, would have embarrassed them. I should have added that they reacted awkwardly when they saw the judge walk into the mediation room: to have a daughter insisting on child custody when being divorced was difficult to articulate to a stranger.

Cultural biases, when combined with the financial pressure of raising a child, are powerful in persuading divorcing mothers to give up child custody. In the Oil Refinery Worker's Case, the sister had said that "a boy needs to go to college, and bride-price, etc. How can you support all these?" In the Attempted Rape Case, the mother had said "we might reconsider had it been a baby girl." This was because of financial concerns, as explained by the woman's grandfather: "If it were a girl and their side did not want it, we could consider it. With a girl, she could be remarried: we could just lower our bride-price. The girl would become a relative, since she would be married out once she had reached adulthood. A boy needs housing, a bride-price, and other costs when married. She alone will never be able to support that, no matter how hard she works, and the boy, once grown up, would complain to her for the rest of his life." Aware of this, the woman clarified herself in order to address the financial concerns: "The child's medical condition is not serious. The doctor said some kids with similar problems only need a single operation." However, her grandfather insisted: "Who will marry her with a sick child, and especially a boy?"

In these two cases, most of the language infused with cultural bias had been uttered by the divorcing women's natal family members. These relatives, accompanying the plaintiff through the legal process, were supposed to protect and help the plaintiff. Yet, it turned out that they had persuaded the plaintiff to give up child custody. This indicates

how engrained cultural biases are. Most of the time, the judge had remained reticent; she just did not interrupt them. The judge later told me
that she herself might not have been able to say all these blunt words
to the plaintiff. However, the judge also realized that the women were
determined to get child custody. To reach a successful settlement, the
judge had allowed the relatives to use blunt language to pressure the
wife. Put differently, the judge did not do it herself. Similar to another
case documented by Ng and He (2014), the judge had made the best use
of the participants in the mediation, whether it be the relatives of the
plaintiff or the other party. As it turned out, only with these altercations
(and some sobbing) did the plaintiff release her agony and give up child
custody. This was exactly what the judge had expected as the outcome.
In other words, the judge, by remaining succinct or reticent, had orches-
trated the mediation session. She took advantage of, if not intentionally
marshaled, the pressures from the natal family members. This strategy is
reminiscent of those adopted by judges in prereform mediations (Huang
2005).

Resisting Mediation Pressure

When facing pressure from judges, most women, though torn by their
child custody battles, became reticent and obedient. Many turned
emotional (Li 2009; Chen 2007); only a few fought back. Sometimes
resistance was fierce. However, in all cases that I encountered, with one
exception, the women succumbed to pressure. In the exception, the
mother resisted pressure in the mediation and was awarded custody of
her daughter in the subsequent adjudication. She paid a heavy price for
this victory, though. Her rare success, compared with other failed cases,
suggests that financial independence is crucial in the battle for child
custody.

In the Strategic Policeman's Case from Shaanxi, the defendant, a policeman in his early thirties, had originally been discharged from the
army. The plaintiff claimed that their personalities did not fit and that
the man had ignored her and their three-and-a-half-year-old daughter
during most of their marriage. She was determined to get a divorce, but
both parties fought for custody of the daughter. In the pretrial mediation between the judge and the plaintiff, the judge focused on financial

disparities: "Living in your mom's home, you don't have a job or income. Now that you are requesting child custody, with what will you raise her? In other words, you might not even be able to support yourself. How can you support your child? She has reached a stage that costs a lot."

The judge first mentioned that the woman was unemployed. This contrasted with the defendant, who worked as a policeman. "You may not even be able to support yourself. How can you support your child?" This rhetorical question highlighted the woman's precarious finances. The plaintiff responded: "The reason why I do not work now is the defendant. He keeps giving me a hard time, so I cannot work normally. I can work. I used to work in a kindergarten. It is true that I am poor, but my parents are not. My father works abroad, with a monthly salary of 20,000 yuan, and they have two apartments in the city. I am their only daughter. All these assets will be mine."

The plaintiff attributed her unemployment to the man because "he keeps giving me a hard time." That means her unemployment was unrelated to her ability to work, and her financial situation would change after divorce when the man stopped troubling her. She continued to refute the judge by stressing that she, though unemployed, was not poor; as the only daughter of the family, she would inherit her parents' wealth. In other words, she had the financial capability to raise the child.

The judge continued to push: "These conditions may be temporary. Your parents can support you now. But when they are aging and cannot earn that much, can they still support you and your child?" The plaintiff responded: "But I do not lack money now. Who can guarantee what will happen in the future? And, I will be fine if the defendant pays part of the costs of raising the child." With these responses, the woman refuted the judge's points. She emphasized that she had money now and that it was the current, not future, situation that the judge should consider. Furthermore, the defendant would also have to pay child support.

Once the judge realized that the pressure based on financial disparities had been unsuccessful, she turned to the child's future: "In fact, the court determines custody of the child based on which party will be more conducive to the child's development, who can better protect her, and offer her a stable, healthy, and safe environment. A child is not an asset. Child care takes a lot more than money. The child, if awarded to the defendant, can be raised by his parents. And together with his sister, they can help take care of the child." The plaintiff retorted: "That is exactly the problem. He will not take care of the child if he gets child custody. As a policeman, how can he have time for our child? For the four years of our marriage, all my time has been devoted to rearing the child. On the contrary, how many days has he spent with the child? I should get child custody."

The plaintiff was not distracted by the judge's points on the child's future or on the availability of the defendant's relatives to care for it. She persisted on the point that the defendant lacked the time to take care of their daughter and that *she* had already spent a lot of time doing so. She also raised the point that the daughter would prefer to stay with her instead of the father. She continued: "I meet all these conditions. You may ask my child who she likes living with. I have money for my kid and that is it. Why do you have to look into whether the money was originally earned by me or by my parents? Please have a look at all these goods I bought for my child from Taobao." To corroborate her statements, she pulled a stack of receipts out of her purse and showed the judge the kid's stuff that she had bought. Realizing that she could not convince the woman to give up child custody, the judge stopped the mediation session.

The plaintiff's resistance is powerful. In many regards, this woman was exceptional. She was the only daughter in a well-off family and demonstrated a willful personality. When the judge raised financial issues, the woman suggested she would be fine. The most powerful resistance came from her rhetorical question: "I have money for my kids and that is it. Why do you have to look into whether the money was originally earned by me or by my parents?" She had the support of her parents. A key to her success was her financial situation, which allowed her to refute the judge and placed her at an advantage. When the judge asked about other factors about the child's future, she said she had invested most of time taking care of the child and thus was in a better position to get child custody. Furthermore, because the future was uncertain, her care would be a more decisive factor. Living in the suburbs instead of an isolated village, she was less subject to the cultural biases seen in the other cases.

Not every woman was this successful. In the Oil Refinery Worker's Case, several factors tilted the balance: the difficulty of raising a son, the bleak prospects of being remarried with a son, and the woman's low earning capacity. During pretrial mediation, she had been assertive about child custody, but after her aunt and sister lambasted her, she wavered. Tears in her eyes, she hid in her coat scribbling in a comic picture in her cell phone cover. It was a difficult decision for her to give up the child. Eventually, however, she backed down from her request. Raising her head and looking at the judge with eyes red from sobbing, she asserted: "The child can be theirs, but I will pay the child support, otherwise they will never allow me to see the child." This forfeiture is similar to the "internalized disempowerment" found in court-sponsored mediation sessions in the United States (Ricci 1985).

In the Attempted Rape Case, the woman's family members were from rural areas, neither well-educated nor cosmopolitan. They addressed the judge as "comrade," an archaic title common only before the 2000s. This term unveiled the isolation of the family's living environment. When her relatives pushed her to give up child custody, the woman invoked her financial capacity and her means to fight cultural biases: she first mentioned that the financial burden to treating the boy's medical condition was not prohibitive. With the land requisition compensation, if agreed by the man's family, she would be able to raise the boy herself. She argued that "the land requisition compensation was distributed to me, and why shouldn't I have it? It is my money and I will not let them have a penny! Otherwise, I would rather not have this divorce." As to cultural biases, she first asked: "What is wrong with the boy?" She even suggested not remarrying but instead living with her son for the rest of her life. The courage and determination of this twenty-five-year-old mother was palpable. She even suggested that to rent an apartment in the city would be a way to overcome cultural bias. By so doing, she would not have to bother her parents.

Nonetheless, her resistance was unsuccessful. Without compensation from the man's side, her arguments were weak; she had little in her arsenal with which to fight back. Her only bargaining chip against the plaintiff seemed to be refusing to agree to a divorce, which was not feasible given the tension between the two families. This is why (as will be detailed later), out of desperation, she told the judge of the father-in-law's attempted rapes. Financial dependence is thus the most fundamental reason for gendered child custody judgments. Other studies have corroborated this. In Li (2009: 183), when a judge suggested that a mother drop her child custody claim, the mother resisted: "I am greatly concerned with his psychological development, especially his character." However, the mother made immediate concessions when the judge invoked a financial point: "It is so expensive to pay the tuition and other costs for extracurricular activities, can you afford it? Why bother?" This is also why in urban areas (where women's financial situations have improved), they are more likely to be awarded child custody.

Adjudication: Using Child Custody to Strike a Balance

Indeed, the pressures from judges during mediation are less visible in developed and coastal areas: when the economic development level increases, cultural biases decline. Many women from well-off families, or who have decent jobs, are more willing to overcome material and cultural barriers—as long as they can stay with their kids. All these factors thwart the judge's mediation. Some judges fall back on rhetoric such as the following: "Eventually the child belongs to society. Raising . . . him will not change the fact that you are the mother. Why do you have to fight so hard?" One judge said to a divorcing woman: "Divorce cannot deny the fact that you are his parents, because you are his parents forever" (Li 2009: 183). As true as these statements are, they do not address the concerns of most parents fighting for child custody. They care more about the emotional attachment to the children, the opportunities, and the time they can spend with them (Xiao, Gao and Wang 2014). Hollow rhetoric is thus ineffective in persuading women to give up child custody through mediation. Then, the judges must adjudicate. As mentioned, a divorce judge's paramount concern is whether the marriage can be maintained. Other concerns, such as determining child custody, the division of marital property, and compensation for domestic violence, are all subordinate. In one judge's own words: "Child custody is a secondary issue."

In this section I provide three adjudicated cases in different times and regions to illustrate how women's rights become bargaining chips in contested divorce litigation. The first two are from the Shaanxi Court, one from 1991 and the other from 2018. The contrasts and similarities will show how the rationale of the courts has survived the massive social and economic changes over the decades. The third case is from the Pearl River Delta Court, in which the judge was courageous enough to grant child custody to the mother. However, her efforts to rescue the child were sidelined when the appellate court reversed that decision. Taken together, the three cases offer a picture of entrenched court practices thwarting the laws' implementation.

In the Railway Worker's Case (1991), a railway worker, originally from Sichuan but based in Shaanxi, was sued for divorce by his wife, a worker living in Sichuan. The judge, or the clerk (书记员), responsible for the case,[2] had traveled all the way from Shaanxi to Sichuan to investigate the reasons for the divorce. She found that because the couple were geographically separated, an arrangement common in China at that time, their four-year-old boy had been raised in Sichuan by his mother. The couple had a huge fight during Spring Festival, their once-a-year meeting. The conflict intensified when the mother-in-law picked a fight with the woman. The trigger for the divorce petition was that the woman had not received her remittance from the man.

The woman insisted on child custody during the judge's visit. She had raised the boy most of his life. She had a stable job with a decent income, and her parents, living in the same town, could lend a hand. In contrast, the man, living afar, with a job with the railway company, never had a fixed residence. This would prevent him from tending to the child. Should the court award him custody, the boy would be sent to his paternal grandparents. The boy, according to the memory of the judge, was adorable. He always hid himself behind his mother when she talked to others. It seemed that his mother's body had been a protective wall for the boy.

According to the judge, the trial was quite a scene. Enraged by the divorce petition, the man vehemently opposed it using vulgar language. He insisted on child custody if a divorce had to be granted. The trial ended with the woman sobbing. The judge, a novice at the time, sought advice from a senior colleague, who told her:

> The marriage cannot be maintained. But child custody should go to the man. Look at his angry face, and how mean he was to the woman in front of all of us. For a man living far from home, a divorce decision means that his home is gone. Awarding child custody to the woman means that the man would lose his child, a double whammy. All of sudden, he would

lose both a family and a son, [and] you never know what he might do to us. And he would not let go of the woman. You must find a way to let him win a battle. Otherwise, a divorce denial would be safer.

The young judge was nonetheless touched by the woman's resolve to end the marriage. A divorce denial would have been too brutal for the boy, who had lived with his mom since birth. Should the man get child custody, the boy would have to live with his paternal grandparents, with whom he was unfamiliar. However, the judge also realized that, even with a divorce denial, there was no reason to continue the marriage. Eventually, she granted a divorce and awarded child custody to the man; the woman had to pay monthly child support of 25 yuan. No appeal was filed, but the woman mailed the court a stack of materials protesting the child custody decision. Six months later, another petition from the woman arrived. It stated that ultimately the man had not taken the child. Apparently, the man did not have the capability to care for his son. This time, the woman asked the man to pay her 25 yuan as child support. This request went nowhere: the court could not initiate such an order after the case had been closed.

When the judge looked back and reflected on this case, which had occurred almost three decades before, she felt guilty about the decision. She felt it had been unfair to the woman, because her right to child custody had been deprived in order to offer psychological solace to the man. The father had been awarded child custody despite the time that the mother had spent nurturing their son, her stable job, her family's support, and the connection between her and her son. According to the law, these factors overwhelmingly favored the woman. That is why the young judge was puzzled and sought the advice of a senior judge. The senior judge understood the law but was also versed in the institutional concerns of the courts. The father was awarded child custody simply because he had opposed the divorce, as revealed by his crude manner and obscenities during the trial. Furthermore, when the father did not actually take the child, the court could do nothing to reverse the child support decision. Ironically, the mother had to take care of the son *and* pay child support. It was not the father but the mother who suffered the double whammy. The laws had given way to concerns for social stability.

"Over almost three decades, has the court's rationale changed?" I asked. "Barely," the judge answered. "If anything, we have only more tilt toward social stability maintenance." Nowadays, judges rarely travel for investigations, because the cause of divorce is no longer its focus. The novice judge is now a powerful official of the court. Her salary had increased from 90 yuan in 1991 to more than 7,000 yuan in 2018. Inflation in China over these years had rendered the 25-yuan child support payment insignificant. The courthouse had changed from a shed rented from a local factory to a grand, fully decorated, and well-equipped building, with CCTV covering every corner. The procedures of court operations are now printed on the wall in the case filling division. Today, the court receives ten times as many cases as it did three decades ago. She continued: "If a case is filed today, I would say, 100 percent, the court would render a divorce denial. This is the safest way for the judge and the court. For a first-time petition, there is no point for the judge to get into child custody battles, a can of worms. It is the woman who has to figure out what to do."

The words of the judge were verified in the Primary School Teacher's Case filed in 2018. Aged thirty-two, the wife, a primary school teacher, had wanted a divorce, custody of their four-year-old daughter, and 5,000 yuan as compensation for domestic violence. The man was a jobless hooligan with a bad record: domestic violence, collective fighting, and alcohol abuse. She once called 110 (the equivalent of 911 in the United States) when the man beat her. After the divorce proceeding began, he had given the woman a hard time. At one point, he objected to divorce, and at another point he said it was okay. One moment he did not want child custody, then at another moment he insisted on it. Later, his parents were also involved in the fight and claimed they did not want to give up child custody. The real reason seemed to be that the man would receive huge demolition compensation if he got custody. At one point, he even suggested that as long as he got child custody, he would not ask the woman for child support. He admitted to the domestic violence but would not pay a penny in restitution. Neither party was legally represented.

The woman satisfied all the legally stated conditions for child custody: she had a decent job with a stable income, was well-educated, and had spent much time nurturing the daughter and would be willing to continue doing so. In contrast, the man had little education, no stable income, and records for domestic violence and bad habits. Since he rarely spent time with the daughter, had he been awarded child custody the daughter would have been taken care of by his parents. In the initial settlement, the judge convinced the woman to give up child custody. However, when the man and his father negated the original deal and requested an additional 500 yuan per month in child support (because "she has a job with a stable income, but he does not"), the woman was so angry that she decided not to settle.

The judge was in a dilemma. She tried to talk the plaintiff into a settlement: forgo child custody and get a divorce first. But the mother's position on child custody was unwavering: she could not let the man destroy her daughter's future. She argued that on all fronts the man was not a suitable parent for child custody. For the sake of child custody, she would be willing to give up the land requisitions from the man's village committee, including the daughter's share. She requested only 500 yuan for child support.

The judge was hesitant. In her late twenties, she herself had a daughter the same age as the couple's and was sympathetic toward the plaintiff. She also realized that the woman had made significant compromises and that keeping her in such a marriage was unfair. She was unsure, however, how the man would react to an adjudicated divorce. Would he do something horrible to the woman or to the judge? She approached the plaintiff for another arrangement: the man would officially receive child custody, but in reality the woman would take care of her on behalf of the man's family; the man would take guardianship back when the daughter was older. As a go-between, she tried convincing the woman: "In essence the man does not really want child custody. He won't do much after this period. Once the daughter grows up, she will have her own opinion. If she doesn't stay with the man, she won't want to live with his family. And I do not think the man can do much to change that. Then you can initiate another lawsuit to change child custody." The plaintiff was reluctant to accept this deal. She agreed only to sacrifice more property rights. Then, she encountered the typical response of the court: stalling. Three months later, she decided to accept the proposed deal on the condition that the man allowed her to take care of their daughter.

The adjudicated outcome seemed acceptable. Though the woman was not awarded child custody, child support was only 300 yuan, lower than the expected 500 yuan. In the original settlement, there had been no compensation for domestic violence. However, the judgment now adjudicated 5,000 yuan for the woman. Of course, it was unrealistic to expect the hooligan to pay, but she could now deduct this part from her child support. The woman was happy about the decision and thankful. After she obtained the judgment, she paid the judge a special visit, bringing a cake to show her gratitude. For the man, the child custody decision suggested that he had also secured a victory in the litigation and that the judge had been fair.

This approach seems to have become a pattern: facing a man who had a quick temper or was physically violent, women usually find withholding consents for divorce understandable: as long as they can stay with the child, they accept that the man gets custody. Separating de facto and de jure rights is another innovative but pragmatic solution for hard cases in light of the institutional pressures judges face.

Similar to the Saleswoman's Case depicted at the beginning of this book, the thankful sentiment had been misplaced. While both parties' concerns were addressed and balanced, the woman's legal custody rights had been sacrificed, as were the rights of her child. Staying with her mother would have been the most beneficial to her future; now she had to live with her hooligan dad or paternal grandparents, with whom she was not comfortable. The judge later advised the woman that she could also file a separate suit to alter child custody after one or two years if the man was unfit for the role. This seemed like another soothing message, but nothing was guaranteed. The man might take a stronger position in the child custody lawsuit. Once again, the laws were not implemented as intended, and women's rights were trampled.

Such a balanced approach is also seen in cases involving *guanxi* (social connections) to judges. An outrageously unfair decision may trigger the other party to protest. To prevent this, the judge would rather make a neutral decision. The party with *guanxi*, contrary to the conventional belief, may not be favored. Exactly because the connected party often comes with trust, it is sometimes easy for the judge to persuade the connected party to accept such a decision, as shown in the Case with *Guanxi*.

The plaintiff seeking divorce was a lady in her early forties. She has been doing quite well economically and socially, and her husband, a laid-off worker, was taking care of their eleven-year-old son at home. Her aunt, a clerk at the court, had a close relationship with the judge. Due to this relationship, the plaintiff wanted not just the divorce but also the house and custody of their son.

With this *guanxi*, the judge would favor the plaintiff in many ways, especially in advising her what evidence to collect and how to collect it (He and Ng 2017). As to the economic compensation and child custody, however, the judge's position was firm. She said to the plaintiff: "You know that I am very close to your aunt. But for divorce cases, the capacity of the judge is limited. The key is how you two handle the issue, because this is your life. The defendant said that your emotional affection did not break down and he had no fault in this process. He even insisted us to investigate [by mentioning this the judge hints that the plaintiff is having an affair]. All I can help is one thing—divorce. But the house and the custody will be his." The judge then replied to the aunt, who was in court: "The plaintiff is not coming for economic compensation and the house. She has money—look at how she dresses herself. All she needs is a divorce certificate." Her balanced decision was accepted peaceably by the plaintiff because of the existence of a trusted relationship.

A major concern in such a decision is the unbalanced situation between the two litigating parties. The plaintiff is having a new relationship, and she is doing very well economically and socially. Her life is full of hope. But the husband suffered a double whammy: he already lost his job, and now his wife and family. Without a stable income and career, their son might be his only hope. If the judge made a decision favoring the plaintiff, it is likely that the defendant could not accept it and thus would protest. He may even commit suicide or launch petitions. The judge will also feel uncomfortable pushing such a miserable man over the cliff's edge.

Most judges facing such a dilemma follow the safest route: a divorce denial or a divorce decision with child custody awarded to the man. Nonetheless, there are outliers. Judge Ming, in her late thirties, was the director of the Family and Adolescence Division at the Pearl River Delta Court. She was well trained in the law and was gender-conscious. There was a divorce case in which the couple had an eleven-year-old son; the woman had an adult daughter from her previous marriage (see chapter 4, the Case of the Coerced Video). The man, a college professor, opposed the divorce. He said that he would not let go of her. At every step in the proceedings, he made trouble. One example was a claim of domestic violence. While the woman presented evidence from police reports and hospital records, he claimed it was *she* who had beaten *him*. Both parties also fought over custody of their son. There were four interview testimonies between the judge and the eleven-year-old in the files. The first one read:

> JUDGE: If your parents get divorced who do you want to live with?
> MINOR: If I pick one, the other will be mad. I think it's better for the judge to make the decision.
> PLAINTIFF (MOTHER): You name one. We will all leave the room.
> MINOR: I will not say. If I say one, the other will beat me. It is better for the judge to make the decision.

The minor changed his words from "the other will be mad" to "the other will beat me" after both parents left the room. Apparently, at least one party had threatened to beat him.

In two other testimonies, the judge asked the child who had spent more time with him and who he really wanted to stay with. The minor said "Mom" but immediately asked the judge not to show his father the testimony for fear of being beaten. The judge nonetheless showed it to the man. In the fourth testimony, recorded fifty days later, the minor described how the man had beaten him and subsequently forced him to record a video in which he said that he would stay with his father.

Based on the behavior of the man and all the evidence and testimonies, the judge was determined to rescue the mother and the son from a violent father. She granted the divorce petition and awarded child custody to the woman. As the judge expected, the man appealed. Apparently, he also gave the appellate judge a hard time. Eventually, the appellate court reversed the child custody decision, citing:

> First, the woman earned 5,000 yuan per month, while the man earned 7,000 yuan and had an apartment. The man's financial situation was obviously superior. Second, from the viewpoint of the child's future, the man

was a college professor, thus in a better professional position to mentor the child. Third, the rules of the SPC suggest that one party has the priority for child custody if the other already has a child. The plaintiff has a daughter from a previous marriage while the man, 44 years old, has a very low chance of having another child.

In addition, the appellate court also mentioned that the son's opinion was only for reference and thus "cannot be the sole basis for a decision." When interviewed, the trial judge could not conceal her contempt for the appellate reversal: "A college professor, thus in a better 'professional' position? Give me a break! Why did they not mention that he had beaten the child and the woman? Then the man, a forty-four-year-old, would have had a low chance of having another child? Nonsense again. The only reason was that the man was such a troublemaker and the appellate judge bowed to him."

The case files corroborate the trial judge's observations. At the very least, there is no legal basis to award child custody based on one's profession. The SPC (1993) mention educational opportunities provided by the parent as only one factor when considering child custody. Common sense suggests that entering one profession could not guarantee a better position for educating children. Being a college professor does not mean that the man would have been a caring father. Indeed, the man was not, given the domestic violence that he had committed, the threats to his son, and the video he coerced his son to record. The other two reasons for the reversal were equally shaky. The income gap between the two was 2,000 yuan. This may have made a slight difference, but it could have been remedied with child support. The man had an apartment subsidized by his work unit, but that should have been regarded as matrimonial property. The man's financial situation was better but not "obviously superior." The third reason—that the woman had another daughter—was also problematic. The daughter, from the woman's previous marriage, was already an adult by the time of the trial. The weight of her presence should have been minimized when considering the minor's custody. Further, a woman at forty-four may have difficulty getting pregnant, but most men at that age are likely physically capable of fathering a child. None of the three points had been strong enough to trump the man's beatings of both the son and the woman. The only explanation for reversing the decision was that child custody had been used by the appellate judge as a bargaining chip. The man had vehemently opposed the divorce, and the judge wanted to satisfy some of his requests.

The decision-making pattern of the appellate court was clear. In a different case in which the man's domestic violence had been established, Judge Ming both granted divorce and awarded child custody to the woman. The disgruntled man appealed, as he had threatened to do. In the appellate court, both decisions were reversed. The appellate court, citing that this had been a first-time petition and that the man had insisted on reconciliation, ruled "no divorce" for the couple, taking the safest route. The appellate court's decision had not mentioned domestic violence. As demonstrated in chapter 4, as long as the case ends in mediated reconciliation, domestic violence is destined to become an afterthought.

These two cases indicate that, in a backhanded way, an outlier judge is unable to change the entrenched patterns of judicial practice. These patterns are rooted in the systematic incentive mechanisms for all judges. Even though the trial judge had been determined to protect the woman and her son from a violent man, the appellate judge was not on her side. The analysis shows that the appellate judge was not superior at interpreting the laws. Was he simply more bureaucratic? Fed up by the mess created by the man, he eventually chose the safest route. Why should he take the chance? Legally speaking, there were two children in the family. One child awarded to each divorced party was the best solution. It would appear equal to the parties and to the general public. The man, as vengeful as he was, was also satisfied with the victory and the torture he had brought upon the woman.

Child custody thus becomes an instrument that judges use to strike a balance. In their own words, "We want a case closed without lingering effects." The man is physically stronger in that he may thwart the judgment's enforcement, hurt the woman, or harass the judge. The judge has to assess the risk and address his concerns. In this process, the laws become twisted, and so do the principles intended to protect women's interests and those of the children. Balance is achieved, but the weaker party, usually the woman, sacrifices child custody. The rationale is that squeaky wheels get more grease (Michelson 2006; He 2009a). The judge often exerts more pressure on the weaker party. Thus, laws that are intended to protect women's interests are slighted, traded, dispensed, or marginalized.

Strategic Behavior

One consequence of the court's *modus operandi* is that some litigating parties behave strategically to perpetuate gendered outcomes. Once the parties become aware of the court's approach, especially with a lawyer behind them, they may claim they want child custody even though they do not. They will refuse a divorce even if they are sure that the marriage has fallen apart. They may ask for a greater share of marital property, even if they do not deserve it. The reason behind these exaggerated claims is straightforward: with more claims and more intense resistance to the divorce, they will have a higher stack of bargaining chips and thus are in an advantageous position to negotiate. While both parties in divorce litigation may show this tendency, women are more willing to heed men's claims. This is because women, financially and physically, are usually in an inferior position and are thus unable to compete with men. Financially, for example, men can provide better living conditions and education for the child. Moreover, more women than men want to break free from their marriages, as more women than men are divorce plaintiffs (Brinig and Allen 2000). To make matters worse, women shoulder the primary responsibility for day-to-day child care. Due to their links with the children, they seem more willing to sacrifice other rights in order to secure child custody. Li (2009: 157) has documented this in a mediation session: "I would like to suggest that if he let me raise the child, the apartment on XX road will be his. I can give him that apartment if I can have the child."

The Strategic Policeman's Case exemplifies the strategic behavior and its gendered consequences. When the judge interviewed the policeman before the trial, he had not yet hired a lawyer. While he was reluctant to be divorced, this reluctance subsided once he realized that the woman was determined. This man also did not have a strong opinion on child custody. As a policeman, he needed to be on standby for work at any time and frequently shifted guards. It would have been difficult for him to care for the child, and his parents were also reluctant to take care of the child for him. He seemed fine with allocating 25 percent of his salary as child support should child custody be awarded to the woman. As for the property, he also seemed honest. He admitted that the electronics had been a bride-price from the woman's family, and his parents had borrowed 20,000 yuan from the woman's family to invest in a restaurant. The only thing, he said, was that he did not have so much cash on hand. He might need more time to repay it.

As was shown, the judge's mediation efforts had been unsuccessful because of the woman's resistance. While the trial was under way, the judge was informed that the man had hired a lawyer from a local law firm. On the day of the trial, the man changed all his positions: He disagreed with the divorce; if the court rendered an adjudicated divorce, he insisted on child custody. His reason for seeking child custody was that this was his parents' first granddaughter (a patrilineal claim) and he also had a stable income (a financial claim). Apparently coached by his lawyer, he repeatedly emphasized that the woman had neither a stable income nor a permanent home. When the woman said that she had found a job as a kindergarten teacher, the man said that the income was only 1,100 yuan per month, much lower than his 4,500 yuan. He also produced evidence for his salary. As for the home electronics, he claimed that they had been bought after the marriage certificate had been issued and that he had paid for them. Thus, they should be regarded as marital property instead of the bride-price. He denied that his parents had ever borrowed the 20,000 yuan from her parents. He also claimed that all the charges on her credit card were for her personal expenditures. Since his income was enough to support the family's living costs, there had been no need for her to charge these items on the credit card. In addition to these oral claims, a written statement, apparently prepared by the lawyer, was presented on the spot. The judge, not to mention the plaintiff, did not have the chance to see it prior to the trial.

The plaintiff, a woman in her late twenties, was caught off guard. It seemed that she had not expected such a dramatic position change from the defendant, nor had she ever experienced any legal battle like this. Carrying only her cell phone, she did not even have a pen with her, let alone documents. When the judge asked her if she had any evidence of the marriage, she said "no"—she even failed to mention their marriage certificate. Instead, she continued fumbling with her cell phone to relieve her anxiety. When it was her turn to present evidence, she only mentioned that a WeChat message proved the existence of the 20,000 yuan debt. However, the man denied that the message was from his account. Then, she had nothing with which to fight back. When another judge in the collegial panel suggested she present evidence of the breakdown of their emotional relationship, she replied, "I don't have any." The calmer the defendant was, the more nervous she became. Only when asked if she had any advantageous conditions for raising the child did she catch her breath and say that her parents could help and that she had just found a job.

The man's changed positions were strategic. His real concern had been the property, and the child custody request was merely tactical. He rarely spent time with the daughter and would have little time to do so in the future. In contrast, the mother was determined to get child custody: the daughter had basically been raised by her, and her parents were happy to lend a hand. The child had already been integrated into their lives. They were willing to continue raising the child despite the high costs involved.

Considering the man's landslide victory in the trial, the judgment had favored him. While the woman was awarded child custody, the electronics were regarded as marital property, not as the bride-price. More important, the claim to the 20,000 yuan debt was not supported because the woman could not produce any evidence.

Both parties seemed happy with the decision. The woman got child custody, which she had desperately wanted; the man was ecstatic. He had contributed little to the family but received a great deal of monetary rewards. Advised by the lawyer, he had behaved strategically. The court had responded to these strategic behaviors as they had expected. To render a divorce decision against a party unwilling to be divorced, the court must compensate that party on other issues such as property or child custody. In this case, in which the fight over child custody had been strategic, the woman's property rights were compromised. In this way, a balance had been struck. Indeed, when the man's position on divorce changed from "yes" to "no," the judge adopted the Normal Procedure and formed a collegial panel of three. This is because when one party is unwilling to divorce, the court, to play it safe, usually does not adopt the

Simplified Procedure, which is more efficient but only entails one judge. This change, in itself, is another practice demonstrating that the judges and courts prioritize efficiency and stability.

In many ways, the judge could have rendered a decision favorable to the woman. First, she could have instructed her to provide evidence for the property claims (e.g., records of credit charges for items such as milk and toys for the child), which would have constituted mutual obligations. During the trial, the judge could also have suggested that the woman present evidence about other valuables at the home. Second, the electronics could have been regarded as her property, even though she could not provide evidence. This was because it was a local norm that the groom pays the bride-price to the bride. Finally, the starting point for child support could have been set at the moment the two separated, instead of when the judgment went into effect.

The judge, however, did none of the above. She had no incentive to do so. The wife was already satisfied with her child custody victory. Given her poor performance in the trial, the outcome could have been worse. She should have felt lucky that child custody had not been sacrificed. Had the policeman resisted the divorce, or had a propensity for violent reprisal, the divorce petition likely would have been rejected. Alternatively, a divorce might have been granted, but child custody would have been awarded to the man. The basis for this decision could have been that the man's finances were in better shape, thanks to a higher and more stable salary and the apartment. From the perspective of either the law or the general public, these were sufficient, despite the fact that the man was not suitable for being a parent or even willing to take on the responsibility. Eventually, neither appealed. The judge was able to dispose of the case.

The man's strategic behavior had made a difference. Li (2015) argues that there is entrenched gender inequality on the part of lawyers at the case filing stage. This chapter has demonstrated that inside the courtroom, the judges, in concert with the lawyers, encourage this strategic behavior and reinforce gendered outcomes.

Conclusions

In this chapter, I have demonstrated how courts perpetuate gendered outcomes in child custody battles. Due to judges' performance assessment criteria, their priority in divorce cases is to resolve cases without any lingering effects. As a result, whether a marriage can be amicably resolved becomes their topmost concern. The issue of child custody is thus marginalized and often becomes a bargaining chip to achieve a balanced result. Financial disparities between the two genders and cultural biases against women are often used as tactics to coerce women to give up child custody. Most women cave in to the pressure. Successful resistance is rare, and when it does occur it is from those who are financially independent. As a result of the courts' approach, strategic behavior is encouraged. Women, however, have to sacrifice their child custody rights for divorce. Men's chances of being awarded child custody, however, can be enhanced when a divorce is denied.

Judges in more developed and progressive coastal areas are less effective at coercing women to give up child custody compared to those in the hinterlands. They must adjudicate. In this sense, both economic development and social progressiveness will improve gender disparity. However, the rationale of the courts, driven by their incentives, remains the status quo in adjudication. Child custody is used as a bargaining chip for the judges to strike a balance in their decisions. Given the balanced approaches of the courts and their tendency to bow to financial disparities and cultural biases, when a family has two children, it is likely that each parent will get one.

The gendered child custody outcomes in China appear more serious than those in court-sponsored mediation in the United States. In the US setting, judges are not forced to reach a settlement. They merely try, based on the belief that parents are forever and that both parties are able to reorganize their private lives (Schepard 2004: 50–67). It is ideal if they can facilitate a settlement, but failing to do so would not affect their job performance or prospects for promotion. Without such pressure, child custody is not regarded as a secondary issue in divorce cases. At the very least, child custody is not used as a bargaining chip. Nowhere would these mediators have mobilized such intense pressure to cajole, persuade, and coerce the litigating parties into a settlement. The internalized disempowerment problems found in the US setting are nothing compared to what this chapter has demonstrated in regard to the Chinese system. In the United States, mediation has been criticized because women, with fewer financial resources, were more likely than men to compromise for the sake of their children. Thus, they became easy targets for unscrupulous manipulation (Bryan 1994). Yet this problem has been ameliorated ever since federal legislation has required states to adopt child support guidelines based on parental incomes. The guidelines have created clarity and certainty about parents' financial obligations to children after divorce, reducing the potential for manipulation during negotiations (Mnookin and Maccoby 2002). While financial disparities between men and women no doubt persist, mediation has increased the likelihood that child support will be paid (Maccoby and Mnookin 1992). Both men and women perceive mediation as fair and valuable (Gordon 2002). In Chinese courts, the judges orchestrate and facilitate such maneuvering. They allow economic inequalities and cultural biases to penetrate the deal; by so doing, they can close the case in a way consistent with their own concerns.

6

Property Division and Male Advantage

In this chapter, I turn to the relationship between judges' institutional constraints and litigants' resource disparities. The division of conjugal property illustrates how judges, under institutional constraints, have let the "haves," mostly men, come about ahead. The term "resource disparity" is derived from Galanter's seminal paper "Why Do the Haves Come Out Ahead? Speculations on the Limits of Legal Change" (1974). Galanter argues that despite the institutional arrangements to guard against particularism, private power, and inequality, the haves still come out ahead in the US court system. Even if ideal legal arrangements—such as judicial independence, due process, ethical and competent judges, and so on—are in place, the haves benefit because the stronger party's advantages are inevitable.

Situating the discussion in the US context, Galanter assumes that the judges making the decisions are neutral. When his original thesis on resource disparity is tested in other countries, the assumption becomes untenable. For example, Haynie (1994) demonstrates that in the Philippines, the laws and policy may favor the "have-nots" because social stability is an important concern; Dotan (1999) argues that the Israeli High Court may have an ideological preference toward the have-nots. In other words, the laws and the judges may be biased. A broader theory has been proposed by Wheeler et al. (1987) and refined by He and Su (2013). They have suggested three sets of elements—relating to the law, the courts (judges), and the litigating parties' characteristics—to explain Galanter's proposition that the stronger party wins more often. The first set of elements suggests that there may be a normative tilt of the law toward or against the stronger party; the second proposes that the court itself—specifically the judges—may be biased; the third stipulates that the stronger party typically commands greater resources, has more experience, or is in a better strategic position (cf. Albiston 1999). Indeed, based on an empirical analysis of about 3,000 cases from Shanghai courts, He and Su (2013: 139) find that "in Chinese litigations, the impact of party resources deployable in the courtroom may only be the tip of the iceberg." In some areas, the laws bluntly favor the haves. In others, the judges are influenced by "the form of constraints on the behavior of the judges." Furthermore "the judges' consideration of their own career and the larger political implications may have an impact on the litigation outcomes" (He and Su 2013: 139).

This may reflect how, during divorce litigation, common marital property is divided in China. Women's rights advocate and the lawyer Guo Jianmei commented of the famous divorce case of Li Yang, the founder of Crazy English (Tatlow 2013): "It's a huge flaw in the system. The state doesn't intervene to force rich men like Mr. Li to reveal their true assets, and it doesn't allow lawyers like us to do it either, it doesn't give us the rights. The is a society that doesn't control those with money or power. It doesn't see things through to the end."

When women face off against husbands in divorce litigation, they are the weaker party. For a long time and for various reasons, the earning capacity of women has been lower than that of men. Socialism did not liberate women. "Chinese women endure educational, *economic*, political, and cultural inequities that are international features of women's secondary status" (Stacey 1983: 4; emphasis added). If the financial disparity between the genders was narrower during the first three decades of the People's Republic, after the marketization in the mid-1990s, women, particularly middle-aged women, became financially more vulnerable compared to their male peers. Until recently, they had been required to retire ten years earlier than men, and women were also more likely to be laid off or forced into early retirement during the wave of privatization. Furthermore, the earnings gap between husbands and wives in absolute terms has only increased (Gilmartin et al. 1994; Shu and Bian 2003). Fincher (2014) points out that as far as the gender wealth gap is concerned, the right place to focus on is residential property. According to her (2014: 5), "[M]any Chinese women have been shut out of China's explosion of housing wealth because urban homes appreciating exponentially in value tend to be registered solely in the man's name." According to a survey she cited (2014: 7–8), only 30 percent of marital home deeds in the most expensive cities in China list the woman's name, whereas 70 percent of women contribute to the home purchase. A legal consequence is that a woman faces a heavier burden of proof to show that she has equal shares in the communal property, even if her name is on the deed. In a famous case, the court awarded only 30 percent of the home value to an abused wife, even though she was the joint owner (2014: 72).

How, exactly, do the judges divide property between men and women in divorce litigation? As will be shown, the legal stipulations favor men. Yet, I focus more on how the laws have been implemented than on how the laws should be revised. Can the existing promises of the laws protecting women's interests be fulfilled? Have the court practices exacerbated a situation where the laws are already unfair? In this chapter, I contend that throughout the proceedings, the judges' concerns for self-protection and efficiency have further disadvantaged women in property divisions. Women often have to give up their property rights in return for a divorce or obtaining child custody. Delaying an unavoidable divorce decision, and the bidding process for a wife who has no other place to live, contribute to women's distress. Additionally, judges are often indifferent to the generally substandard legal services that women receive.

Property Division

Consistent with the state's policy orientation empowering citizens to dissolve unhappy marriages, property divisions have surfaced as a key issue for marriage and divorce during the reform period. A rather unique characteristic in China's divorce law is that there is no alimony or maintenance, either for or from either side. Article 42 states that at the time of divorce, if one party has difficulties supporting himself or herself, the other party must render appropriate help from her or his personal property such as the residence. Specific arrangements are to be made between both parties through consultation. This means that once the communal property is divided, the couple will no longer get any financial support from one another. This legal arrangement only intensifies the fight over property division, especially for the financially disadvantaged party. If he or she cannot get a better share at the time of settlement, that party may struggle after divorcing.

While the 2001 landmark amendment to the Marriage Law makes divorce easier to obtain, it also clarifies that when dividing matrimonial property, the court is supposed to take good care of women and children. Article 39 stipulates that in cases where an agreement cannot be reached, the People's Court is to make a judgment in consideration of the actual circumstance of the property and on the principle of caring for the rights and interests of the wife and children. It launches procedures that aim to recognize fault and provide compensation for blameworthy marital conduct (Palmer 2007). It also introduces legal penalties by defining civil and criminal liabilities. Behaviors that justify divorce could entitle an innocent party to claim damages (Art. 46). Further, by recognizing significant gaps between men's and women's financial standing and social status, the state acknowledges its obligation to protect women's rights in marital and familial conflicts.

Nonetheless, individual property rights have been strengthened. In contrast to Article 13 in the original 1980 Marriage Law (both spouses have equal rights to manage a couple's jointly owned property), Articles 18 and 19 of the 2001 Marriage Law define individual property within marriages and elaborate how prenuptial or other notarized agreements between spouses can designate legally enforceable claims. Accordingly, all property acquired before marriage is presumed to be individual, unless otherwise agreed, as is the case for all items that one party deems to be for his or her personal use. Article 19 stresses individual ownership in emphasizing how agreements to designate separate ownership are binding for both parties. This marks what Davis (2014: 558) terms "the turn away" from China's longtime advocacy and support for a conjugal property regime.

This tendency has become clearer since then. For more than a decade, the Supreme People's Court has promoted property-related marital regulations. The SPC's first batch of Interpretations of the 2001 amended Marriage Law focused on property divisions more than any other issue. In 2003, the court promulgated the second batch of Judicial Interpretations. Of the twenty-nine articles, twenty were property-related. Of significance was a provision that courts could not withhold divorce from the party at fault if affection had broken down. It specifies and supports individual property rights within a marriage but leaves protection of marital property vague. For example, Article 22 of the 2003 SPC Interpretation specifies that absent other arrangements, parents investment before a marriage should be seen as a gift to their child alone; investments after the couple are married are considered gifts to the couple. In contrast to the First and Second Interpretations, the Third Interpretation, in 2011, undermines the latent protections of communal property. It privileges parents' investments in married children's residences if the parents had invested and registered the residence in their child's name before the marriage (Art. 7). The Third Interpretation elaborates that in cases where parents of both the husband and the wife have invested in the purchase of the home, absent other arrangements, ownership will be apportioned on the basis of the parents' investment. An underlying theme in this process is separating affection from property.

Scholars have lambasted this position in the amended Marriage Law. In examining the "disparate impact of some of the facially-neutral provisions," Ogletree and Alwis (2004) argue that the Marriage Law fails to address many problems in determining women's property ownership, both during the marriage and following divorce. Because the law fails to "account for the experience and values of women . . . the law may actually disadvantage women" (254). The procedural weaknesses of the law, the wide discretion given to a poorly educated male judiciary, and the difficulty in meeting the requirements of proof all undercut the ostensible gains women secured through the 2001 amendments. They also recognize that even when wives gain title to property, they lack the financial resources to realize their legal rights. In sum, Ogletree and Alwis find that "equitable property distribution in the context of inequality between two parties does not produce equal results" (281). In terms of protecting women's welfare, the revisions were mostly symbolic. Margaret Woo (2003) is less pessimistic. She believes that the 2001 amendments redressed some of the disadvantages by clarifying the grounds for divorce, defining what constitutes conjugal property, and elaborating on child custody and visitation rights. She concludes that the 2001 revisions "swing the pendulum back" (133) toward more collectivist arguments that ultimately may protect women's interests. However, she also finds that because women have fewer economic resources than men "to make their stories heard" (132) in more evidentiary based judicial decisions, the new emphasis on contractual arguments and burden of proof disadvantages most women.

Scholars are even more critical of the SPC Interpretations on property division. They argue that under the Interpretations, only emotional issues are still covered by the Marriage Law and the courts; in terms of property, the SPC Guidelines look more like contract law. Davis (2014) argues that the 2011 SPC Interpretation turns away from established norms of the communal property regime, favoring formal over substantive equality. The prenuptial arrangement has an important role in determining the division outcome should a divorce ensue. Some Chinese scholars have even suggested that the Marriage Law has been changed into property law. They predict that the laws, when implemented, will lead to more gender inequality and even revert back to the feudal period. According to Davis (2014), the logic of the voluntary contract has been extended to intimate relationships, and there is a trend toward the "privatization of marriage." Jiang (2011) asserts that these SPC guidelines will turn back the clock to when the stronger party (most likely the man) openly preyed on the weaker party (usually the woman) in property division. Protecting vulnerable parties in marital disputes has lost momentum; greater attention has been diverted to the personal freedom to dissolve unhappy marriages and the codification of individual property rights through divorce settlements. The law and the judiciary thus recognize more of the individual property rights and are more attuned to citizens' property rights.

More clear is the changed orientation of the law; less known are the actual operations of the courts and their decisions' impact on the two genders. Most analyses have been based on the letter of the law; few have touched on the law in action. One exception may be Li and Friedman (2016), who document the predicament of a rural woman who, after years in an unhappy marriage, was resolved to sue for divorce in court. They state (2016: 161): "Preoccupied with its own priorities and interests, the grassroots courts system is insensitive to rural women's marital suffering and unsupportive of their pursuit of legally endowed rights upon divorce. Instead of following the law as it appears on the books, judges often cut corners, skip judgment on property division and conjugal 'fault,' and, in effect, reduce divorce litigation to merely a matter of marital dissolution." They contend that the judges also allow long-standing patrilineal values and property regimes, coupled with norms of patrilocal residence after marriage, to permeate their decision-making process. This exacerbates married women's inferior status within their conjugal communities and their weak claims to matrimonial property.

Their study suggests that rural women often get little financial compensation, property, or alimony from divorce litigation. But their husbands retain control over conjugal property.

The other exception is the survey conducted by Chen et al. (2018). They examine the outcomes of property divisions in 360 divorce cases sampled from three years in a district in Chongqing. They find mixed results as to gender equality. Some suggest improvements, but many others aggravate inequality. For example, they find that that in 34.8 percent of the cases men were assigned more communal property, whereas in only 16 percent of the cases did women get more (Chen et al. 2018: 112).

While these studies provide insight, many questions remain unanswered. On which aspects does the decision-making process become gendered? What are the judges' concerns on these issues? If the laws have already disadvantaged women, how have the judges, through their behavior, exacerbated the situation?

Women Trading Property for Child Custody and Divorce

In Li's (2015) study on how legal workers in rural Sichuan interact with their divorce clients, she finds that the they often prod female clients to forgo their property rights. She argues that this gendered pattern is derived from the institutional structure of the service fees collected by the legal workers: they usually charge a lump sum for a case, and thus they want to finish processing cases as soon as possible. While this explanation makes sense, questions remain: Why don't the legal workers press their male clients more? The following sections will show that this gendered pattern stems from the judges' approach: it is the judges who press females to give up their property. In many cases, the legal workers are simply conduits, relaying these pressures to their clients.

In chapter 5, I demonstrated that women's child custody is used as a bargaining chip to strike a balance. This rationale applies equally to women's property rights. They are two sides of the same coin. As in child custody, the weaker party's property rights are more dispensable because judges are unwilling to confront the stronger party. The difference, if any, is that property rights are more likely to be forfeited than child custody, since nowadays people care more about child custody rights. After all, personal rights seem more important when financial resources are more abundant.

A pattern thus emerges: if one party wants a divorce or child custody, he or she has to sacrifice property rights. There is a trade-off between property and personal rights: one needs to pay for personal rights. A lawyer with twenty years of experience in Shenzhen explained to me:

> Whoever initiates the divorce process will get the short end of the stick. This is because the initiator is usually more eager to get divorced. The other party could take advantage of this and respond with a firm opposition, so as to force the initiator to compromise on other aspects such as property or child custody. If the initiator refuses to make concessions, the courts usually grant a divorce denial on the first petition. Then, the divorce decision will be delayed, imposing, at least, psychological pressures to the initiator. To get the divorce earlier, and to be freed from the marriage, many are willing to compromise, trading money for time.

In the Autistic Daughter's Case, a female defendant yearned for custody for her two daughters. She opposed divorce in the first petition and was supported by the court. The man unsuccessfully reversed the decision on appeal. Six months later, he filed another petition. At that time, the couple had already been separated for two years. During the trial, both parties agreed to divorce but fought over other elements, including child custody and property. The seven witnesses summoned by the woman alone indicated the intensity of the fight.

As mentioned, when a divorce case involves two children and both parties fight for child custody, courts usually offer each party one child. This may be the best way to show a judge's evenhandedness. In this case, of his several claims, the man had requested custody for one child, even though, because he was working for a remote production and construction corps in Xinjiang,[1] he was not in a good position to raise her. However, the woman, for reasons which will be explained momentarily, wanted custody of both children despite being unemployed. The morning after the trial, the woman came to the judge:

I want both children. The property is far less important. I cannot separate the two. You know, how great would it be for them to grow up together! This is because my elder daughter has autism. Her nursery [school] teacher said that she always quietly stays in the corner, without talking to anybody. It is worrisome. A doctor later confirmed that it was autism, though not serious. She is getting better now, and she can go to school by herself. Now that I agree to a divorce, as I said in the trial, I want both children. He does not love the children; he only wants a share.

With such a significant compromise being proposed, the judge soon helped reach a deal: the woman gave up receiving support for one child, reimbursement for money borrowed (debts) for raising the children, and any appreciation in value of the conjugal apartment. The apartments' value had tripled from 3,400 yuan to 10,000 yuan per square meter since they had bought it. For the 120-square-meter apartment, she had lost 400,000 yuan, equivalent to ten years of her salary (3,000 yuan per month)! She would live with the two children in a suburban apartment originally owned by her parents.

This is the trade-off that the woman had to accept. The family had two children, a result of the relaxed birth-control policy effective since 2015. As mentioned, the courts' usual practice is to allocate one child to each side. To achieve a result diverging from this usual practice, significant concessions are necessary. The woman had originally wanted a divorce, child custody, and property: she had summoned seven witnesses to support her positions. She opposed the divorce on the first petition, trying to offer the kids a seemingly intact home. However, to secure custody of both daughters, instead of just one, she had to forfeit her property rights. The woman's desire to gain custody of the two children put her in a disadvantaged negotiating position. She said to the judge: "I can give up everything as long as I have the two children with me." Her daughter's autism seemed to be the key to her decision.

Similarly, when the divorce itself is in dispute, women often have to forgo property rights to obtain their own freedom. In the Strategic Policeman's Case (see chapter 5), when the woman filed the divorce petitions, she also sought child custody, payback of a 20,000-yuan debt, and division of the marital property. In particular, she insisted that the husband repay 20,000 yuan borrowed from her parents. At the pretrial interview, when the policeman was not yet represented by a lawyer, he had been amenable to the divorce and repayment of the debt. In the pretrial mediation, the woman, assuming both parties had agreed to divorce, insisted on child custody and the property rights. Thus, she had successfully resisted the judge's pressure regarding child custody.

In the trial, the policeman behaved more strategically, and the original dynamics changed. He opposed the divorce and sought child custody. Moreover, he denied the debt's existence and fought every item of property, from bride-price to baby formula. Taken aback, panicking, and nervous, the woman did not know how to respond. She had to fight for the divorce and child custody, two items that she had earlier taken for granted. She almost forgot the issue of property division. Realizing how poor her performance had been during the trial, the day after she took the initiative to approach the judge despite their unpleasant pretrial mediation session. This time, she made it clear to the judge that all she wanted was a divorce and child custody. She was ready to give up the communal properties and forfeit the 20,000-yuan debt. Still uncomfortable, she asked her relative, a prosecutor who knew the judge well, to act as a go-between (on *guanxi*'s impact on judicial decision-making, see He and Ng 2017).

With this U-turn in the wife's position, it became an easy case for the judge, who had always been focused on how to end cases peacefully and efficiently. In the judgment, the judge did not even bother to mention all the small electronics that should have belonged to the woman, who already felt grateful for being awarded the divorce and child custody. The judge later told me that had she taken this position in the pretrial mediation session, then the case would have been settled quickly.

In this case, the woman had been more eager to get rid of the man than vice versa. Her original positions for the property during the mediation had been based on the assumption that the man would be willing to divorce and give up child custody. Her bottom line, however, was revealed once the divorce and child custody were contested. Then, the only bargaining chip she had was the property. That was why she eventually made significant compromises on that issue.

This rationale seems equally applicable to both genders, but why are females' property rights more often slighted? First, women are both financially and physically weaker within Chinese society and thus easier to persuade. Second, mothers spend more time with their children and thus have a closer link, as shown in the Autistic Daughter's Case. To get child custody they may have to forgo property rights. Finally, it is women, not men, who initiate the majority of divorce lawsuits (Xu 2007; Chen, Zhang and Shi 2018; Wang 2007; Li 2015: 175, footnote 7). If she is the initiator of a divorce, the woman often has a strong desire to leave the marriage behind. This consideration is subjective, dependent on individual preferences and values, and thus cannot be quantified in monetary terms. Nonetheless, the woman is often more eager to dissolve the current marriage and move on. Often she is more willing to compromise. When the man is more resistant to divorce, the judge will press the woman on other issues. That is why it is women who disproportionally bear the brunt. The gendered pattern creeps into property division.

Disparate Impacts of Delayed Decisions

As I demonstrated in chapter 2, delaying divorce decisions has become routine for both first-time petitions as well as those intensely contested. This is done to address the courts' concerns over efficiency and stability. This section explores the financial impacts of these approaches. It contends that a delayed decision often disadvantages women in terms of property division. One common exit strategy for divorcing couples is to transfer their communal property (see e.g., Fincher 2014: 150). But a delayed court decision paves the way for men—usually the holders of conjugal property and in a financially superior position—to hide, transfer, or squander the property. When the divorce is finally granted, there is little property left for the woman. The man may have experienced a change of heart because of the protracted battle and accumulated resentment. He therefore is more likely to wage a full-scale war and refuse to compromise. In other words, the bureaucratic and political concerns exacerbate women's already inferior position in terms of property rights.

This pattern is exemplified in cases that are initiated by men but resisted by women. As in chapter 2, in this type of case men usually have developed a new romance or have become economically better off. For those who are eager to leave the marriage behind, they could compromise on the property division. However, when their requests are persistently denied, their counterstrategies are to transfer, hide, or squander the communal property. They may simply go ahead and start a new life without finalizing the divorce, since they cannot get it from the courts anyway. A denial decision from the court, ostensibly supporting the requests of the woman, actually places her in an irreversibly miserable situation. This deals another blow to her already disadvantaged position.

In another Shaanxi case (the Distraught Woman's Case), the husband, a construction contractor, had become involved in a new romance and sued to divorce his wife, who was a housewife. According to the woman, the man had committed domestic violence against her. More unbearable for the woman, the man's new love kept texting indecent, insulting, and humiliating messages to her. With his new love, the man, after moving out of the original apartment, had vandalized the defendant's home. Insulted, the woman vehemently opposed the divorce. In her own words, she would not let go of such a scoundrel. The law should be on her side.

It seemed that the man had made a fortune by taking subcontracted projects in Beijing. However, the woman knew nothing about the details of these assets. It was from her brother, who worked for the man's company as a driver, that she learned about the man's fortune. Regardless, this had not been her focus; she argued that their mutual affection had yet to break down. The man, then, perhaps eager for an expedited divorce, or out of guilt or sympathy, proposed to compensate the defendant 50,000 yuan. Of course, there was room for negotiation if the woman was willing to go that route. Determined to oppose the divorce, the woman ignored the offer.

Because of the defendant's stance against divorce, and because it was a first-time petition, the judge, a man in his forties, was unwilling to waste time on mediation. He soon took the best strategy: an adjudicated denial. The law seemed to be on the woman's side.

Six months later, the man initiated a second petition for divorce. This time the woman's position changed. While she still opposed the divorce, she was willing to negotiate financial compensation. She even provided two bank accounts under the man's name and 5,000 yuan for the court to conduct an investigation, hoping that the court could uncover the profits from his projects. This indicated that she was ready for divorce should the husband's earnings be found and equally divided. After all, by then the couple had been separated for almost two years. The man, during the trial, also admitted that he had 150,000 yuan in savings. The outcome hinged on the amount of compensation.

While the woman provided two bank accounts under the man's name, it was the judge's job to identify the conjugal property. This time, the case was in the hands of a different judge. This judge, in his fifties and near retirement, was not in good health and had been known for not making extra effort in cases. He only perfunctorily checked the two accounts provided by the woman and found no money. Apparently, the money earned by the man during the marriage had been transferred or hidden in an unknown account. Since the woman's expectations for compensation had been high and the man was defensive, the conflict between them was hard to reconcile. When the two parties could not reach an agreement on monetary compensation, the judge rendered another adjudicated denial. As the subsequent developments would reveal, a decision seemingly fulfilling the wife's requests had in fact been nothing less than a steep blow to her prospects.

After being rejected twice by the courts, the man gave up requesting a divorce through the court. It seemed that the woman had won the legal battles because the courts had supported her requests. However, she got nothing more than a marriage in name only. The man never returned home. Instead, he lived with his new lover in a location unknown to the defendant. Rumors suggested that they had even had a child.[2] The man fulfilled none of his responsibilities as a husband. The court seemed to side with the woman, but the decisions earned her little material benefit. The adjudicated denials seemed to identify the couple's problems yet provided no solutions. They were akin to a medical report that detected the cause of a disease but failed to identify a cure. Eventually, the man's strategy was effective. Four years after the second petition, the woman, realizing that a divorce denial decision did no good for her, initiated a petition as plaintiff. The woman, tortured by the experience, became distraught. Easily agitated, she could not even focus when communicating with others. At the time she filed the petition, she had been working as a part-time security guard in a college dorm and was barely supporting herself.

Six years had passed since the man initiated his first divorce petition. When they met for the third trial, little mutual affection remained between the two. The man's position was clear: he agreed to divorce, but he had no savings left and could not compensate the woman for any cause. He also insisted on custody of their fifteen-year-old daughter because the wife, given her mental status and job security, was unfit for guardianship.

This time, the judge was a recent graduate with a master's degree from a prestigious law school.[3] From a well-off family, he did not need the job to support himself, and he had little aspiration to be promoted. His work attitude was not much better than those of his predecessors. Since both parties agreed to divorce, the judge focused on child custody and property division. As the only conjugal property that the wife had proven was the apartment bought for 40,500 yuan seven years earlier, the judge divided it in half according to the SPC guidelines. The husband bid 100,000 yuan, higher than the wife's offer. As a result, the husband received ownership of the apartment. The wife received half of the bidding price—50,000 yuan—and moved out of the apartment. The judge also awarded custody of their daughter to the man because of the wife's unstable mental condition and insecure employment status.

This marathon of a divorce fight finally came to an end. She had won some early battles but lost the war. The two delayed decisions on divorce—two adjudicated denials—seemed to support the claims of the wife. In reality, however, they had cost her the best opportunity for better financial compensation. If an adjudicated denial was an obvious choice and a routine practice for the first petition, the second adjudicated denial had been financially disastrous for the woman. The man had been a contractor of his own transportation business. He was the business's operator, but the woman knew nothing about its operations, let alone its profits. Thus, the man easily transferred the profits to unknown accounts.

It was difficult, if not impossible, for the woman to prove the existence of those assets. If the first denial offered an opportunity for the couple to recover, the second denial was completely unnecessary. The man was already cohabitating with another woman, and he never came home. The only communication between the nominal husband and wife were the insults hurled at one another. How could such a marriage be rescued by an adjudicated denial? After that legal encounter, the man felt that the woman had intentionally blocked his request for a divorce.

So he simply gave up pursuing a divorce in the courts. He opted for co-habitation with his new love, a common phenomenon in China today. At that point, his original sympathy and guilt toward his wife vaporized. That was why he had taken a firmer stance in the third trial. In the division of the conjugal apartment, he went for a higher bid, squeezing the woman out of a living space.

The judges understood that the collapse of such a marriage was inevitable. After the divorce, the man would move on with the new love, perhaps with the daughter from the previous marriage; the woman would live in a small rental apartment, employed or unemployed, at least temporarily. The judges of the first two petitions nonetheless chose adjudicated denial to end the cases. This was also the best way to protect themselves. The judge in the third trial simply granted the divorce and divided the property following the routine practice.

This case is not unique. As documented elsewhere, judges facing such cases may explain the consequences to the bereaved wife, but they do this primarily to facilitate a settlement. In the Case of Mrs. Li documented in chapter 3, I demonstrated how a judge, through pragmatic discourse, urged a wife to accept a divorce settlement when the husband was still in a position to offer some financial compensation. She stated that "once the husband's heart was not in the family anymore, what is the difference with and without a husband?" The judge had wanted to bring about a settled outcome, which would have been consistent with her own interests. However, her advice was also important for the estranged wife: she might be financially better off by accepting a divorce and settlement. Further delays would only cost her, without offering any bargaining leverage, eventually sinking her into financial distress. Indeed, in the Distraught Woman's Case above, the judge in charge of the first petition had also attempted to mediate. However, that effort had been more than enough to pacify the irritated wife. The judge abandoned any mediation and rendered an adjudicated denial. A fundamental question is: When women raise requests that may eventually hurt their own interests, do judges lend them a hand? These cases each demonstrate that because of efficiency concerns, the judges have little incentive to help out impoverished women.

Of course, in cases in which men oppose the divorce, similar consequences exist. However, men's financial status and earnings power are higher compared to women's. The impact of such a decision pattern will be less destructive for men than for women. Most men are in a position to control the family's finances and thus avoid falling victim to a wealthy wife. A report by Peking University's Women's Rights Research Center (2001) states: "Despite the facially neutral safeguards in the law, in reality, women have little knowledge of what property is actually owned and have little recourse to tracing property when it is illegally transferred to a third party by a spouse" (quoting Ogletree and Alwis 2004: 261). Ogletree and Alwis (2004: 262) stress that "the challenges surrounding providing ownership or concealment of property constitute an insurmountable burden to women in China." While the law provides that neither side can transfer property without the other party's consent, women are often unable to gather real evidence on property transfers or to compel witnesses to testify to the existence of concealed property. They may be unaware of the full extent of the property; even if they do have knowledge of it, they are rarely able to submit proof. If the plight of women is rooted in procedural laws that require litigants to provide evidence, the judges' approach to divorce cases only makes matters worse. As the Distraught Woman's Case shows, the court's strategy of delay provides an opportunity for men to conceal and transfer property. A delayed decision, or an adjudicated denial, offers a safe haven for the judge. The consequence for women, however, is the loss of her last opportunity for compensation. For example, in her second legal battle against her husband, the distraught woman provided 5,000 yuan for investigation fees. Yet, she got nothing in return, partially because of the judge's laziness and incompetence. However, a divorce denial is not the trademark of only those judges who are ill-suited for the job; it is shared by *most* judges because of the courts' incentive mechanisms.

Indifference to Substandard Legal Services

The importance of legal representation in China's litigation system has been demonstrated by scholars (He and Su 2013). Indeed, whether or not a party obtains legal representation is a key indication of resource equality: inferior financial capability often means inferior legal representation, in terms of both availability and quality (He and Su 2013). In the context of divorce litigation, no hard statistics for legal representation are available. However, given the financial disparities between men and women, and the access barriers women face (Li 2015), women likely enjoy fewer and less competent legal services. However, a more relevant question for our purposes is: When women's lawyers or legal representatives provide unprofessional advice, sometimes detrimental to their interests, or when women suffer from a lack of legal representation, do the judges help?

To answer this question, one should look again at the judges' incentives when facing unprofessional legal representation in the courtroom. As long as efficiency and stability concerns are addressed, why should judges care? As detailed in the Strategic Policeman's Case (chapter 5), when the policeman hired a lawyer after failing to reach a settlement, the judge did nothing to help the woman even though she could have done a lot.

Indifference is also the reaction pattern when judges notice substandard legal services being rendered on behalf of women. In the Distraught Woman's Case, the woman had no legal representation during the first two trials (other than her uncle, a retired official). At the third trial, when she had made up her mind to divorce, she hired a citizen legal representative (for more on citizen legal representatives in China, see Li 2015; Liu 2008); she could not afford a professional lawyer. With the help of these amateur representatives, she made six requests in her filing statement:

> First, divorce from the defendant; second, 100,000 yuan for emotional injuries due to the indecent text messages and other faults committed during the marriage; third, 50,000 yuan for property damages for vandalizing the plaintiff's home by the defendant and his lover; fourth, the division of the conjugal apartment; fifth, custody of their daughter; and finally, the litigation fees born by the defendant alone.

To a trained eye, this was an unprofessional statement. Item three claimed compensation from the man's lover, a third party to the litigation who lacks privity. Since this was not allowed under the procedural laws, the woman dropped the claim at the suggestion of staff in the case filing division. This, however, was not necessary. Had she received more professional advice, she could have simply crossed out the lover's name.

In that case, she would have kept the claim and might have received some compensation for it. Item two looked just but was unrealistic. The courts have varying criteria on issues of emotional damages, but the amount is connected to local living conditions, and any award is generally meager. According to the guidelines and practices of local courts, the maximum emotional compensation for a wrongful death was 20,000 yuan at the time; how could 100,000 yuan be realistic for insulting language? Exaggerating claims is also common among inexperienced lawyers and legal workers. They mistakenly believe the more claims, the better. Any hyperbolic claims, however, mean only more litigation fees. The distraught woman's last point, on litigation fees, though commonly raised in commercial lawsuits, was also ludicrous in divorce litigation: the courts rarely hold one party solely responsible for all litigation fees.

Most important, the dispute over property division was supposed to focus on the bottom line of the man's company, yet the woman had not claimed this.[4] It was during the trial that she presented a contract for a project, trying to prove the existence of the husband's earnings. However, the court is bureaucratic: it does not make judgments on claims unstated in the filing statement. When a plaintiff falls short of staking out specific claims on marital property, the court avoids any ruling on such matters (Li 2015: 171–72). To add more claims, a litigant has to go through another round of the case filing procedure, which usually means additional litigation fees. Indeed, it was common for unprofessional legal workers to advise clients to make new claims during the trial, hoping the issues could be adjudicated without paying litigation fees. This advice is popular among clients because it seems to save them litigation fees. However, the courts rarely delve into added claims. An exceptionally responsible judge might make further efforts—perhaps explaining the court's requirements and investigating hidden or transferred properties (He and Ng 2013c)—but most of the rank and file never bother. That was what had happened in this case. The young judge with the well-off background made no efforts in this regard. He merely ensured that the procedures followed were consistent with the law. The final judgment stated that the claim was rejected owing to a lack of evidence, a vague statement common in China's civil judgments.

Indeed, the woman's uncle and her legal representative during the third round of litigation had not been competent enough to locate the assets accumulated by the husband. During the second litigation, providing two bank accounts and expecting the courts to conduct a thorough investigation had been idealistic during a time when judges were facing heavy caseloads (Woo and Wang 2005; He and Ng 2013b). According to Ng and He (2017a), judges only occasionally conduct investigations, usually after the litigants or their legal representatives have paved the way. If legal representatives cannot do most of the preparatory work in locating evidence, it is unrealistic to expect much from a judge.

If this is the situation for adjudicated cases, indifference is even more pronounced in mediated cases. The preference for mediation trumps women's interests. In the Shanghai Migrant Worker's Case, for example, the judge even talked to the lawyer in private, asking him to persuade the female plaintiff to withdraw her case. As documented by Ng and He (2014), a judge may even dissuade the lawyer from performing legal duties if doing so helps achieve a mediated settlement. Li and Friedman (2016: 161) state:

> Judges in charge of divorce lawsuits frequently circumvent adjudication and resort to mediation, a shortcut that protects them from challenges to their rulings by litigants or other state agencies. During the mediation sessions, judges rarely pushed for equitable division of property between spouses. Instead, they tend to persuade and even pressure the wife to relinquish her claims to conjugal property in hopes that such a compromise would facilitate subsequent negotiations with the husband. To expedite divorce settlements, some judges went as far as to encourage the wife to buy off her husband, leading to even more unequal litigation outcomes. Although in this situation a wife might successfully secure her husband's agreement to the divorce, she did so at the cost of relinquishing her claims to conjugal property while also paying out a significant amount of cash.

Echoing the existing literature, the Bride-Price Case shows the judge's approach to a bride-price dispute, a frequent occurrence in rural China. A man had filed for divorce because the woman had "refused to live with him." Both parties agreed to divorce, and the remaining issue was the bride-price. The man's family had paid 130,000 yuan as the bride-price, a large sum of money for the family. At trial, the woman admitted the bride-price but said she had no money to repay it. Note that she did not say she would not pay, only that "she had no money to repay." A formal Interpretation by the SPC (2003, Art. 10) stipulates that the bride-price must be returned if the couple never lived together. However, this law did not apply to this case because the couple had lived together, though only for several days. Then the judge turned to the legal worker hired by the woman for an opinion. A professional lawyer would have responded with a clear-cut "no," because the law does not apply to this situation. Instead, the legal worker responded that "they can return some of the bride-price, but the amount should be determined by the judge." From this response, the judge saw an opportunity for mediation. He summoned a lay assessor for help. The assessor, a retired village official in his seventies, understood what the judge wanted. He said to the woman, her legal representative, and her natal family members that "this might have constituted marital fraud. If so, it would be a criminal case instead of a civil one. Then, the situation would be far more complicated than returning the bride-price: the whole family might be incriminated. You'd better return the bride-price! Next time I will find you another man, and will get a larger amount of bride-price." The legal worker, wearing an uneasy smile when passing another cigarette to the lay assessor, said that these comments made sense. Simultaneously scared and enticed by the lay assessor's statement, the woman's side immediately agreed to settle. Consistent with what He (2016) finds, the lay assessor served as an instrument of the judge in facilitating mediation. The judge, of course, was pleased with the assessor's performance, since the latter disposed of the case by mediation. The result, however, was that the woman "agreed" to pay back all the bride-price, despite the law saying otherwise.

Losing Through Bidding

For most urban families, the most important assets are the apartment, which is usually co-owned by the couple. Thus, the apartment's division often is the only issue when awarding property. Article 20 of the SPC's second batch of Interpretations on the Revised Marriage Law states that when a couple cannot agree upon their apartment's ownership and value, the court is to allow a bidding process in order to make a determination. This stipulation has invited much criticism because it assumes equal bargaining power between men and women. On the

Interpretation's promulgation, Zhao (2011) asserts that the party with less cash flow would not be able to outbid the other party and thus would suffer. Ogletree and Alwis (2004: 266) predict: "Women usually do not have the money to reimburse husbands, so the house automatically goes to him. Even though Article 42 of the Revised Marriage Law states that a party who is having problems subsisting at the time of divorce should be helped by the other party, this provision, without any corresponding enforcement mechanism, remains merely symbolic and an attempt to inculcate moral values."

What I will demonstrate, however, is that in reality the courts not only "allow the usage of bidding when the couple cannot agree upon the apartment's ownership and value" as the SPC Interpretation stipulates; they also push for its usage regardless of a unfavorable outcome for the financially weaker party. Between the lines, the SPC Interpretation suggests that bidding is not the only way to determine ownership. As long as a party objects to such a mechanism, judges can and should arrange an alternative, most likely a market appraisal. Due to efficiency concerns, however, in more than thirty trials involving apartment division that I observed, the bidding process was adopted. Indeed, all my judge interviewees confirmed its widespread usage. The judges stressed the efficiency of determining an apartment's value through bidding. Market-value appraisals, the alternative to bidding, could cost as much as 10,000 yuan for one apartment, depending on the local costs of living. Few litigants want to pay for this. With the judges' emphasis on costs, eventually all litigants followed their advice, and in most situations the man secured ownership with the higher bid. What the judges did not mention is that a successful bid by two parties would save the judge a lot of time and procedural hassles. An appraisal could take three to five months to complete. No wonder judges are fans of the bidding process. It simplifies their job. However, this convenience incurs expenses, usually borne by women, the financially weaker party in the divorce process.

This is exactly what had happened in the Distraught Woman's Case. Working only part-time as a security guard, and after six years of divorce battles, the woman was so distraught that she was unable to carry on a meaningful conversation; she was not in any position to compete with the man in the bidding process. Her own survival depended on her natal family. How could she have enough cash to outbid the husband? At trial, as the judge recalled, she could not even focus her attention, and many of her answers did not make sense. In contrast, the man controlled a transportation company, and along with his resentment toward the woman he had all the determination and financial resources to outbid her, thereby kicking her out of the apartment, her only shelter. In the trial, the man was candid in his contempt toward the woman, behaving as if she did not exist. Before the bidding started, the outcome had already been determined.

Under the guidance of the judge, they quickly agreed to adopt a bidding process to determine the value and ownership of their apartment. The judge started from 50,000 yuan and asked the parties to bid: whoever bid the highest price would get the apartment. When the defendant bid 100,000 yuan, the distraught woman could not raise further, so the value was established. The defendant got ownership; half of the bidding price—50,000 yuan—was to be paid to the plaintiff. The market price of the apartment was around 130,000 yuan. The gap between the market price and the lower (bidding) price stemmed from the bidding process itself. There were only two bidders, whereas in a competitive market there could have been numerous offers. Thus, the weaker party could not afford to bid the market price. As a result, the party who loses ownership—usually the woman with less cash on hand—suffers in the bidding process.

In another Shaanxi case, the husband, a driving coach, sued to divorce his wife in her mid-fifties, a laid-off worker from a State-Owned Enterprise. To pay for their daughter's education, she had bought out (买断) her job at the SOE for 20,000 yuan ten years before. The consequence of the buyout was that she had lost all her pension.[5] Now she was working ten hours a day for a supermarket, earning 1,800 yuan per month. The couple had a small apartment, the family's only major asset. The husband had moved out a year before. According to the woman, he was in a new relationship and was already cohabitating with his lover. Nonetheless, the wife opposed the divorce. She said that he would return home once he had fooled around enough. She would keep waiting. Presenting the man's receipts for medicine and a cell phone, she, without legal representation, wanted to prove that they did and could live together. With a lawyer behind him (again, resource disparity), the man suggested dividing the apartment through bidding. He was honest enough to admit that he had 20,000 yuan in his stock brokerage account.

The woman was lucky enough to have a sympathetic judge, a middle-aged woman. The judge did not give the man an opportunity to bid for the apartment because she knew that it was this woman's only lifeline. Instead, she denied the divorce, fulfilling the woman's request (and simultaneously addressing efficiency concerns). The judge later told me that she hoped the marriage could last until the daughter got married; then she would have new hope in life (addressing the judge's stability concerns). However, it was expected that the man would soon initiate another divorce petition. At that point, a divorce and the bidding process, would be inevitable. The woman would likely lose the apartment, since she could not pay the man such a considerable amount of cash. It was probable that she, with half of the bidding price, would move out of her current home and rent a smaller apartment for the rest of her life.

Few judges are that sympathetic. For most divorce litigants, trials are traumatic, a marked date on their life calendars. For the judges, however, it is just another day of business. Most judges in charge of family issues have seen too many divorce cases and broken families. They just want to dispose of the cases, as long as their efficiency and stability concerns are addressed. What they have shown is what Weber (1954) calls "institutional apathy." Whether such a practice would do harm to the female is beyond their concerns. As the judge in the Railway Worker's Case said: "It is the woman who has to figure out what to do." As the rank and file, their role is similar to that of most bureaucrats: to fulfill the job requirements.

Such a gendered outcome may not have been intended by the SPC, whose goal is to provide a convenient solution to dividing conjugal apartments. Regardless, men's financial status is inevitably superior, and this puts them at an advantage. Once women lose the bidding, they lose their home. Gone are the conveniences of their original apartment: a familiar living environment, easy access to schools and hospitals, and social connections.

Making matters worse, judges' interests exacerbate the situation. The SPC Interpretation specifies that undertaking a bidding process is conditioned on the consent of both parties. Yet in reality, it operates as if there were no such condition. Whenever both litigating parties claim ownership, the judges push them to undertake the bidding process. This seems to be the only lawful and efficient way to fix the value and determine ownership of conjugal property. Any party who opposes the process appears to be giving the judges a hard time.

Conclusions

As far as the law is concerned, the issues of divorce, property division, and child custody are independent of one another. Each issue has its own governing principles and rules. Divorce is determined by whether or not mutual affection has broken down. Child custody is determined by the best interests of the children. According to the law, the decision on one issue should not affect the other even though, procedurally, only by granting the divorce would the judge determine division of property and child custody. From a judge's perspective, however, these three issues are interwoven. When a party initiates a divorce petition, that person often requests one or more of the three. Most divorce cases involve more than one issue, and the judge has to weigh all these elements in the decision. Whether one agrees to be divorced, for example, may depend on how the other two issues are resolved. For a judge, these are three bargaining chips that can be employed to negotiate with the litigating parties. When the issue of divorce is contested, the other two bargaining chips become useful. If one party is steadfast on child custody, for instance, that party will then have to compromise on divorce or property rights.

In this chapter, I illustrate that, once again, under institutional constraints, Chinese judges adopt approaches that are harmful to women's property interests throughout the divorce process. The existing literature is correct that the changed legislative orientation disadvantages women in terms of property division. To achieve gender equality, laws require revision. Conjugal property should also include intellectual property, honors, or other intangible property, to provide some examples (Su 1999). Yet, judges' concerns have aggravated the situation. To end a case efficiently without lingering effects, women have to forgo their property rights—usually their only bargaining chip—in exchange for either divorce or child custody. Delaying a decision for a divorce that is clearly inevitable, a seemingly neutral approach, disadvantages women more so than men. Due to the gendered financial disparity, women lose in the bidding process for the conjugal apartment. Judges are also indifferent toward substandard legal services detrimental to women's interests. These factors each indicate that in addition to the unfair legal stipulations, institutional constraints have further perpetuated gendered outcomes.

7

Cultural Biases

Cultural bias against women in China has only been touched in the context of child custody determination and property division during a divorce. In this chapter, I highlight how courts perpetuate such bias. It is another aspect that has contributed to gendered outcomes in China's litigation process, in addition to thwarting legal rights and reinforcing economic hierarchies.

Cultural biases against women abound in China. Confucian ideology and the patriarchal family system hold that the wife is inferior to the man (Mencius, quoted in Fung 1963: 25). She is supposed to take care of the husband and run his errands. Wife-beating is taken for granted when she fails to deliver such services or irritates him (Honig and Hershatter 1988: 291–97). In the Saleswoman's Case cited at the beginning of this book, the man defended himself by saying "for all these years, have you cooked for me?" The man in the Case of Changed Procedure refuted his wife this way: "Why did I beat you? You *danced* with other men!" (emphasis added). A saying in northern China goes: the beaten wife is like the flour kneaded. Popular proverbs include "[w]omen are like wheelbarrows; if not beaten for three days they cannot be used" (Belden 1970: 314). Chinese culture has long regarded fights between couples as a natural part of life: "The couple fighting at one end of the bed reconcile at the other." Other adages normalize its presence: "The teeth always bite the tongue" and "a bowl clashes with the pan all the time." I once witnessed a defendant use vulgar language to denigrate his wife during a hearing. When interrupted by the judge, he said that he would have slapped her in the face had they not been in a courtroom, since "before divorce, she remains my wife." Upon hearing this, the wife did not protest. Instead, she acquiesced to the man's demands. The wife's reaction alone speaks volumes about the internalization of such cultural biases.

Women also suffer from patrilineal bias. A woman deserves to be divorced or beaten if she does not give birth to a male heir to carry on the marital bloodline. "There are three things which are unfilial," said Mencius, "and the greatest of them is to have no posterity" (quoted in Chai and Chai 1962: 81, note 3). This was the case with Mrs. Li in chapter 3, as well as the plaintiff in the Singapore Laborer's Case. A wife's main function, many believe, is to bear children for the man. Chastity was the crucial expression of female fidelity (Spence 1979: 100; Ch'u 1961: 198–99). Biases upon the remarriage of a widow still exist, because widow chastity was idealized as an expression of wifely fidelity, the highest feminine virtue in the Confucian pantheon. A *tuoyouping* (拖油瓶, a woman with children from previous marriages) depreciates in the marriage market, since she has already had others' babies.

Patrilocal residence in rural China—married women are expected to relocate from their natal families to live with their husband's family and community—is another bias against women. Traditionally, it is said, "[s]he had few opportunities to escape from her new home. She was not allowed to die in the home of her natal family" (Stacey 1983: 34). Things are much better now thanks to social development and population mobility. But once divorced, women often find themselves isolated in their conjugal communities. Divorced women are more likely to be asked to leave the conjugal home and thus suffer economic losses (Wang 2001). After divorce, the husband, and the relatives from the husband's side, become unfriendly or even hostile. Living in that community could become unbearable, and leaving seems inevitable. Indeed, in traditional agrarian societies, land was the major form of property that passed exclusively to sons through the male lineage (Merry and Stern 2005; Agarwal 1994). At least in some parts of rural China, village exogamy women—that is, those women who move to the home of their husband's family—have found themselves dispossessed upon divorce, with her in-laws reclaiming the land on which they had been working and living, even if it was the husband who sought to terminate the marriage (Alford and Shen 2004). This is why most divorced women would rather return to their natal communities or find jobs in the city. In a word, they are *forced* to leave their homes.

Instead of fighting these biases, most judges regard them as a tool to efficiently close cases. Often they make use of these biases. This is why domestic violence is trivialized and women's efforts to gain child custody are sidelined. The patrilocal practice also marginalizes women when negotiating with the husband's family on property division. Most often, they have to forgo much of their conjugal property because they have to leave the domicile.

Focusing on women's hesitancy to raise gender-related issues, in this chapter I demonstrate how judges, following institutional concerns, turn a blind eye toward female suffering. Judges rarely inform women of their rights; furthermore, they avoid issues even when they learn facts. Occasionally, they use an issue as a bargaining chip to facilitate closing a case. Suffering from this gender bias in court, women fail to voice their claims and are awarded less property or compensation than they deserve. I contend that because of judges' inaction toward the traditional and cultural taboo of women articulating their unfair treatment on gender issues, women are denied fair decisions.

Sex as a Taboo

In 1927, Wen Hsiu famously filed to divorce her husband Pu Yi, China's last emperor, in part because of his sadism and inability to father children. Behr (1987) praised her as courageous, with great willpower. Almost a century later, are Chinese women freer to raise gender- and sex-related issues in divorce litigation? How do the courts and judges respond to the issues?

Recent decades have witnessed a sexual liberation in China. "Sex—in some form of other—has emerged from obscurity to occupy a position of unprecedented prominence in public life in the People's Republic" (Evans 1995: 357). Issues of sexual autonomy and independence have become more frequently examined and debated. As this book goes to print, many social elites have fallen from grace as the #MeToo movement sweeps through China.

Sexual problems have been a factor contributing to China's increasing divorce rates. Extramarital affairs are often cited by litigants in order to gain an upper hand in the courtroom, especially in the more developed areas and when they have a legal representative (Zhang 2017). Common evidence includes intimate text messages, contrition letters, and promises to rectify. After all, extramarital affairs have become a social reality that can now be discussed in public settings.

Yet, despite decades of influence from the outside world, "[t]he two sexes are characterized by different forms of sexual behavior. Normal male behavior is open and outwardly expressive, whereas in the female, it is more hidden and shy. This signifies a difference between male activity and initiative and female passivity, which is determined by sexual physiology and psychology" (Wang 1993: 97). Moreover, the Chinese state has maintained control over sex and sexuality, as part of the agenda toward social harmony (Sigley 2006), and it has to keep sex issues within the family (Sigley 2006).

Evidence suggests that male impotency is a common problem in reform-era China. Discussions of impotence in the media and on the internet are common. Flyers on lampposts along city alleys advertise clinics to treat sexually transmitted diseases and male sexual dysfunction. Commercials appear on TV and in other media touting herbal tonics to cure impotence. In Zhang's words, impotency is an "epidemic" (2015). Nonetheless, a search for publicly available adjudication documents reveals that only a handful of such issues have surfaced in the decisions. Of 1.9 million divorce cases from 2008 to 2018, only 654 petitions filed by women were filed on the basis of male impotence (Lawsdata 2018). Zhang (2015: 123) finds no research supporting the rise in the incidence of divorce resulting from male impotence. At least in these public sources, the instances in which women file petitions based on male sexual impotence are disproportionally low.

Consistent with the search results, my fieldwork investigations and interviews with judges confirm that topics related to sex, such as male impotence, marital or domestic rape, and homosexuality are rarely raised in the litigation process. In one sensational case, the wife dismembered her husband because she could not stand his violence against her anymore; she did not tell the judges and lawyers of the situation until her death sentence was reviewed by the SPC, when two experienced female lawyers intervened (Luo 2019). "Only at that stage she told the lawyers that she was often burned by cigarette ends, hit by iron clothes hangers, and forced to have sex right after an abortion surgery. She once hinted to a cadre of her residence neighborhood committee that her genital was hurt, but nobody paid attention to it." This taboo is especially true in rural and hinterland areas where these topics remain, by and large, taboo. Mentioning husbands' impotence seems to imply women's indecent desires, falling into the stereotype of licentiousness. Any open talk of male impotence seems embarrassing, contrary to the image of a decent wife or woman (Ho et al. 2018; cf. Safronova 2019). The traditional picture of the female body remains passive: she never initiates sex, nor does she demand satisfaction (Zhang 2015: 123). These matters, although central to most marriages, become almost invisible during the legal battle. Even in cases where this is the real issue, most female litigants are reticent to talk about it. Both parties ostensibly focus on other issues. At most, they hint at it before brushing it off.

Inhibited Women

The four wives described in this section were the exceptions among the victims of the inhibited sex problem. Indeed, the judges had learned about the situation inadvertently during the mediation process. None of the sex issues was mentioned in the case filing statements; nor had the wives raised any during the trial process. The courts never recorded anything either, of course. In a way, this revealed the cultural obstacles facing women articulating this problem. The female litigants—often the victims of the cultural bias—had to overcome psychological barriers just to speak out.

In the Shandong Waitress's Case, a twenty-five-year-old woman from a village in Shandong was married to an optimistic and outspoken lorry driver from an SOE in Shaanxi. She had met him through her uncle, an executive at the SOE, which employed his parents as well. Her uncle had been well-intentioned. He had hoped the marriage would enable his niece, along with her father (his elder brother) and her mother, to come live with him in Shaanxi. With his help, his niece had been assigned to work as a waitress in the SOE's canteen, and both of her parents got temporary jobs with the SOE.

Two years later, after the unexpected death of the uncle, the marriage went sour. According to the filing statement of the divorce petition, the trigger for the petition had been intensifying conflict between the couple's parents. They had even gotten into a physical altercation just two weeks before she had filed the petition, and he had threatened to kick her parents out of his home. Her main request, in addition to divorce, was compensation for her contribution to their matrimonial apartments, which had been subsidized by the SOE because of his employment.

The judge, a middle-aged woman, tried to settle the case with the standard inquiry into the cause of the divorce. It was during the pretrial mediation session that she accidentally uncovered the genuine reason for divorce: the judge had suggested that family disputes would subside once they had a child. When pressed, the plaintiff said that it would be impossible for them to have children.

Surprised, the judge pushed further, "Is it related to your health?"

The plaintiff looked around, making sure that nobody was in sight and that the door was closed. She then lowered her voice, as if it were a secret buried for ages:

> No. He has problems in that regard. Having been married for two years, we are like never married. Impotent, he cannot have a child. I have known the marriage was not sustainable since its very beginning. Half a year after being married I told my mother, who stopped me from telling anybody else. She was afraid that my uncle's family would become aware of it. One year later, our conflict intensified, and I told my aunt [her uncle's wife] about it. Initially skeptical, she was eventually convinced by my mother-in-law. Indeed, without informing me, my husband went to a big hospital in the capital city for treatment. But it was not cured. My aunt persuaded my mother to accept this: it was not easy to find a trustworthy family; perhaps adopting a child would do. Because back then my whole family had relied on my uncle, my mother was afraid to say no. For that period, I basically lived with my parents, as he was pulling gambling all-nighters, without coming home.

None of this was mentioned during the formal trial. In front of the defendant, a collegial panel of three, a clerk who took notes of the trial process, two lawyers representing her and one lawyer for the defendant, and ten witnesses, she was more inhibited. The trial focused on her claims regarding the man's gambling practices (a so-called pernicious habit) and the family discord. When the man agreed to divorce, the focus soon switched to who was the real owner of the apartment and whether the woman, along with her natal family, had deliberately encroached upon the man's property by marrying him.

Male impotence is a taboo subject. The man had also been reluctant to let anyone know of his condition because this concerned his manly dignity. He had not let his wife know about his efforts for treatment. For a young wife, it was also hard to speak out. Indeed, the woman was pressed by the judge, who pushed for the real reason for divorce. The woman had been afraid that, unless she told the judge the truth, her efforts to get financial compensation be jeopardized. The woman had to overcome significant psychological barriers. She had not told her mother until half a year into the marriage. Only after a year had passed did she tell her aunt, the most important relative in her family. Furthermore, this had occurred only after the young couple's conflict had become unbearable. Also buoying her courage was her experience in the suburban areas where she had worked for two years. Still, she remained cautious. She looked over her shoulders when she told the judge about this. Nowhere in the filing statement was it mentioned. It is possible she may have not even informed her two young lawyers. Her inhibition was consistent with that of her mother. When informed, her mother had advised her "not to tell anybody else." She had been afraid that the uncle's wife, the mastermind of the marriage and most important relative in Shaanxi, would have been embarrassed. Similarly, her aunt's reaction after learning this had been to cover it up and look for alternatives, despite the woman being only twenty-three years old. Her advice was to adopt a child. These individuals had shared the understanding that male impotency was an embarrassing topic unsuitable for open discussion.

Such an inhibited tendency was found in the Bride-Price Case, in which a migrant worker in his mid-twenties had filed for divorce because the woman, also a migrant worker, had "refused to live with him." In the filing statement, the man stated that they had met through a matchmaker and got married the fifth time they saw each other. One caveat is in order: this was not a love-at-first-sight story. The first three times they met, the couple talked. They were engaged on the fourth meeting, in which the man paid a 130,000 yuan bride-price.[1] Then, on the fifth meeting they applied for their marriage certificate. The woman then kicked him out of their bedroom the week they were married, and they never lived together. In the official response, the woman stated: "I agreed to a divorce. For the year we were married, I rarely lived with the man, and we did not have much to talk about. He was not capable of making money."

However, they could not reconcile the issue of the bride-price, and the woman also refused to return the living expenses that she had received from the man while they had been married. The responsible judge, a man in his forties, while attempting to mediate the case, was puzzled: Why did she not want to live with the man? He then asked a female judge from the district court, also in her forties, who happened to visit the dispatched tribunal where the case was filed, to talk to the woman. Taking the woman to another room, she proposed that the wife continue to live with the man so that he would withdraw the petition. The wife responded:

> It was not me who did not want to live with him. It was him who was afraid of living with me. When I took off my clothes, he would tremble, rolling himself into a ball. Every time it was like that; he was unable to do it. For the whole year, we never slept together. In front of so many people, I cannot speak this out.

Similar to the Shandong woman, she had revealed the truth only in a private conversation with the judge, when pressed to reconcile. Her formal responses to the man's allegations had been that they did not have much to talk about and rarely stayed together. She had been unwilling to refute the man because "[i]n front of so many people, I cannot speak this out."

Equally reticent was the plaintiff in the Shanghai Migrant Worker's Case, in which the young wife—already leaving home for work in Shanghai and separated from her husband for more than two years—had filed a divorce petition. The filing statement mentioned that she had been beaten only by her mother-in-law. Throughout the pretrial mediation sessions, she had been reluctant to reveal the truth, even after being grilled by the judge over why she wanted to divorce the man whose family was in economic distress. Her response: "But we still quarrel every day, every night." "Every night" was emphasized. She continued: "I left for Shanghai as a migrant worker since I could not stand it anymore." Her sobbing continued. She also denied that she had been having an affair. Puzzled and impatient, the judge amplified her voice, urging her to withdraw the petition.

At this moment, her lawyer approached the judge, pulling at her sleeve, hinting for a private talk. After they walked to the staircase in the corner, the lawyer whispered:

> The boy has that kind of disease, thus cannot have a normal sex life. As a young man, the way he released his desires was to scratch girls' genitals. She could not sleep the whole night. Her genitals had been injured to the extent that she could not even get out of bed, let alone walk. It was so serious that the girl returned to her natal home and was afraid to go back. After the man stalked her in her natal home, she went to Shanghai. This is the main point for the divorce petition, but the girl is unable to speak up herself.

Then, the judge wondered why the couple had a child. The lawyer responded: "The boy is four years old now. The man got the disease, perhaps, two years ago. It was unclear why a young man got such a disease. He had been unwilling to see a doctor. At this young age, he was eager to do it, but he couldn't. So he did not allow the lady to sleep. She was so tortured and her whole body was trembling when she mentioned this."

The judge was not convinced—that is, until the woman agreed to withdraw the petition under her lawyer's advice that a divorce would be impossible this time. Happy to learn of the withdrawal, the man pleaded with the woman to go home with him, a common patrilocal practice: since the divorce is not granted, the wife is to return home with the man despite the fact she filed a divorce petition. The wife grew agitated: "We fought every night. Do you believe we can live together? I feel scared when I see you now!" Upon hearing this, the man's face froze. He stood still, embarrassed.

In the presence of the husband, the judge, and her lawyer, the woman did not mention her husband's sexual problem. She only said that "we fought every day and every night." She tried to use the nightly fighting as cover for the embarrassing topic of male impotency. When the judge pressed her on whether she had another man, she did not reveal the secret. She would have rather taken the moral blame that she was divorcing him for economic reasons. Her response was to sob.

Even after the wife withdrew the case, she avoided mentioning her husband's impotency. Instead, she said: "We fought every night. Do you believe we can live together? I feel scared when I see you now!" When the man's family tried to take her home upon knowing that she had withdrawn the case, she sprang from her chair and cried, "I will not live with you! I will never go to your home! I will file another petition in six months!" Without knowing the real reason behind the fighting, these statements are hard to comprehend. The woman was still trying to use the fighting and other vague language to cover up her husband's impotency. The man, knowing what was implied by her words, turned pale in embarrassment.

Despite living in Shanghai for two years, she was silent on the impotency issue, in both her testimony and written filings. She used all kinds of language to cover it up, even when pressed by the judge. She only shared this with her lawyer, perhaps because she had learned that her original reason—being beaten by her mother-in-law, who had psychiatric problems—was not enough to obtain a divorce, or because she realized that the financial distress of the family would make the divorce petition more unlikely to succeed. One thing was clear, though: the cultural bias against openly discussing male impotency is widespread: Even the lawyer had only "whispered" it to the judge in the staircase in the corner and used "that kind of disease" to refer to the problem; he did not break the stalemate until the judges urged his client to drop the divorce petition.

Similarly, the young woman in the Attempted Rape Case had been initially inhibited by this cultural bias. She had met her husband while working in the city as a migrant worker. Her husband, a lorry driver, claimed that for more than a year she had never been home, abandoning their son and refusing to do any domestic work. Both parties agreed to divorce, but they fought over custody and property (see chapter 5). The wife insisted on the 80,000-yuan land requisition compensation, which would have been her share. The husband's family, however, agreed to compensate her only 10,000 yuan and insisted on child custody with child support.

A private caucus was conducted between the judge and the husband and his legal representative, but the husband did not appear to have the final say. He consulted his father on every issue. When the judge said

20,000 yuan was too low, given that the land compensation of her share had already reached 80,000 yuan, the husband's legal representative stepped out of the judge's office, once again, to call the husband's father.

At this moment, the woman went into the office alone. She had gotten into an argument with her natal family members, who had urged her to give up custody and lower the monetary compensation. She calmed herself: "I have important things to tell you, judge. During the first month after the boy was born [坐月子, or "postpartum confinement"], his father tried to rape me. . . . He pushed open my door, rushed to my bed, embraced me forcefully, kissed me, and wildly fondled my breasts. I resisted frantically, screaming." She later explained that no family members had been around: Her mother-in-law was shopping in town; her husband was working, driving the lorry. She continued: "This happened three times in total. I took preparatory measures the second time. He held me from behind, and took off my pants. I resisted vehemently, kneeing down to hold his legs and threw him off. I sprang up faster than he did, running out of the home. The third time he almost got me. Unexpectedly, my mother-in-law came home. He had to set me free."

Asked by the judge if she had told anyone about it, she responded: "My mother-in-law did not say a word. She was not in a position to confront my father-in-law, who is the king at home. He beats her all the time. My husband did not trust my words. He said that I had slandered his father and that I had picked a fight with him." She continued: "I called to tell my mom. She said that I should not tell anyone, to preserve my good reputation. She agreed to take me back to my natal home once the first month was over [according to local customs, it is unacceptable to live in the bride's natal home for the period]. I intended to say this to you but my parents prevented me from doing so. But I believed I should let you know."

Attempted rape is a serious crime. It is easy to understand how this young woman had been hurt: fear, humiliation, panic, and frustration, with nobody to turn to. This was why she had left her conjugal home right after the child's first month. The divorce had not been because she was lazy, as the husband had claimed, nor had she been ambivalent toward her child: she had insisted on child custody, despite his illness and the stigmatization of *tuoyouping* (a woman with children from previous marriages).

Despite the allegation of such a crime, initially the woman did not make the judge aware of it. As her own mother had suggested, spreading the word about the rape would have damaged *her* reputation and jeopardized her bride-price if she were to remarry. Even her natal family tried to prevent her from revealing this to the judge. She made up her mind to speak out only when the others had left the judge's office. Apparently, she had been waiting for the right moment. She had sought help from both her husband and her mother-in-law, but both had turned her away. These incidents underscore the cultural bias endemic to this issue.

Among the four victims we discuss, this woman was the only one to have taken the initiative to speak out to the judge. She had also hoped to claim more financial compensation. The other three women, by revealing the problem either directly or indirectly, had merely tried to end their marriages. None realized that the damages they had suffered also warranted compensation. Was the woman in the Attempted Rape Case the rule or the exception? In several aspects, this woman was unique. The first was her strong personality. Energetic and upbeat, she was willing to disobey her natal family members, including her father and grandfather. Second, she was a victim of attempted rape, for which damages were arguably more serious than male impotency. However, only she had been in the position to understand the fears, panic, and humiliation she suffered. Third, the husband's family's offer was laughable. When both parties negotiated the settlement, the position of the husband's family had been firm: they agreed to compensate the woman only 10,000 yuan, despite the fact that her land requisition compensation had already reached 80,000 yuan. Even the judge suggested that this offer was too low. In the wife's calculus, the compensation she demanded was not only her land compensation, or her contribution to the family welfare, but also the damages that she had suffered. When her demands were opposed—not even her own natal family members were on her side—she had nobody to turn to. Eventually, she overcame the cultural barriers: she had the vague intuition that revealing the truth to the judge would better position her in the negotiation.

These four victims each spoke out in the context of mediation. This pattern exists for three reasons. First, mediation often offers a private caucus in which cultural bias is minimized. Even in the Shanghai Migrant Worker's Case, the lawyer took the judge outside of the conference room and told her the genuine reason for the divorce. Second, in mediation, judges always bring pressure to bear. To resist them, victims must speak out. Finally, the judge was also a woman, and women appear more comfortable discussing such embarrassing topics. Indeed, I never heard similar stories from a male judge.

Judges' Inaction

When female petitioners overcame the cultural bias and finally revealed the truth, how did the judges respond? To what extent are these stories factored into final judgments? How have social norms affected the courts' decisions, and how do law, gender, and sex interact?

In all four cases, the judges were surprised or shocked upon hearing the wives' stories. In some circumstances, they were only half-convinced of their truth. A clear pattern, however, was that no further actions were taken—no verifications, no further investigations, and sometimes not even any further inquiry.

In the Shandong Waitress's Case, the female judge, in her late forties, was herself embarrassed by the topic. She had been trying to talk the plaintiff into withdrawing the case. Upon learning the truth, the judge realized that her proposed solution would not work. After that, she no longer attempted to persuade the plaintiff to maintain the marriage. The conversation came to a halt, and the plaintiff did not raise it in trial— nor did the judge. As is documented in the literature, in divorce cases the courts forgo the former practice of investigating the real basis for seeking the divorce. This had been the convention during the Mao era and the early period of reform (He 2009a). In most cases, judges focused only on the issues claimed, and more important, only on those integral to their final decisions (He and Ng 2013b). In this case, the woman never claimed that the man's sexual impotency had been the reason for divorce. Even though the plaintiff had confided this to the judge in private, her goal was to resist pressure from the judges to reconcile. That goal had already been achieved: the judge stopped pushing. Moreover, the man agreed to a divorce, and so the issue of whether to divorce was settled. Why should the judgment hinge on an embarrassing issue unrelated to the final resolution of the case? Why bother to verify or conduct further investigation?

This inaction persisted into posttrial mediation. Even though the two parties had difficulty reconciling property division, the judge never even hinted to the man that it had been his erectile dysfunction that had overshadowed, if not caused, the divorce. Had she invoked this issue, she could have expected a denial from the husband. To defend his dignity, he would have fought any such allegations. Then to resolve the issue, the court would have had to conduct further investigations. Again, why bother?

The pattern of inaction was also revealed in the Shanghai Migrant Worker's Case, as the judge skirted this issue. It was in the pretrial mediation session that the problem was revealed, in private, through the lawyer. Nothing had been raised in the formal filing statement. For the same reason, why should the judge bother to look into it? The judge had been convinced only by the conversations and body language between the couple and the man's embarrassed facial expressions. While the revealed reason might help her understand whether or not the marriage could be preserved, any further inquiry seemed redundant as far as the final decision was concerned. She continued her mediation efforts by informing the lawyer that a divorce outcome for such a first-time petition would be impossible. Thus, she coerced the plaintiff to drop the petition. Similar in the Bride-Price Case, the judge, upon learning the real reason for divorce, stopped pressuring the woman and instead pursued mediation on the bride-price.

The Attempted Rape Case had been somewhat different. Upon learning of the father-in-law's attempted rape of the wife, the judge did nothing to verify the claims. Nor did she report the case to the police, even though she herself, based on the reaction of the husband's legal representative, had believed the woman's account. Instead, she used it as a bargaining chip to pressure the husband's family. She did not encourage the woman to report it to the police or file a criminal case, because that would not have been necessary for her to dispose of this case. To convict the father-in-law, the evidence would have to come not only from the victim but also other sources. The woman, when attacked, had been with her weeks-old baby. In panic and fear, how could she have preserved evidence? As long as the father-in-law denied all the accusations, which was likely, the case could probably not be substantiated. The father-in-law could argue that the woman had framed him. Had that happened, the woman would have lost both face and her reputation, embarrassing herself and her natal family members even more. Indeed, an attempted rape often leaves little trace. Encouraging the woman to file a criminal lawsuit might have backfired.

Moreover, the strong-willed father-in-law seemed to enjoy absolute authority within the family. He often beat his wife, and his son was so obedient that he sought instructions during the negotiation. He exemplified the patriarch in China's tradition. He attempted to rape the daughter-in-law three times, perhaps because of the traditional belief that "[a] father-in-law could rape his daughter-in-law with impunity" (Ch'u 1961: 198–99). At the very least, he knew that she would be unlikely to disclose this. He must have been surprised when she did report it to the judge, a symbol of judicial power and public force. He might not have had a clear idea of whether the judge would take further actions. For him, the best strategy was to compromise and to terminate the marriage as soon as possible. This aligned with the judge's goal. Using the incident to force the father-in-law into a financial compromise, in a way, she had supported the lady. After all, that was all she had asked for.

This was why the judge had utilized this revelation as a bargaining chip. No matter how much she hated the father-in-law, or how sympathetic she was to the lady, her goal was to close the case. She was unconcerned with whether she could also help the lady. Even if the judge and the victim had managed to locate evidence, the ultimate goal would still have been to end the case. As long as this objective was achieved, any evidence uncovered would have been buried. Obtaining this evidence would have been helpful, but not crucial, to achieving the judge's ultimate goal.

Gendered Outcomes

Judges' inaction is understandable; encouraging victims to speak out or taking an assertive role would upend the balance between the litigating parties. Then, the judges might not be able to achieve the mediated outcomes that fit their interests. The inaction, nonetheless, takes a toll on women's interests.

In the Shandong Waitress's Case, upon learning the real cause for her seeking divorce, the judge did not tell the waitress that this might be a favorable litigation strategy. Had the woman explicitly stated that sexual impotency had been the real reason for divorce, the dynamics of the trial would have changed. By not clarifying this, the woman, as the plaintiff in a divorce, could focus only on trivial issues—such as the man's gambling and his reluctance to support the family—to prove the breakdown of mutual affection. As a result, the husband's side became more emboldened in staking out a position. Throughout the trial and the mediation, they never mentioned impotency. While they agreed to divorce, they staged a show of property encroachment between a poor, greedy rural family and an honest, affluent urban household. They summoned three witnesses, each well-respected in the region, to prove that the man's family was the owner of the apartment. The man's father, a midlevel manager at an SOE, requested a meeting with the judge to detail the purchase process in which he, in order to buy the apartment, had borrowed money from friends and relatives. A divorce rooted in male impotency had thus been transformed into a righteous defense against a greedy encroacher, locating the husband's family on the moral and legal high ground. Had male impotency been disclosed at trial, the overconfident position of the man's family would have been upended. Of course, it was expected that the man would have fought such allegations, but the law and the evidence would have been on the woman's side.

If the husband's condition had been disclosed, the adjudicated outcome would have been better for the woman. It seemed that the man, already aware of his impotency, still decided to marry the woman, and the marriage had continued for three years while the condition remained uncured. This may have constituted deceit, with damages resulting for the woman. According to Article 10 of the Marriage Law, a marriage is void when there is an existing medically confirmed disease inappropriate for marriage that is not cured after the marriage. While impotency is not explicitly listed as a disease inappropriate for marriage, infertility is a serious concern for most families. In judicial practice, Article 10 usually forms a basis to void marriages. This is also widely understood and accepted among the general public. Furthermore, based on Article 39, the court will then partition the conjugal property in the woman's favor, because the man had concealed his condition before the marriage.

With his impotency disclosed, the man's position during the posttrial mediation would have been compromised. With an unfavorable adjudicated decision pending, he might have been willing to make significant concessions. Without the open disclosure of his condition, however, the woman's private conversation with the judge served only to resist the judge's pressure for mediated reconciliation. Since the man was not opposing the divorce, the disclosure accomplished little.

If the Shandong waitress did not get what she deserved, the woman in the Bride-Price Case suffered a significant financial loss. As illustrated in chapter 6, when the judge ran out of ideas to reconcile the two sides, the lay assessor, a retired village official in his early seventies, stepped in to talk to the woman, her parents, and her incompetent legal representative: "Look! The other side offering such a big bride-price, the only purpose was to get a daughter-in-law. Your girl kicked the groom out the third day after being wed, and rented a room herself—still refusing to live with him. How would you feel if you were in their shoes? Staying in the man's family for less than fifteen days, this might have constituted marital fraud. It would be a criminal case instead of a civil one. Then, the situation would be far more complicated than returning the bride-price: the whole family might be incriminated."

Fraudulent sales of women as "brides" are common in China. After making handsome payments, those men soon found that their "brides" had disappeared, along with bride token (Li 2021 forthcoming). Of China's population of 1.4 billion, there are approximately 34 million more males than females, a demographic nightmare stemmed from the longtime One Child policy and engrained cultural preference for sons over daughters (Denyer and Gowen 2018). The shortage of brides is further exacerbated by village women's migration to cities during the reform period (Choi and Peng 2016). Some families have to pay off human traffickers to locate daughters-in-law for their unmarried sons. According to Li (2021 forthcoming), "[E]stranged husbands who are caught up in divorce suits often turn into outraged defendants, taking out their marital frustrations on judges in charge of their cases. Adjudicating divorce thus comes with a set of occupational hazards, harassment, verbal abuse, threats of violence, threats of suicide, revenge aimed at one's family members. . . . The list can go on in terms of the pains angry men can inflict on their judges."

Upon hearing this, the woman's side was rattled. They immediately accepted a deal to return the full 130,000 yuan bride-price, even though initially the man had asked for only 110,000 yuan. As analyzed in chapter 6, the law states there is no need to return the bride-price under these circumstances, because she had indeed lived with the man (SPC 2003: Art. 10). The situation would have been more ambiguous had the judge told the woman to raise the man's erectile dysfunction during the litigation process. Once again, she had been preoccupied with getting a mediated result. The lay assessor, aware of what the judge wanted, had volunteered to threaten the woman's family with a criminal charge, coercing her side to compromise (c.f. He 2016). Since this was consistent with the judge's interests, she had turned a blind eye toward the unfair settled outcome.

In the Shanghai Migrant Worker's Case, the judge had been skeptical of the lawyer's story but was convinced by the man's facial expressions and the couple's interactions. The judge had told only the woman's lawyer that a divorce was impossible, and that the family needed time to accept the woman's departure. When the lawyer resisted by saying that the wife had been away from home for two years, and that the family should have been prepared for this, the judge continued:

> That was before the formal divorce petition, which was not understood by the court. This is the first time she has formally filed the divorce petition. This is also the first time for the man's family to understand that she truly wants to leave them. This is different. You have represented numerous divorce cases. Think about it: under such a family background, how much pressure can the little young man take? He said to us that he would rather die than be divorced. Such a threat is realistic, should a divorce be granted now. So, this time, even if we have a formal trial on the case, the outcome would also be rejecting the woman's divorce petition. That is why I hope you can cooperate with us and help persuade the woman to withdraw the petition. She could, of course, file another petition in six months, if she still wants to divorce him then. This divorce petition would be considered when the next petition is adjudicated.

Given the shortage of potential brides in China, anxieties over finding a second partner following divorce are palpable, especially for an impoverished family. The judge sensibly found a solution: voluntary withdrawal. The woman gained nothing by revealing the damages she had suffered through her lawyer's private conversation with the judge. A divorce denial was more to address the judge's stability concerns and to allow the man's family more time to prepare for her departure. The judge, realizing the inevitable collapse of the marriage, resorted to the safest strategy: no divorce for the first-time divorce petition, whether it was withdrawn or adjudicated. She used the excuse that, for the first time, both the court and the man's family knew there would be a divorce.

Such an outcome was not inevitable. Had the judge told the woman and her lawyer to add this reason to the formal filing statement, she could have cited domestic violence—she had been injured to the extent that she could not walk—and rendered a divorce with financial compensation. Since the issue of the case had been divorce only—not property division—the woman had not suffered financially. However, she had wasted at least six months in a meaningless marriage.

In the Attempted Rape Case, the outcomes were indeed changed by the judge's behavior. In the posttrial mediation, the husband and his legal representative, after consulting the husband's father several times, decided to increase the compensation from the initial offer of 10,000 to 25,000 yuan. This was still well below the woman's demand of 80,000. The judge asked the man to leave the office and then spoke to his legal representative in private:

> 50,000 yuan, and no child support. The father-in-law attempted to rape this woman three times. As you see, she just asked me to deal with this matter. I was pondering whether to report this to the police. Why shouldn't I? Now you call your friend, the father-in law, and see if the woman's requests can be met.

Ten minutes later, the legal representative returned from the call without uttering a word. His facial expression, however, confirmed the accusations. A settlement was struck: the husband's family agreed to pay 40,000 yuan, in response to the judge's 50,000 yuan suggestion, and the woman gave up custody of their child.

This appeared to be a triumph for the woman. The negotiation process had been painful. The father-in-law, who had the final say for his son's issues, was resolute. After several rounds of back and forth, he was willing to increase the compensation only from 10,000 to 25,000, on the condition that the woman payed 500 yuan per month in child support. Nothing suggested that he would cave on this issue. The patrilineal and patrilocal biases against women also placed him in an advantageous negotiating position. That is also why the initial mediation had been a stalemate.

The father-in-law might never have expected the woman to disclose the rape. This was why he had attempted to rape her repeatedly and held such a firm position in the negotiations. He believed that she had to sweep this ordeal under the rug in order to protect her reputation. Despite his expectations, the woman did disclose it to the judge. While the judge may not have been in the position to criminally prosecute him, she represented official public power. Indeed, it was never clear whether the father-in-law, a peasant, could tell the difference between the court and the police. For such a man, there is likely information asymmetry between what he thought a judge could do and what the law authorizes a judge to do. In his mind, a formal investigation of the judge might have put him in jail. Thus, such a disclosure to the judge was intimidating enough. Under these circumstances, his best strategy was to settle as soon as possible.

Nevertheless, such a triumph was limited because of the judge's indifference. Its net value was 15,000 yuan, and the woman had to give up custody of the child (see chapter 5). The woman could have gained more had the judge been more assertive instead of settling on an easy solution. She did not need a police report; she could have simply pushed a little harder. However, she did not even fight for the original suggestion of 50,000 yuan. As mentioned, the land compensation for the woman's share had already reached 80,000 yuan, not to mention her trauma from the attempted rape and her other contributions to the family. Moreover, the man's side had the money to pay (from the land compensation and from the man's regular job as a lorry driver). Indeed, threatening a party with jail time is an effective tactic for a judge to force one party to strike a deal. Su (2000: 243–47) has documented a physically intimidating man who confronted his neighbor after seducing his wife. Upon hearing a criminal threat from the court, he had been willing to increase the compensation and serve legally baseless jail time. In practices of criminal reconciliation, similar compromises abound (Ng and He 2017a).

In sum, even in those rare cases in which victims overcome the cultural barriers to speak out, the final outcomes are gendered because of the judges' inaction or indifference. Coming clean to a judge is not useless, but the impact is limited. The outcomes are only slightly tilted in victims' favor. Had the judges been more assertive, the women would have been treated more fairly. The judges' *modus operandi* thus reinforce gendered outcomes.

Female Infertility

If judges are indifferent to male impotency, how do they react to female infertility? The contrast will help illustrate gendered outcomes here as well. Generally, judges find this issue understandable: in most situations, the man gets what he wants. Often, men have little inhibition to make a claim and file to divorce an infertile wife. The judges simply endorse their rights, which are etched into China's cultural tradition. After all, a moral, responsible Chinese woman produces a "quality" child at the right time—soon after marriage (McMillan 2006). As Handwerker (1995: 366) notes, it is women who are invariably blamed for infertility. Both the state's population policy and Confucian gender ideals assume that the normative female body, not the male body, is and should be fertile.

In the Anesthesiologist's Case, a thirty-five-year-old man, his family's only son, sued to divorce his wife, who had recently become seriously ill. With anasarca spread to her face, she had been too weak to finish the pretrial conversations with the judge. Two years older than the man, she looked like his mother. After six years of marriage, they still had no children. The formal divorce filing stated that the foundation of the affection was shaky and that there was personality incompatibility. However, the genuine reason for the divorce, as the man's legal representative stated at trial, was the woman's infertility. They had tried to treat her condition, but to no avail. The man's father, on his death bed, had nagged him to find another woman who could bear him a child. For the father, this seemed the only way to extend the lineage. The judge's brief investigation found that all of the man's family members, including his parents, had been fond of her. After he had been laid off from a local SOE, she had supported his education in Shanghai for three years. This had qualified him to become an anesthesiologist. She had also tended to her father-in-law for nine months in the hospital before he died. After the man had found a new job, and with his parents gone, he initiated the divorce petition.

Helpless, the woman said to the judge: "No matter how much I did, I did not deliver an heir for their family. That is my fault. Being so ill, there is no chance for me to be pregnant. I am a burden for the family." A divorce outcome seemed both inevitable and understandable for this ill woman: "For all the housework I did for the family for so many years, I only requested a place to stay after the divorce—that is, the forty-square-meter apartment subsidized by his original work unit." Since the man had inherited a large apartment from his father, the case was settled soon after the man agreed to the woman's request.

As shown, to obtain a divorce, men usually include additional reasons for seeking the divorce, such as the incompatibility of personality, family discord, or a lack of mutual understanding before marriage. However, once the issue of infertility is brought up, both litigating parties, and other participants, including the judge, all know the genuine reason underlying the divorce petition. Unlike male impotency or other sex-related male conditions, which are often buried without a trace, female infertility, regarded as a physiological and cultural defect, is openly discussed in trial and recorded in the adjudication documents. There is no privacy. By taking this position, the judge and the court endorse the male-dominant culture.

In the above case, even though it was a first-time petition, there was no resistance to the divorce. The man was not blamed for his heartless action: filing to divorce the woman when she was gravely ill, and right after he had landed a job that, without the long-term support of the woman, would have been impossible to get. The man also made no compromises on property division. He got the large apartment, and the woman got the small one. Both apartments had been marital property and should have been equally divided. The judge never raised this point in the mediation, even though Article 2 of the Marriage Law stipulates that women and children's property rights should be favored. The woman was willing to accept the small one because she felt guilty for not delivering a child for the family. Why bother? The woman blamed herself for not fulfilling the responsibility of continuing the lineage and thus for the "breakdown of mutual affection." She said to the judge: "This is my fault . . . I am a burden for the family." Internalizing this cultural bias, she had forgone any leverage on the issue of property division. This was why she asked only for the minimum living conditions: basic shelter.

As far as the judge was concerned, she was glad to facilitate such a settlement. Female infertility is regarded as a strong basis for the breakdown of mutual affection, thus meeting the standardized legal criteria for divorce. A divorce, even with property division favoring the man, was the expected outcome.

Conclusions

Cultural biases, as reflected in the discourses (Conley and O'Barr 1990), are an obstacle toward gender equality in court. Similarly, traditional biases against women exist in China. As illustrated, these biases inhibit women in speaking out about personal suffering. Moreover, judges, even when women do speak out, turn a blind eye toward the suffering.

Under such a *modus operandi*, the cultural biases against women in Chinese society, especially in rural areas,[2] find their ways into the judicial decision-making process and further disadvantage women's property rights in divorce litigation. These biases include, but are not limited to, patrilineal ideologies, patrilocal practices, and women's roles in issues related to sex. Engrained in Chinese society, these biases marginalize women and result in diminished property rights. Consistent with the cultural biases, judges rarely broach the issue of sex. In the few exceptions in which sex-related issues are revealed to the court, judges brush them off. Suffering from such sexual bias in court, women fail to make their claims and thus receive less property or compensation than they deserve. Another layer of gendered outcomes is perpetuated.

Judges' inaction and indifference toward issues related to sexual problems are consistent with their behavior patterns toward domestic violence (He and Ng 2013a). After all, male impotency and rape also result in damages. The difference is that Article 10 of the Marriage Law does not explicitly provide protection against male impotency. Due to the incentive constraints, judges are even more reluctant to take actions for male impotency than for domestic violence (He and Ng 2013a). This explains why we see the perpetuation of cultural biases.

Judges' indifference and inaction also perpetuate gendered outcomes, since these revelations in private do not make a difference during the litigation process: victims are more reticent, unwilling to share their suffering with the judges. Furthermore, turning a blind eye has ripple effects outside the courts. When rural women go to great lengths to seek legal assistance for marital rape, Li (2015) found that legal workers only state "what he did was lawful." Li (2015) contends that the legal workers could help the victim make a claim based on personal injury, even if marital rape is exempted under Chinese law. However, even if the claims had been presented to the court, the judge would have asked: What is the evidence? The rapist would be even more confident because the issue is usually difficult to prove. Ultimately, it is judges' behavior that shapes the legal workers' approaches. If judges became more proactive in protecting women's interests, lawyers might change their own behavior accordingly.

Epilogue

Gendered Divorces in Chinese Courts

With painful episodes in their lives unfolding, divorcing couples fight their most intimate battles in public. Divorce court is where litigants and other participants conceptualize people's legal rights and moralities. It is where the state overwhelms society, often with resistance along the way. Through the lens of divorce cases, in this book I address how law, gender, and society intersect in China today compared to the past.

Despite a substantial increase of public awareness regarding gender inequality in China, Chinese women—through a mass of legislation combating domestic violence, decades of activism, important scholarship, and relevant training—face tremendous difficulties obtaining fairness and justice in the divorce courts. Laws meant to protect them, compensate them, and deter further harms all fail in that forum because of the institutional environment in which judges are embedded.

Gendered outcomes in divorce cases are not new. For decades, news reports and scholarship in China have documented them; existing studies have attributed these outcomes to incomplete legislation, resource disparities, and cultural biases. This was my starting point. In this book I contend that the courts' institutional constraints, interacting with those factors identified in the existing studies, play a central role in generating gendered outcomes. I demonstrate the systematic failure of China's judiciary to achieve gender equality in divorce litigation from two perspectives. First, many laws protecting women's rights have not been implemented: Judges regularly ignore actual or alleged domestic violence; protection orders are rare; women's rights to child custody are routinely sacrificed; and women disproportionately bear the brunt when courts deny divorce petitions. Second, judges do not alleviate the existing economic and cultural biases against women.

Instead, they take advantage of these biases to facilitate their own goals, thereby aggravating the gendered treatments. Through property division, judges help men (the "haves" in terms of economic capabilities) come out ahead. On sex-related issues, judges reinforce cultural biases. Taken together—despite the facts that gender equality has become an integral component of human rights and that gender equality has been enshrined in both China's Constitution and its domestic laws—gendered outcomes are systematically adjudicated through routine court practices and decision-making. Note that most cases (twenty-three out of twenty-nine, or 79.3 percent) analyzed in this book were handled by female judges (see appendix), higher than the percentage of female judges presiding over divorce cases across the country. If female judges are usually more sympathetic toward women, as some claim (Haire and Moyer 2019), the overall outcomes of China's divorce litigation should only be more gendered.

China's situation thus offers an opportunity to examine the limited role of law in achieving gender and social equality. Why is the law's impact curtailed in courts? Is this phenomenon confined to divorce litigation? What light can China's example shed on the nature of the judicial system in a modern authoritarian state? What should be done? What does this study say about China's legal developments?

Three Contradictory Goals

In the context of divorce cases, the Chinese state has three goals. First, it aspires to implement the laws legislated by the congresses. The laws reify justice, which is always a main tenet of the judiciary. This goal is best realized if the judges follow the letter and the spirit of the laws. By implementing the laws, it hopes to ameliorate the principle/agent delegation problem (Ginsburg and Moustafa 2008). Second, the state wants to maintain social stability. Social control is an integral function of the judiciary expected by the state (Shapiro 1981). In China's context, the state wants to ensure that court decisions resolve disputes and end grievances. Third, the state wants efficiency. It requires courts to respond to cases within a reasonable time frame. These three goals are related to the state's ultimate concern: legitimacy. In President Xi Jinping's own words, it is to "let the people feel justice in each case" (figure A.14).

While fairness and justice are mentioned explicitly, the concerns for stability and efficiency are implied. Had the masses experienced justice and fairness, how could social stability be threatened? Similarly, without efficiency, how could the masses experience justice and fairness?

Achieving these three goals simultaneously is ideal but unrealistic. Often they are incompatible and even contradictory. As demonstrated throughout my analysis, the twin goals of following the law when maintaining stability may clash when judges, by following the letter of the law, grant divorce decisions to female plaintiffs while male defendants protest and threaten extreme action. The efficiency goal also contradicts with the stability goal. In some cases, a six-month cooling-off period is constructive to pacify the distraught parties and to prepare both sides for the inevitable outcome. It gives both sides room to accept that the marriage is over and that it is time to move on. A cooling-off period, however, is not an "efficient" decision, time-wise. When the stability goal prevails over the efficiency goal, the result is to stall any further adjudication. Is not justice delayed merely justice denied? By the same token, judges often cannot pursue justice and efficiency simultaneously. This is why they encourage litigants to adopt a bidding process to fix the price of marital property and compensate one party. Denying divorce petitions, which is at the root of several gendered outcomes, stems from efficiency concerns because judges want to avoid litigating property division and child custody. To increase efficiency, they steer simple and complex cases toward Simplified and Ordinary Procedures, respectively. These classifications predetermine outcomes. Once again, the goals of efficiency and justice clash. Due to the internal contradictions of these two goals, some courts openly prefer efficiency over justice.

This is why the judges cannot decide cases according to the laws alone. Rather, they become slaves to bureaucratic and political concerns and are simultaneously influenced by social and economic forces. Judges have to make sure that legal effects of their decisions are compatible with the social effects. These constraints prevent jurists from formalistic legal interpretation and implementation. They must consider whether their decisions are acceptable to both parties. Often they are unable to impose the decision that they view as legalistically proper. In these situations, they have to gauge the potential reactions of the parties. Will they take extreme actions? Bargaining with other litigants, the judges behave more like another litigating participant instead of the ultimate arbiter. As in criminal proceedings, justice in divorce cases is negotiated (Baldwin and McConville 1977; Ng and He 2017b). To refer to Bourdieu's "juridical field" (1987: 850), external changes are reflected in Chinese courts, where internal conflicts within the field are decided by external forces.

A Governance Dilemma in the Authoritarian State

Such gendered outcomes reflect a governance dilemma. An authoritarian state is always ambivalent toward the rule of law and protecting individual rights through professional lawyering (Ginsburg and Moustafa 2008; Sarat and Scheingold 2006; Halliday et al. 2007; Gallagher 2017; Van Rooij et al. 2016; Jiang 2019). It needs legal systems for instrumental purposes, yet it cannot trust them. It therefore also needs to find a way to control judges, an important cohort of legal actors (Solomon 2007). The Chinese state wants to resolve disputes, but it relies on judges to handle them. To incentivize and guide these actors, the state establishes a series of assessment criteria. The judges then have to balance following the law against meeting these criteria. Often, the latter prevails because of concerns over self-protection and administrative convenience. Gender equality is the principle of the law, but it may not be the judges' priority. Instead, judges must render a decision that avoids provoking extreme reactions. In doing so, they would rather allow social, political, economic, and cultural inequalities to permeate the process.

These gendered consequences seem more intrinsic to an authoritarian regime when compared to liberal democratic states. In the United States, for example, even though Fineman (1991) argues that equality remains an illusion, her analysis targets the social workers rather than the judges or the judiciary. While US judges can certainly possess gendered biases in the courtroom (Resnik 1996; Epstein and Goodman 2018), Chinese judges are torn between the goals of efficiency and stability versus the "neutral" implementation of the law. In a broader context, social movements toward gender equality in China have been repressed (Fincher 2018).

In this sense, the authoritarian state better fits MacKinnon's (1989) definition of the "repressive state." MacKinnon emphasizes the repressive legislative process, in which men dominate the process and implement rules that disadvantage women. Men no doubt dominate within a democratic process. In the authoritarian state, men dictate the laws: the legislative process already disadvantages women. Making matters worse, the laws' implementation further harms women's interests. Many Chinese judges, because of their bureaucratic and political concerns, are unwilling to help victims, even when they discover domestic violence or rape in divorce litigation. Women's injuries are buried and their voices are muffled in a context of bureaucratic apathy. As the institutional inequalities are permitted to operate in court (like the behavior the laws prohibit), the laws protecting women's rights are systemically resisted.

In his classic book *The Faces of Justice and State Authority*, Damaska (1986) classifies court procedures through two dimensions: the authority type, and the state's goal. One dimension of his two-by-two table is whether the authority is hierarchical or coordinated; the other is whether the state's goal is to implement policies or resolve disputes. If the United States fits better with the coordinated authority with the goal of dispute resolution, China is diagonal to the United States in the two-by-two table. With a hierarchical authority, implementing policies is emphasized over resolving disputes.

As mentioned, the Chinese state's policy goals in divorce litigation include family harmony and social control, in addition to dispute resolution. The policy goals are often in tension with justice and fairness, the paramount goal of the law. If the goal of the law is to achieve gender equality, then the judiciary cannot focus on it, because it has other goals to fulfill. Furthermore, civil procedure in China offers plenty of room for judges to twist the legal goals, as seen in the ubiquity of mediation. This is why women's rights and dignity are often sacrificed during the litigation process.

Gendered outcomes in divorce litigation are therefore linked to the civil procedure of a given political regime. All else being equal, the authoritarian nature of China's state adds a layer of gender bias against women that does not exist in the United States. If the repressive state and lack of gender consciousness are the reasons behind gendered outcomes in the United States, these factors are equally as salient in China (Yuan 2005). However, once the law's goal is set as achieving gender equality in the United States, judges are less distracted by the bureaucratic and political concerns than are their counterparts in China; US judges can focus on dispute resolution. In contrast, China's political goals and its bureaucratic machinery compromise the law's goal of gender equality. In short, changing the law's orientation toward gender equality is an insufficient condition for achieving a gender-neutral outcome.

This is perhaps why prereform China did not deliver on its promises of gender equality (Stacey 1983: 2–4). Other than a few brief periods when the state's policy goal was to attack the traditional patriarchal family systems,[1] it sought to stabilize a repressive social order (Johnson 1983; Wolf 1985; see, however, Diamant 2000). In 2001, when the 1950 Marriage Law (an explicit assault on China's patriarchal family system) was amended, social inequality between women and men persisted. Most Western feminists, who had been enthusiastic about China's prospects to liberate women, eventually regarded China under socialism as a failure. If Stacey's (1983) study focuses more on the socioeconomic structure, my analysis illustrates how the promise of gender equality becomes disillusioned during the divorce litigation process. The policy goals of the state are internalized into the institutional constraints of the courts. This has taken a toll on the legal promise of gender equality.

Beyond Divorce Cases

Institutional constraints influence the judicial mind in contemporary China; this finding is not limited to divorce cases. The impact of these constraints is conspicuous in divorce cases because judges in that arena enjoy vast discretion (Cai and Qi 2019). In other cases, it is more subtle. The phenomenon of the squeaky wheel getting more grease is widespread in court decisions. In dealing with medical malpractice disputes, for example, judges tend to hold hospitals at least partially responsible, even if evidence suggests they are innocent of causing harm. After all, the injured party has already suffered in the process of the medical treatment and is likely to become a squeaky wheel: if they gain nothing in litigation, it is possible they will appeal or complain. But hospitals have greater resources: holding them responsible is unlikely to generate appeals or complaints. Rendering a judgment acceptable to both parties thus strikes a balance (He and Su 2013). Of course, judges also benefit from so doing: they have not only resolved the dispute but also protected themselves from liability (He 2012). This method is common in disputes involving traffic accidents and unpaid worker salaries (He and Su 2013), as well as in the notorious "married-out women" disputes in which women in rural areas claim land compensation from their village committees (He 2007a; Chan 2019).

While the combination of both legal and social effects has become a cliché in the rhetoric of the Chinese judiciary, the real message conveyed is that the courts have to consider whether a balance can be achieved and whether the judgment is acceptable to the parties; this in turn has much to do with institutional constraints. Some of my informant judges even explicitly said that an effective way to control appeal rates would be to increase the costs of appealing a decision, that is, to award some benefits to the losing party even though there is no legal basis for so doing. When the losing party gains something, it has less motivation to appeal. After all, the goal of appealing a decision is usually to gain some benefit. If this goal is satisfied beforehand, appeal is less likely. In this sense, the "haves" might not always come out ahead in contemporary China. Although China's balanced treatment of disputes is tied to the legitimacy and ideological concerns of the judges, as found in the Philippines (Haynie 1994) and Israel (Dotan 1999), it has a more direct correlation with institutional constraints.

When facing a significant and complicated case without a clear-cut answer from the law, Chinese judges frequently seek instruction from upper-level courts. According to traditional wisdom, this happens because both the state and the upper-level courts want to control the judiciary. For a long time, most students of Chinese law have uncritically focused their attention on the undue external or internal influences on judges; to them, judges have always appeared passive under the pressure of the decision-making process. Yet from the perspective of institutional constraints, judges in lower-level courts seek instruction from higher courts to avoid potential liability for answering these legally difficult questions. Judges in the lower courts are the ones who seek instruction from other, more powerful political forces to avoid any potential liability. Because this practice has been widely criticized for displacing the principle of appeal and interfering with judicial independence, upper-level courts have become reluctant to offer opinions. Seeking guidance from and reporting back to higher-level authorities responsible for evaluating their performance has become an entrenched practice (Chen 2016: 214;

Tang 2016). When in recent years individual judges have been authorized to handle cases more independently, the courts and the judges have used internal directives—speeches from court leaders, members of the ruling party, and/or government officials, as well as and minutes from the meetings of high-ranking officials—as the basis for deciding legally difficult questions. When these resources are not available, judges have even tried to rely on the precedents of upper-level courts, even though they know those precedents have no official legal effect. Some rely on the decisions of courts in other jurisdictions (Liebman and Wu 2007). They do so because those precedents provide some shelter for avoiding potential criticism and scrutiny. At the same time, depending on the local contexts, they ignore some Guideline cases that, legally speaking, they are required to follow (Ahl 2014). This is because they are more immediately subject to local political and bureaucratic constraints (Liu 2019). By the same token, judges tend to rigidly interpret and apply statutory articles to new situations regardless of legislative intent, even though such applications are problematic.[2] They also tend not to apply abstract legal principles because such applications are not supported by clear statutory articles and thus might be struck down as wrong. It is unclear whether, given greater discretion, they would apply the law more independently in accordance with its provisions, yet it is clear they have employed various self-protective measures. Engrained in the behavior patterns of the court staff is the logic of institutional constraints: the greater the discretion Chinese judges enjoy, the more likely they are to succumb to the pressures of the assessment criteria.

Local variations across China have strengthened the argument that institutional constraints sway the judicial mind. For example, in areas where caseloads are low—meaning that efficiency is not an looming goal for local courts—high mediation rates have once again become an important standard for assessing the performance of the court staff. Judges and courts in these areas mobilize all potential resources and employ both creative and stereotyped strategies, repeatedly cajoling divorcing couples to reconcile (Gao and Zhou 2006; Xiong 2015). Thus, the baseline for divorce petitions has shifted back to mediated reconciliation: courts are reluctant to render any decision unless and until the couple signs a reconciliation agreement. Judges handle divorce petitions this way not because they care about the couple's future or about social harmony, but ultimately for their own interests: mediation helps avoid protest petitions, scrutiny, appeals, and complaints (Gao and Zhou 2006: 71). Anecdotal evidence also suggests that in courts where the expected working style is "busy," judges tend to render more adjudicated divorce decisions because those decisions make them busy (or at least look busy). In some courts where the judges have low salaries and there is no effective way to check corruption, adjudicated divorce has also become a common choice because it offers them an opportunity to divide matrimonial property and consequently greater opportunities for rent-seeking. Court decisions thus become a function of many elements, whereby the raw number of completed cases, the completion rate, the appeal rate, and the complaint rate each play a significant role at a time when justice and efficiency are the themes of the bureaucratized judiciary. Instead of weakening my overall thesis, these local variations corroborate the finding that under certain incentive structures, self-interest rules judges' behavior, and self-protection or self-preservation are themes inherent to China's judiciary.

Policy Recommendations

As MacKinnon (1989) argues, only when judges act can equality promises be invoked. To reduce gendered outcomes, an important step would be to reveal the imbalance and unfairness resulting from judicial implementation of the gender-neutral principles and rules. Focusing on the courts' institutional constraints, in this book I offer an alternative reform agenda. An effective judicial intervention is needed (Epstein 1999). An immediate remedy to reduce gendered outcomes in the litigation process would be to adjust how judges are assessed. A fundamental approach is to alienate the bureaucratic and political concerns from the legal goals embedded in the judicial process. The assessment criteria of the judges' performance need an overhaul.

First, mediation should be used more cautiously. As demonstrated, the pursuit of a high mediation rate has been the major source of gendered outcomes. Despite its positive functions, mediation trivializes domestic violence, sacrifices women's rights to child custody, and ignores cultural and economic biases against women. Mediation also allows, and even encourages, the trade-off between divorce versus child custody and property; it is the platform for and the conduit to perpetuating gender inequality. In the common jurisdiction (Gu 2010), mediation is used to settle family disputes, but its role is limited. In light of China's practices, there is reason for this limited role.

Eliminating all mediation from divorce cases may be unrealistic. Looking toward the intimate relationship between litigants in family cases, in 2015 a nationwide "family cases trial reform" sought to preserve and reconcile marriages through intensive *mediation*. The courts in Gansu Province, for example, "push for reconciliation and not divorce" (*The Paper* 2019). The Guangdong High Court (2018) stresses the priority of mediation and the setting up of mediation before the hearing in family cases. The SPC Notice (2018) on protecting the safety of litigants and family members also emphasizes mediation. In reality, however, some courts in the more developed areas have deepened the division of labor in the courts because of caseload pressures: the judges adjudicate while nonadjudicating personnel mediate. Some judges I interviewed suggested that the role of mediation had declined in their courts. Different trajectories notwithstanding, mediation will likely persist in China's family law practices.

As long as mediation is still allowed in divorce proceedings, judges should inform litigants of its gendered implications before they accept a settlement. Judges should also inform victims that domestic violence will not be factored into mediation. A fundamental step would be to once and for all bar mediation for cases involving established domestic violence. Judges should warn plaintiffs that, through the mediation process, their rights may be traded for the other party's consent to the divorce. Judges should also determine child custody independent of any other concerns rather than use it as a bargaining chip. For sex-related issues, judges should inform litigants of the pros and cons of disclosing embarrassing private matters in the hearing (as opposed to in mediation).

Second, courts should be more cautious when pursuing the goal of efficiency. Given the explosion of caseloads in many courts, there is a pressing need to process cases efficiently. Such a pursuit, however, often comes at the expense of women. Using the bidding process for the couple's apartment is one example. The parties need to be informed of the pitfalls when choosing bidding as a way to divide their apartment. When one party is short on cash, bidding may not be in their best interests, even if it is free (whereas the alternative, a fair-market-value appraisal, results in more costs). In this sense, adding more judges to the judiciary might be helpful.

As demonstrated, protection orders are underutilized partly because they create more work for judges. One solution would be to adjust the incentive mechanism, incorporating it into the formula for evaluating judges' performance. A more direct solution would be to simplify the approval procedure, for example, by lowering the threshold for evidence. After all, a protection order is just a warning; even if it is not later substantiated by facts, such an order would cause little harm.

Third, judges should not be penalized, or their careers threatened, because of "malicious incidents" resulting from their decisions. As the regime responds to the demands of society, judges are responsive or even overresponsive to the threat of malicious incidents. However, this creates a vicious cycle. Many litigants take advantage of the courts' concerns. Squeaky wheels get more grease, but social stability may not be maintained. Thus, the courts' approaches sometimes backfire.

Fourth, judges' gender consciousness needs enlightenment. While the SPC guidelines (2008) already required judges specializing in divorce cases to receive at least twelve hours of gender education and eighteen hours domestic violence education (Art. 20), it is unclear whether all the requirements have been implemented. Many judges do not even realize that their approaches are gendered. Many may not realize that they fail to understand victims' experiences and narratives (Epstein and Goodman 2018). They should overcome hostility toward domestic violence complainants; they should treat domestic violence as any other crime (Epstein 1999: 13). Furthermore, when they are inundated by institutional concerns, they may lose sight of the cultural and economic biases against women, as shown in the cases related to patrilocal, patrilineal, bride-price, and sexual issues. More gender consciousness training is needed, in addition to replacing the current institutional concerns with concerns that prevent gender biases.

And last: laws should be revised to protect women's interests. The current standards may not be enough in light of the courts' institutional constraints. For instance, the standards for domestic violence need clarification. The SPC guidelines (2008), issued by its Applied Research Center, should be turned into a formal judicial interpretation. The SPC should eliminate any formal Judicial Interpretations that carry gender biases.

Should these proposed changes be implemented, gender equality will increase. Nevertheless, reforms implemented inside the courts alone are inadequate because gender prejudices are prevalent in society at large. After all, the gender consciousness of the public and traditional biases cannot be altered overnight. It is a matter of fact that societal forces permeate the courts. Moreover, it is unlikely that courts would be able to provide remedies for issues that are best handled through the police, the All-China Women's Federation, and/or other political or administrative channels.

Looking Ahead

By exploring the gendered consequences in divorce cases in this book, I provide a counterpoint to the importance of the safeguards in the American constitutional design: only under institutional structures, such as separation of powers, can one take the view that rational action theory is limited in predicting judicial decisions (Cohen 1991: 187, 192, 193; Epstein 1990: 827, 838; Posner 1993; Sisk et al. 1998: 1498). When these incentive structures are removed or altered, self-interest rules behavior. I thus offer an endorsement of the theory of self-interest: as external constraints are inappropriately imposed, legal decisions will be affected, if not twisted, in such a way that judges maximize their own welfare. Furthermore, greater judicial independence or discretion will not guarantee that judges will decide cases in accordance with the norms of the "original tenor" or "original meaning" of the legislation, as assumed by some economists (Landes and Posner 1975: 885). These considerations suggest that incentive structures remain significant in studying judicial behavior.

In addition to shedding light on the functioning logic and behavior patterns of Chinese judges and courts, this book raises questions about the future development of Chinese laws protecting women's interests, in addition to other areas of the legal system. How have the institutional constraints of Chinese courts affected the development of China's legal reforms? Whether one can design a reform plan and implement it in China is beyond the scope of this book. To ensure that legal principles or rules achieve their intended results, however, examining the institutional constraints of the courts should be prioritized. As shown, the oversimplified incentives of "efficiency" and "stability" are misplaced: it is these incentives that have led to such routine treatment of contested divorce cases. My analysis points to a more realistic and useful research agenda: Will it do greater social good for these incentives to be mitigated in the Chinese judiciary? How can a balance be struck between making judges more accountable for law, on the one hand (Gong 2004), and freeing them from the pressures of the bureaucratic and political measurements on the other? What side-effects will the assessment measurements bring? Is the state incentivized to create an elite group of judges in the administration process in accordance with the law (Zheng et al. 2017)? Do balanced decisions in light of the incentives of the judiciary not conform to the interests of the state? If the state's paramount goal in China's legal reform is to preserve social stability, does the state have sufficient incentive to overhaul the institutional constraints of the judiciary? Answers to these questions will enlighten our understanding of the Chinese judiciary and court decisions' impact on gender equality.

As this book goes to print, another round of judicial reforms is under way, including: the lay assessors' reform, the judges' quota reform, the establishment of circuit tribunals (Wang and Chen 2019), the decoupling of judicial salary and administrative rank, and the centralization of judiciary budgets. Furthermore, changes to judicial accountability, integrity, and professionalism have also been debated (Woo 2017; Zhang and Ginsburg 2019; He and Su 2014; He 2021 forthcoming). A special Family Division with a unique set of procedures is to be implemented across the country. According to some measures, judges have more room to make their own decisions, and courts have become more professional and rules-based. How would these changes affect divorce law practices? What are the gender implications?

Some reform measures may improve the situation. The creation of the specialized Family Division, for example, may increase the response of judicial apparatuses to domestic violence (Epstein 1999). The criminalization of domestic violence may also deter such offenses and raise public awareness (see, e.g., Hanna 1996). The training for family-case judges will also enhance their gender awareness. Having said that, the overall situation is not sanguine because of the political climate and the judicial environment.

The slogan now is: "Let those who hear the cases adjudicate, and hold the adjudicators responsible." The most dramatic change so far has been that a judge may make a decision without the approval of the supervising division head or other court officials, which heretofore has been an entrenched practice in Chinese courts (Ng and He 2017: 114–18). The latter part of the slogan, however, means that judges have "lifetime" responsibility (终身责任制) for any "mistakes" stemming from their decisions. Article 25 of the Several Opinions to Perfect the Judicial Responsibilities (SPC 2015) stipulates that the judge is held responsible for the quality of the cases handled for life. This covers not only issues of corruption, factual mistakes, and inappropriate legal applications but also any procedural and paperwork flaw that "causes serious consequences" (Art. 26.5.). This could be either intentional or grossly negligent. These stipulations leave much space for interpretation. For example, what constitutes "serious" consequences? Inside the court, these mistakes can be traced from cases reversed on appeal or remanded for retrial by superior courts, internal case checks, and letters and in-person complaints (Art. 34; Wang 2016).

As the political ideology and the court's role to serve the general public have been stressed, the disciplinary and political departments have been quick to respond. Because the departments want to avoid being labeled as politically sluggish, a tiny issue can trigger a serious investigation. Many judges have been held responsible for technical problems or inconsistencies in procedural niceties. When a litigant complains, the Party's Disciplinary Department, buoyed by the political atmosphere emphasizing loyalty to the Party, eagerly initiates a formal investigation. In one case, a judge was punished because of a typo in his adjudication decision, even though the typo had been made by his inexperienced clerk (*Sina News* 2018). Detained in the investigation camp reserved for corrupt officials under *shuanggui* (双规 or "double stipulations") (Sapio 2008), some judges have been treated as criminal suspects. They have been pressed to "confess" under threats from the Disciplinary

Department to initiate a full-fledged investigation into all cases they handled. During the investigation, they have no procedural rights or the rights to remain silent or to consult a lawyer. With the role of the adjudication committee having shrunk, the traditional mechanism of diluting responsibilities has become less available and less effective (He 2012). One judge told me: "We are pushed to the front line in the battle against all the rising disputes, but we are not equipped with any weapons, not even those for minimum self-defense."

While it is too early to make a comprehensive assessment, some signs already suggest that as the Party-state continues to influence the courts politically and ideologically, judges are trapped in an institutional environment laced with pressure and uncertainty. These changes may reinforce rather than undermine the bureaucratic and political nature of Chinese courts. Under the new political environment and the ideological turn under the Xi regime, judges are becoming only more cautious, and thus the patterns documented in this book may become further entrenched unfortunately. Judges strive to leave no trace of error that might come back to bite them. They are more afraid of complaints from litigants and thus are more responsive to their requests. Given the heavy caseloads and the pressures for efficiency, no judge can pledge an impeccable procedural track record. The threat from the Party's Disciplinary Department is always looming and formidable. Gender equality may simply create more incentives for accommodating bureaucratic and political concerns. We can predict more denials for first-time petitions, less recognition of actual and alleged domestic violence, an incremental increase in the number of protection orders (if any), and continued ignorance of cultural and economic biases. Gender equality, both outside and inside the courtroom, remains a challenge.

In *Sexual Democracy*, Ferguson (1991) points out that underdeveloped countries like China have two problems in providing gender equality programs: patriarchal culture, and weak material resources. Ferguson is right. The strong patriarchy, especially in China's rural and underdeveloped areas, still dominates. And the lack of economic opportunities renders women unable to voice their own choices. Often they succumb to economic necessity and thus forfeit their child custody rights and continue to suffer domestic violence in silence. What Ferguson does not mention, however, is that these two elements work together with the institutional constraints of the Chinese courts in divorce cases. Chinese judges follow an institutional logic of their own. It differs from those identified by Htun and Weldon (2018), but it joins forces with social hierarchy, cultural biases, and economic inequality.

ACKNOWLEDGMENTS

For more than a decade, I have been trying to learn as much as possible about this topic. This book represents the outcome of those efforts. Numerous intellectual debts were accumulated along the way. Song Feng provided inspirations that, back to 2008, ignited my interests in divorce cases in China. As both a judge and a lawyer, his command of the operations of Chinese courts is masterful. When I started my courtroom research and fieldwork, my late classmate and friend Ju Xiaoxiong embraced me with open arms at his court. Several other Chinese judges also provided indispensable data access and sources of information. For the judges, litigants, and lawyers who allowed me to study their cases and kindly agreed to interviews, I am most grateful.

Many friends and colleagues took time to read earlier versions of the manuscript and offered me invaluable suggestions and comments: Cheris Chan, Hualing Fu, Jed Kroncke, David Law, Shitong Qiao, Marco Wan, and Angela Zhang. Specifically, two longtime collaborators, Yang Su and Kwai Hang Ng, have shaped the book's structure and sharpened its arguments. They and Guang Lei got into heated debates on which title to choose. Lawrence Friedman read parts of the manuscript and provided encouragement and advice during the publication process.

Parts of the manuscript were presented at the workshop "Chinese Family Law in Action" on April 27, 2019, at the University of Hong Kong. I am grateful for the helpful feedback received from the participants. Specifically, Michael Palmer, with his profound knowledge in the field, enthusiasm, and humor, has been of great help. Ethan Michelson, who also conducts research on this topic, provided detailed and insightful suggestions for improvement. Ke Li generously offered suggestions and an innovative way to amplify the impact of my research and writing. Rui Huang, a former judge who specializes in divorce cases in China, provided interesting and helpful feedback as well. Huina Xiao provided useful comments, in addition to her extraordinary research assistance.

I also presented talks on the subject at Bond University, Durham Law School, the Center for Gender Studies at Cambridge University, Jilin University, the Sociology Department of Macau University, Nanjing Normal University, Shanghai Jiaotong University, Southwestern University of Political Science and Law, Stanford Law School, and Zhejiang University. I benefitted from audience comments, including those offered by Yuqing Feng, Weidong Ji, Meng Hou, Ye Meng, Xifeng Lin, Xin Liu, Guiguo Wang, Eddie Wei, Xingzhong Yu, and Ge Zheng. Among his other help, Donald Clarke had a long conversation with me on the title. I thank them all and have been diligent in implementing their suggestions in whole or part.

My exploration of this project was initially supported by the General Research Fund in Hong Kong (project no. 142013). Subsequent funding and teaching relief were provided by the Humanities and Social Sciences Prestigious Fellowship in Hong Kong (project no. 37000819). Clara Platter, the editor at New York University Press, has been enthusiastic about the book project. Kege Li, Benjamin Ross, Phoebe Siu, and copy editors at New York University Press provided valuable editorial services.

Passages from earlier publications are used in this volume, all with substantial revisions. My thanks to the publishers for their original publication of my work and permissions. These works include "Routinization of Divorce Law Practice in China: Institutional Constraints' Influence on Judicial Behavior," *International Journal of Law, Policy and the Family* 23(1): 83–109 (2009); "'No Malicious Incidents': The Concern for Stability in China's Divorce Law Practice," *Social & Legal Studies* 26: 467–89 (2017); "When the Cultural Explanation Is Inadequate: The Institutional Constraints of Chinese Judges in Divorce Cases," *Michigan State International Law Review* 28(3): 439–75 (2020). Also: "In the Name of Harmony: The Erasure of Domestic Violence in China's Judicial Mediation," *International Journal of Law, Policy and the Family* 27(1): 97–115 (2013), and "Pragmatic Discourse and Gender Inequality in China," *Law & Society Review* 47(2): 279–310 (2013), coauthored with Kwai Hang Ng.

My father, Tao Xiuxin, always cares about the publication of this book. My son, Tim, has fun reading my manuscript out loud during breaks in his ping-pong practice. Finally, I would like to thank Lucy Chen, who persistently reminds me that academic writing is more meaningful than other obsessions. For this and other reasons, I devote this book to her.

APPENDIX 1

Fieldwork Photographs

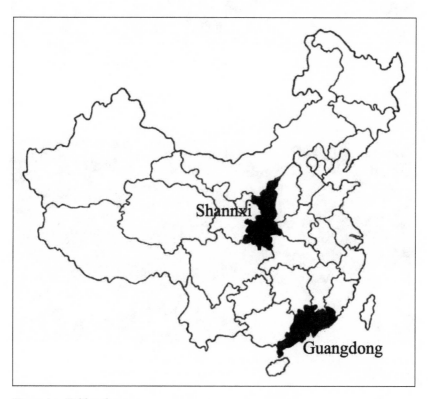

Figure A.1. Fieldwork map.

Figure A.2. The current political wind: The office of sweeping the dark forces and eliminating the evil in a court.

Figure A.3. The gate of a court, with a sheriff's car standing by.

Figure A.4. The case filing division, with the slogan "Virtue and Justice, People Friendly and Supreme Goodness."

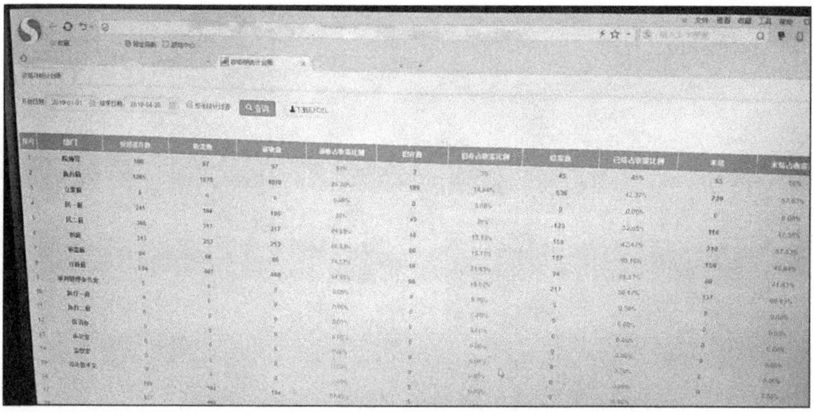

Figure A.5. The progress of cases for each court division.

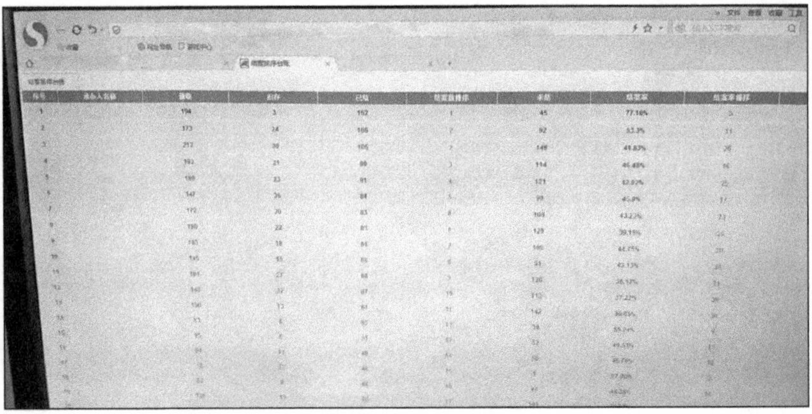

Figure A.6. The progress of cases for individual judges.

Figure A.7. Litigation participants queuing up to enter a courthouse, with a sheriff's car standing by.

Figure A.8. The building of a dispatched tribunal. The slogan reads: "Justice, Integrity, for the People."

Figure A.9. A separate gate with tightened security check for petitioners (访民).

Figure A.10. A judge tries to facilitate a settlement for a divorcing couple. The slogan on the wall reads: "Harmonious and Happy Families Depend on the Collective Efforts of Yours and Mine."

Figure A.11. The office to protect the rights of women in a court in the coastal area, with leaflets: "How to write a petition letter."

Figure A.12. The setting of a trial room, with surveillance cameras from all angles.

Figure A.13. An old man trying to divorce his wife in the hearing, with a legal aid lawyer. The hearing was recorded live and shown on the screen.

努力让人民群众在每一个司
法案件中都感受到公平正义

Figure A.14. "Let the People Feel Justice in Each Case" (Xi's Words) are on the walls of many courtrooms.

Figure A.15. A sandbox therapy room for children in a courtroom.

APPENDIX 2

Fieldwork Cases and Adjudication

1. ALCOHOL SALESWOMAN'S CASE (2014, SHAANXI)
   District court, female plaintiff and judge, first petition, both parties were
   not represented, issue of divorce.
   OUTCOME: Divorce denied after adjudication.
   See chapter 2.

2. ANESTHESIOLOGIST'S CASE (2018, SHAANXI)
   District court, male plaintiff and female judge, first petition, plaintiff was
   represented by lawyer and defendant was not represented, issues of
   divorce and property.
   OUTCOME: Divorce granted after mediation; wife received the smaller
   apartment.
   See chapter 7.

3. ATTEMPTED RAPE CASE (2017, SHAANXI)
   District court, male plaintiff and female judge, more than one petition,
   both parties were represented by citizens, issues of divorce, custody,
   property, and rape.
   OUTCOME: Divorce granted after mediation; wife received 40,000
   yuan for compensation; child custody was awarded to the
   husband.
   See chapters 4, 5, and 7.

4. AUTISTIC DAUGHTER'S CASE (2018, SHAANXI)
   District court, male plaintiff and female judge, more than one petition, both parties were represented by lawyers, issues of divorce and
   custody.
   Outcome: Divorce granted after mediation; child custody was awarded
   to the wife; wife gave up property division and child support for one
   child.
   See chapter 6.

5. BRIDE-PRICE CASE (2017, SHAANXI)

Dispatched tribunal, male plaintiff and judge, first petition, plaintiff was not represented and defendant was represented by citizen, issues of divorce, bride-price, and male impotency.

OUTCOME: Divorce granted after mediation; bride-price was returned.

See chapters 6 and 7.

6. Coerced Video Case (2012, GUANGDONG)

District court, female plaintiff and judge, first petition, plaintiff was represented by lawyer and defendant was not represented, issues of divorce, custody, and domestic violence.

OUTCOME: Divorce granted after adjudication; child custody was awarded to the wife.

See chapter 4.

7. COERCED VIDEO CASE, APPEALED (2013, GUANGDONG)

Intermediate court, male plaintiff and female judge, first petition, both parties were represented by lawyers, issues of divorce, custody, and domestic violence.

OUTCOME: Divorce denied after adjudication; child custody was awarded to the husband.

See chapter 5.

8. DISTRAUGHT WOMAN'S CASE (2011, SHAANXI)

District court, male plaintiff and judge, first petition, plaintiff was represented by lawyer and defendant was represented by citizen, issues of divorce, domestic violence, property, and extramarital affair.

OUTCOME: Divorce denied after adjudication.

See chapter 5.

9. DISTRAUGHT WOMAN'S CASE, SECOND PETITION (2012, SHAANXI)

District court, male plaintiff and judge, second petition, plaintiff was represented by lawyer and defendant was represented by citizen, issues of divorce, domestic violence, property, and extramarital affair.

OUTCOME: Divorce denied after adjudication.

See chapter 5.

10. DISTRAUGHT WOMAN'S CASE, THIRD PETITION
(2017, SHAANXI)

District court, female plaintiff and male judge, third petition, plaintiff was represented by citizen and defendant was not represented, issues of divorce, domestic violence, property, and extramarital affair.

OUTCOME: Divorce granted after adjudication; child custody was awarded to the husband, and property was divided in half.

See chapter 6.

11. DISTRAUGHT WOMAN'S CASE, THE SUPERVISION PROCEDURE (2018, SHAANXI)

Adjudicatory supervision procedure, female plaintiff and judge, plaintiff was represented by citizen and defendant was not represented, issues of divorce, domestic violence, property, and extramarital affair.

OUTCOME: Rejected.

See chapter 5.

12. FISH RETAILER'S CASE (2014, GUANGDONG)

District court, female plaintiff and judge, first petition, plaintiff was represented by a lawyer and defendant was not represented, issues of divorce, domestic violence, and protection order.

OUTCOME: Divorce granted after adjudication; domestic violence was established.

See chapter 4.

13. FISH RETAILER'S CASE, APPEALED (2014, GUANGDONG)

Intermediate court, male plaintiff and judge, both parties were represented by lawyers, issues of divorce and domestic violence.

Outcome: Divorce denied after adjudication.

See chapter 4.

14. OIL REFINERY WORKER'S CASE (2018, SHAANXI)

District court, female plaintiff and judge, first petition, both parties were not represented, issue of divorce.

OUTCOME: Divorce granted after mediation; child custody was awarded to the husband.

See chapter 5.

15. OVERDOSED WOMAN'S CASE (2018, SHAANXI)

District court, female plaintiff and male judge, first petition, both parties were not represented, issue of divorce, domestic violence, and protection order.

OUTCOME: Divorce denied after adjudication.

See chapter 4.

16. PRIMARY SCHOOL TEACHER'S CASE (2018, SHAANXI)

District court, female plaintiff and judge, first petition, both parties were not represented, issues of divorce and domestic violence.

OUTCOME: Divorce granted after adjudication; child custody was awarded to the husband.

See chapter 5.

17. RAILWAY WORKER'S CASE (1991, SHAANXI)

District court, female plaintiff and judge, first petition, both parties were not represented, issue of divorce.

OUTCOME: Divorce granted after adjudication; child custody was awarded to the husband.

See chapters 5 and 6.

18. SALESWOMAN'S CASE (2012, GUANGDONG)

District court, female plaintiff and judge, first petition, both parties were not represented, issues of divorce and domestic violence.

OUTCOME: Divorce granted after mediation; property was divided; domestic violence was ignored.

See preface and chapter 7.

19. SHANDONG WAITRESS'S CASE (2017, SHAANXI)

District court, female plaintiff and judge, first petition, plaintiff was represented by citizen and defendant was represented by lawyer, issues of divorce and male impotency.

OUTCOME: Divorce granted after mediation; wife made compromise on property.

See chapter 7.

20. SHANGHAI MIGRANT WORKER'S CASE (2013, SHAANXI)

District court, female plaintiff and judge, more than one petition, plaintiff was represented by citizen and defendant was not represented, issues of divorce, domestic violence, and male impotency.

OUTCOME: Withdrawal.

See chapters 2, 4, and 7.

21. SINGAPORE LABORER'S CASE (2017, SHAANXI)

District court, female plaintiff and judge, first petition, both parties were not represented, issues of divorce and domestic violence.

OUTCOME: Withdrawal.

See chapters 4 and 7.

22. SOBBING DOCTOR'S CASE (2014, SHAANXI)

District court, female plaintiff and judge, more than one petition, plaintiff was represented by citizen and defendant was not represented, issue of divorce.

OUTCOME: Withdrawal.

See chapter 2.

23. STRATEGIC POLICEMAN'S CASE (2017, SHAANXI)

District court, female plaintiff and judge, first petition, plaintiff was not represented and defendant was represented by lawyer, issue of divorce.

OUTCOME: Divorce granted after mediation; child custody was awarded to the wife; wife gave up property.

See chapters 5 and 6.

24. 100 YUAN CASE (2012, GUANGDONG)

District court, male plaintiff and female judge, first petition, both parties were represented by lawyers, issues of divorce, property, and child support.

OUTCOME: Divorce granted after mediation.

See chapter 4.

25. THE CASE OF CHANGED PROCEDURE (2019, SHAANXI)

District court, female plaintiff and judge, first petition, plaintiff was represented by lawyer and defendant was not represented, issues of divorce, domestic violence, and property.

OUTCOME: Divorce granted after adjudication.

See chapter 2.

26. THE CASE OF MRS. LI (2012, GUANGDONG)

District court, male plaintiff and female judge, first petition, both parties were not represented, issue of divorce.

OUTCOME: Divorce denied after adjudication.

See chapter 3.

27. THE CASE OF THE INFANT (2017, SHAANXI)

District court, male plaintiff and female judge, first petition, both parties were not represented, issues of divorce and child custody.

OUTCOME: Withdrawal.

See chapter 5.

28. THE CASE WITH *GUANXI* (2015, SHAANXI)

District court, female plaintiff and judge, first petition, both parties were not represented, issues of divorce, child custody, and property.

OUTCOME: Divorce granted after adjudication.

See chapter 4.

29. THE SEXUAL DISEASE CASE (2007, GUANGDONG)

District court, male plaintiff and female judge, first petition, both parties were not represented, issue of divorce.

OUTCOME: Withdrawal.

See chapter 2.

NOTES

PREFACE

1   Pu et al. (2015) argue that women suffer more from the institutional pressures on efficiency. They suggest that when "efficiency trumps fairness," judges choose a decision with the least cost, allowing gender biases to enter into their decisions. My arguments, as illustrated below, go far beyond this point.

2   The figures released by various sources are not consistent. The figures released by SPC are the most official.

CHAPTER 1. INSTITUTIONAL CONSTRAINTS

1   According to the SPC Work Report (2018), the SPC, with fourteen government branches including the All-China Women's Federation, has established a coordination mechanism for adjudicating reforms for family issues. And 118 courts in Shanxi, Jiangsu, Guizhou, and Xinjiang Provinces have launched pilot reforms on adjudicating family cases.

2   The Pearl River Delta Court where I conducted fieldwork investigation has outsourced this part of the work by providing psychological therapy for litigants or related children who need such services. The court president supported this project, echoing the need to protect women's and children's rights. Two rooms were set aside for this purpose, despite the limited office space for judges. Experts in the region were invited to provide consultations and treatment for litigants under emotional pressure and those noticeably agitated. Sandbox therapy was provided for children who had suffered from domestic violence or emotional abuse. Another room provided a friendly environment for children to communicate with the consultation providers. While these services might help some litigants, they also created more work for the judges, as they had to liaison with experts and supervise the consultation staff.

3   Because the SPC monitors this practice, some courts have to readjust the received cases in accordance with registered cases, the latter of which will not affect their annual case closure rates (interview with a vice president of an intermediate court in the Pearl River Delta on December 2, 2017).

4   Realizing that marriage and family disputes often trigger violence, threaten litigants' safety, and cause negative social effects, the SPC in 2017 issued the "Notice on Trying Cases Regarding Marriage and Family Disputes in Accordance with

the Law and Effectively Safeguarding the Parties' Lawful Rights and Interests and Personal Safety." This directive exhorted lower courts to pay special attention to the issue.

5 A Hunan judge told me that resorting to family members is a useful tactic because the litigants usually take their opinions seriously (interview conducted on April 30, 2015).

CHAPTER 2. ROUTINIZED APPROACHES

1 Due to the nature of divorce cases and the mandatory requirement of mediation, the mediation rate for divorce cases was 38.5 percent in 2016, much higher than civil cases in general (see table 3).

2 This point is echoed in Zhang (2018: 110). The judge he interviewed said that "sometimes it is difficult to divide property. Some apartments do not have formal certificates or ownership; some litigants have too much property, including companies or shares. When it is difficult to divide, we just issue an adjudicated denial. Then there is no need to divide property."

3 Li (2021 forthcoming) points out the disproportionate impact of the stalling strategy for rural women who are a major group of divorce plaintiffs. They "must foot the bill, including litigation fees (*susongfei* 诉讼费), service fees (if legal counselling is involved), travel expenses, and/or lost wages." Facing a stalling decision, "either they stay put, get through the waiting period, lose their incomes from off-farm employment in cities, and then launch another plea for divorce in front of a judge. Or they travel back and forth between the workplace and the court, as the litigation process drags on. Even worse, they give up divorce altogether." In addition to financial costs, migrant women must endure legal uncertainty, psychological stress, emotional turmoil, and domestic violence resulting from prolonged litigation processes.

4 It stipulates that courts can formally impose a cooling-off period for divorce on two conditions: the period does not exceed three months, and both parties in a divorce suit must agree on the arrangement.

CHAPTER 4. TRIVIALIZING DOMESTIC VIOLENCE

1 In a similar case analyzed by Palmer (1986) more than three decades ago, the court simply rejected the petition. The decisions of the courts on these types of cases have not changed much, though the rationale has changed from patriarchal socialism to social stability.

CHAPTER 5. SACRIFICING WOMEN'S RIGHTS TO CHILD CUSTODY

1 Forty miles is a long distance for rural or suburban areas with limited means of transportation.

2 Until recently, clerks in Chinese courts were new recruits, assisting judges in handling cases. Sometimes they were responsible for handling cases themselves.

CHAPTER 6. PROPERTY DIVISION AND MALE ADVANTAGE

1 The Xinjiang Production and Construction Corps (XPCC), known as Bingtuan (兵团) in Chinese, is a quasi-military and business conglomerate located in Xinjiang. It governs a population of 2.6 million people, of whom more than 200,000 are Uyghurs and other predominantly Muslim ethnic minority groups (Duihua, *Human Rights Journal* 2018). The living conditions there were worse than those in most parts of China.

2 According to the law, this might constitute bigamy, which would offer the wife leverage: to prosecute the man criminally. With rumors only, however, she might not be able to locate where the man and his new lover lived. Neither the court nor the police would have any incentive to initiate this.

3 Until recently, few graduates of prestigious law schools, let alone those from well-off families, have worked for the courts. This situation has gradually changed as the judiciary has begun recruiting new blood nationally (see Ng and He 2017a).

4 In several other cases, women's inexperienced lawyers have inadequately stated the prenuptial properties, failed to obtain credible evidence for the value of the communal property or communal debts, and missed opportunities to press the men. Despite all of these substandard legal services, the judges never uttered a word.

5 For an introduction to this arrangement, see Lam et al. (2015).

CHAPTER 7. CULTURAL BIASES

1 The bride-price system itself is culturally biased against women. Due to the bride-price system, only families that can afford the money have the ability to select a bride. These marriages were often in violation of the desires of the individuals and especially those of women—"as if she were an animal just purchased at market" (Smith 1899: 250). For an analysis of bride-price, see Goody and Tambiah (1973).

2 As Stacey (1983: 237–40) argues, one of the consequences of the socialist reforms is that urban family life has significantly been less patriarchal than in rural China. The traditional culture's impact on divorce litigation will also be less visible in urban China.

EPILOGUE

1 For the Soviet Union's similar policy toward Muslim Central Asia, see Massell (1974).

2 For example, the Guangzhou Intermediate Court sentenced a person to prison for life because he had intentionally overdrawn 175,000 yuan from a dysfunctional ATM (the Xu Ting Case). The statute that the court relied on was Article 264 of the Criminal Law, which was intended to punish those who steal funds from financial institutions. The sentence was so problematic that it caused a media stir, and the appeals court subsequently remanded the decision. See *China Daily,* April 1, 2008.

BIBLIOGRAPHY

ENGLISH-LANGUAGE LITERATURE

Agarwal, Bina. 1994. *A Field of One's Own: Gender and Land Rights in South Asia.* Cambridge: Cambridge University Press.

Ahl, Björn. 2014. "Retaining Judicial Professionalism: The New Guiding Cases Mechanism of the Supreme People's Court." *China Quarterly*, no. 217: 121–39.

Albiston, Catherine. 1999. "The Rule of Law and the Litigation Process: The Paradox of Losing by Winning." *Law & Society Review* 33(4): 869–910.

Alford, William, and Yuanyuan Shen. 2004. "Have You Eaten? Have You Divorced? Marriage, Divorce and the Assessment of Freedom in China." In *Realms of Freedom in Modern China*, edited by William Kirby, 234–63. Stanford: Stanford University Press.

Baldwin, John, and Michael McConvile. 1977. *Negotiated Justice: Pressures to Plead Guilty.* London: Martin Robertson.

Balme, Stephanie. 2010. "Local Courts in Western China: The Quest for Independence and Dignity." In *Judicial Independence in China: Lessons for Global Rule of Law Promotion*, edited by Randall Peerenboom, 154–79. New York: Cambridge University Press.

Barlow, Tani. 1994. *Gender Politics in Modern China: Writing and Feminism.* Durham: Duke University Press.

Bauer, John, Feng Wang, Nancy Riley, and Xiaohua Zhao. 1992. "Gender Inequality in Urban China: Education and Employment." *Modern China* 18(3): 333–70.

Behr, Edward. 1987. *The Last Emperor.* London: Futura.

Belden, Jack. 1970. *China Shakes the World.* New York: Monthly Review Press.

Bemiller, Michelle. 2008. "When Battered Women Lose Custody: A Qualitative Study of Abuse at Home and in the Courts." *Journal of Custody* 5: 228–255.

Best, Rachel Kahn, Lauren Edelman, Linda Krieger, and Scott Eliason. 2011. "Multiple Disadvantages: An Empirical Test of Intersectionality Theory in EEO Litigation." *Law & Society Review* 45(4): 991–1025.

Bourdieu, Pierre. 1987. "The Forces of Law: Towards a Sociology of Juridical Field." *Hastings Law Journal* 38(5): 805–13.

———. 1991. *Language and Symbolic Power.* Cambridge: Cambridge University Press.

Brinig, Margaret, and Douglas Allen. 2000. "'These Boots Are Made for Walking': Why Most Divorce Filers Are Women." *American Law and Economics Review* 2(1): 126–69.

Bryan, Penelope Eileen. 1994. "Reclaiming Professionalism: The Lawyer's Role in Divorce Mediation." *Family Law Quarterly* 28(2): 177–222.

Burstein, Paul. 1989. "Attacking Sex Discrimination in the Labor Market: A Study in Law and Politics." *Social Forces* 67(3): 641–65.

Cai, Yongshun. 2004. "Managed Participation in China." *Political Science Quarterly* 119(3): 425–51.

———. 2008. "Local Governments and the Suppression of Popular Resistance in China." *China Quarterly*, no. 193: 24–42.

Cai, Lidong, and Yingcheng Qi. 2019. "Judicial Governance of 'Fake Divorce' with Chinese Characteristics: Practical Rationality of the Chinese Courts in the Transitional Period." *China Review* 19(2): 99–123.

CCTV. 2017. "25% of Married Women Suffer Domestic Violence in China." http://english.cctv.com/2017/03/02/VIDEsd8TYsYQVyXgo86BjANx170302.shtml.

Chai, Ch'u, and Winberg Chai. 1962. *The Changing Society of China.* New York: New American Library.

Chan, Peter. 2019. "Do the 'Haves' Come Out Ahead in Chinese Grassroots Courts? Rural Land Disputes Between Married-Out Women and Village Collectives." *Hastings Law Journal* 71(1): 1–78.

Chen, Feng, and Xin Xu. 2012. "'Active Judiciary': Judicial Dismantling of Workers' Collective Action in China." *China Journal* 67: 87–108.

Chen, Wei, and Lei Shi. 2013. "Developments in China's Provisions for Postdivorce Relief in the 21st Century and Suggestions for Their Improvement." *Journal of Divorce & Remarriage* 54(5): 363–80.

Chen, Wei, Xin Zhang, and Lei Shi. 2018. "Empirical Research on Protecting Women's Property Rights in Divorce Proceedings in China." *International Journal of Law, Policy and the Family* 3 (1): 109–18.

Chen, Xi. 2008. "Collective Petitioning and Institutional Conversion, Popular Contention in Contemporary China." In *Popular Protest in China*, edited by Kevin O'Brien. Cambridge: Harvard University Press.

Chen, Yilin. 2020. "Trending in China: Domestic Violence Victim Left Paralyzed after Flight Attempt Makes Second Try at Divorce." *CX Tech*, July 28, 2020. https://perma.cc/S8R9-Y3GN

Chin, Jason. 2014. "Psychological Science's Replicability Crisis and What It Means for Science in the Courtroom." *Psychology, Public Policy, and Law* 20(3): 225–38.

China Daily. 2003. "Focus: Domestic Violence on the Rise." September 19. www.chinadaily.com.cn/en/doc/2003-09/19/content_265604.htm.

———. 2008. "Life Sentence Cut to 5 Years in Faulty-ATM Case." April 1. https://www.chinadaily.com.cn/china/2008-04/01/content_6580420.htm.

———. 2012. "Orders on Domestic Violence to Keep Women Safe." http://usa.chinadaily.com.cn/china/2011-11/26/content_14165852.htm.

Choi, Susanne Yuk-Ping, and Yinni Peng. 2016. *Masculine Compromise: Migration, Family and Gender in China.* Cambridge: Cambridge University Press.

Ch'u, T'ung-tsu. 1961. *Law and Society in Traditional China.* Paris: Mouton & Y Co.

Clarke, Donald. 2003. "Empirical Research into the Chinese Judicial System." In *Beyond Common Knowledge: Empirical Approaches to the Rule of Law*, edited by Erik Jensen and Thomas Heller, 164–92. Stanford: Stanford University Press.

———. 2015. "China Legal System and the Fourth Plenum." *Asia Policy* 20: 10–16.

———. 2019. "Book Review: Embedded Courts: Judicial Decision-Making in China." *China Quarterly* 237: 266–67.

Cobb, Sara. 1997. "The Domestication of Violence in Mediation." *Law & Society Review* 31(3): 397–440.

Cohen, Mark. 1991. "Explaining Judicial Behavior or What's 'Unconstitutional' about the Sentencing Commission?" *Journal of Law, Economics, & Organization* 7(1): 183–99.

Cong, Xiaoping. 2016. *Marriage, Law and Gender in Revolutionary China, 1940–1960*. Cambridge: Cambridge University Press.

Conley, John, and William O'Barr. 1990. *Rules Versus Relationships: The Ethnography of Legal Discourse*. Chicago: University of Chicago Press.

———. 2005. *Just Words: Law, Language, and Power*. 2nd ed. Chicago: University of Chicago Press.

Cooke, Lynn Price. 2006. "'Doing' Gender in Context: Household Bargaining and Risk of Divorce in Germany and the US." *American Journal of Sociology* 112(2): 442–72.

Custody of Vaughn. 1995. http://masscases.com/cases/sjc/422/422mass590.html.

Damaska, Mirjan. 1986. *The Faces of Justice and State Authority: A Comparative Approach to the Legal Process*. New Haven: Yale University Press.

Davis, Deborah. 2010. "Who Gets the House? Renegotiating Property Rights in Post-Socialist Urban China." *Modern China* 20(5): 1–30.

———. 2011. "Marriage and Divorce Trends in China." https://soundcloud.com /yaleuniversity/tmr_davis_101911-m4a.

———. 2014. "Privatization of Marriage in Post-Socialist China." *Modern China* 40(6): 551–77.

Denyer, Simon, and Annie Gowen. 2018. "Too Many Men: China and India Battle with the Consequences of Gender Imbalance." *South China Morning Post*, April 24. www.scmp.com/magazines/post-magazine/long-reads/article/2142658 /too-many-men-china-and-india-battle-consequences.

Diamant, Neil. 2000. *Revolutionizing the Family: Politics, Love, and Divorce in Urban and Rural China, 1949–1968*. Berkeley: University of California Press.

Dotan, Yoav. 1999. "Resource Inequalities in Ideological Courts: The Case of the Israeli High Court of Justice." *Law & Society Review* 33(4): 1059–80.

Downs, Anthony. 1967. *Inside Bureaucracy: A RAND Corporation Research Study*. Long Grove, IL: Waveland Press.

Duihua. 2018. "Xinjiang Production and Construction Corps: Safeguarding or Endangering Security?" *Human Rights Journal*. www.duihuahrjournal.org/2018/10 /xinjiang-production-and-construction.html.

Edin, Maria. 2003. "State Capacity and Local Agent Control in China: CCP Cadre Management from a Township Perspective." *China Quarterly*, no. 173: 35–52.

Engel, David, and Jaruwan Engel. 2010. *Tort, Custom, and Karma: Globalization and Legal Consciousness in Thailand*. Stanford: Stanford University Press.

Epstein, Deborah. 1999. "Effective Intervention in Domestic Violence Cases: Rethinking the Roles of Prosecutors, Judges, and the Court System." *Yale Journal of Law and Feminism* 11: 3–50.

Epstein, Deborah, and Lisa Goodman. 2018. "Discounting Women: Doubting Domestic Violence Survivors." *University of Pennsylvania Law Review* 167: 399–461.

Epstein, Richard. 1990. "The Independence of Judges: The Uses and Limitations of Public Choice Theory." *Brigham Young University Law Review*, no. 3: 827–56.

Evans, Peter. 1995. *Embedded Autonomy: State and Industrial Transformation*. Princeton: Princeton University Press.

Ewick, Patricia, and Susan Silbey. 1998. *The Common Place of Law: Stories from Everyday Life*. Chicago: University of Chicago Press.

Felstiner, William, Richard Abel, and Austin Sarat. 1980–1981. "The Emergence and Transformation of Disputes: Naming, Blaming, Claiming . . ." *Law & Society Review* 15(3): 631–54.

Feng, Yuqing, and Xin He. 2018. "From Law to Politics: Petitioners' Framing of Disputes in Chinese Courts." *China Journal* 80(1): 130–49.

Ferguson, Ann. 1991. *Sexual Democracy: Women, Oppression and Revolution*. Boulder: Westview Press.

Fincher, Leta Hong. 2014. *Leftover Women: The Resurgence of Gender Inequality in China*. London: Zed Books.

——. 2018. *Betraying Big Brother: The Feminist Awakening in China*. London: Zed Books.

Finder, Susan. 2016. "China's Evolving Case Law System in Practice." *Tsinghua China Law Review* 9 (2): 245–59.

Fineman, Martha. 1988. "Dominant Discourse, Professional Language, and Legal Change in Child Custody Decisionmaking." *Harvard Law Review* 101(4): 727–74.

——. 1991. *The Illusion of Equality: The Rhetoric and Reality of Divorce Reform*. Chicago: University of Chicago Press.

Fu, Hualing, and Michael Palmer, eds. 2016. *Mediation in Contemporary China: Continuity and Change*. London: Wildy, Simmonds & Hill Publishing.

Fu, Hualing, and Richard Cullen. 2011. "From Mediatory to Adjudicatory Justice: The Limits of Civil Justice Reform in China." In *Chinese Justice: Civil Dispute Resolution in Contemporary China*, edited by Margaret Y. K. Woo and Mary E. Gallagher, 25–57. New York: Cambridge University Press.

Fung, Yu-lan. 1963. "The Philosophy at the Basis of Traditional Chinese Society." In *Ideological Differences and World Order: Studies in the Philosophy and Science of the World's Cultures*, edited by Viking Fund. New Haven: Yale University Press.

Galanter, Marc. 1974. "Why the 'Haves' Come Out Ahead: Speculations on the Limits of Legal Change." *Law & Society Review* 9(1): 95–160.

Gallagher, Mary. 2006. "Mobilizing the Law in China: 'Informed Disenchantment' and the Development of Legal Consciousness." *Law & Society Review* 40(4): 783–816.

———. 2017. *Authoritarian Legality in China: Law, Workers, and the State*. Cambridge: Cambridge University Press.

Gilmartin, Christina, Gail Hershatter, Lisa Rofel, and Tyrene White, eds. 1994. *Engendering China: Women, Culture, and the State*. Cambridge: Harvard University Press.

Ginsburg, Tom, and Tamir Moustafa, eds. 2008. *Rule by Law: The Politics of Courts in Authoritarian Regimes*. New York: Cambridge University Press.

Goffman, Erving. 1981. *Forms of Talk*. Philadelphia: University of Pennsylvania Press.

Gong, Ting. 2004. "Dependent Judiciary and Unaccountable Judges: Judicial Corruption in Contemporary China." *China Review* 4(2): 33–54.

Goodman, Jane, Elizabeth Loftus, Marian Miller, and Edith Greene. 1991. "Money, Sex, and Death: Gender Bias in Wrongful Death Damage Awards." *Law & Society Review* 25(2): 263–86.

Goody, Jack, and Stanley Jeyaraja Tambiah. 1973. *Bridewealth and Dowry*. Cambridge: Cambridge University Press.

Gordon, Elizabeth Ellen. 2002. "What Roles Does Gender Play in Mediation of Domestic Relations Cases?" *Judicature* 86(3): 134–44.

Greatbatch, David, and Robert Dingwall. 1989. "Selective Facilitation: Some Preliminary Observations on a Strategy Used by Divorce Mediators." *Law & Society Review* 23(4): 613–42.

Griffiths, John. 1986. "What Do Dutch Lawyers Actually Do in Divorce Cases." *Law & Society Review* 20(1): 135–82.

Gu, Weixia. 2010. "Civil Justice Reform in Hong Kong: Challenges and Opportunities for Development of Alternative Dispute Resolution." *Hong Kong Law Journal* 40(1): 43–64.

Ha, Jin. 1999. *Waiting*. New York: Pantheon Books.

Haire, Susan, and Laura Moyer. 2019. "Gender, Law, and Judging." *Oxford Research Encyclopedias*. https://oxfordre.com/politics/abstract/10.1093/acrefore/9780190228637.001.0001/acrefore-9780190228637-e-106?rskey=BvLwyJ&result=11.

Halegua, Aaron. 2008. "Getting Paid: Processing the Labor Disputes of China's Migrant Workers." *Berkeley Journal of International Law* 26(1): 254–322.

Halliday, Terence, Lucien Karpik, and Malcolm Feeley, eds. 2007. *Fighting for Political Freedom: Comparative Studies of the Legal Complex and Political Liberalism*. Oxford, UK, and Portland, OR: Hart Publishing.

Han, Sulin. 2017. "China's New Domestic Violence Law: Keeping Victims out of the Harm's Way?" https://law.yale.edu/system/files/area/center/china/document/domesticviolence_finalrev.pdf.

Handwerker, Lisa. 1995. "The Hen That Can't Lay an Egg: Conceptions of Female Infertility in Modern China." In *Deviant Bodies: Critical Perspectives on Difference in Science and Popular Culture*, edited by Jennifer Terry and Jacqueline Urla, 358–86. Bloomington: Indiana University Press.

Hanna, Chery. 1996. "No Right to Choose: Mandated Victim Participation in Domestic Violence Prosecutions." *Harvard Law Review* 109(8): 1849–910.

Haynie, Stacia. 1994. "Resource Inequalities and Litigation Outcomes in the Philippine Supreme Court." *Journal of Politics* 56(3): 752–72.

He, Xin. 2007a. "Recent Decline in Chinese Economic Caseload: Exploration of a Surprising Puzzle." *China Quarterly*, no. 190: 352–74.

———. 2007b. "Why Did They Not Take on the Disputes? Law, Power and Politics in the Decision-Making of Chinese Courts." *International Journal of Law in Context* 3(3): 203–25.

———. 2009a. "Routinization of Divorce Law Practice in China: Institutional Constraints' Influence on Judicial Behavior." *International Journal of Law, Policy and the Family* 23(1): 83–109.

———. 2009b. "Enforcing Commercial Judgments in the Pearl River Delta of China." *American Journal of Comparative Law* 57(2): 419–56.

———. 2011. "Debt Collection in the Less Developed Regions of China: An Empirical Study from a Basic-Level Court in Shaanxi Province." *China Quarterly* 206: 253–75.

———. 2012. "Black Hole of Responsibility: The Adjudication Committee's Role in a Chinese Court." *Law & Society Review* 46(4): 681–712.

———. 2014. "Maintaining Stability by Law: Protest Supported Litigation and Social Change in China." *Law & Social Inquiry* 41(1): 212–41.

———. 2016. "Double Whammy: Lay Assessors as Lackeys in Chinese Courts." *Law & Society Review* 50(3): 733–65.

———. 2017. "'No Malicious Incidents': The Concern for Stability in China's Divorce Law Practice." *Social & Legal Studies* 26(4): 467–89.

———. 2021 (forthcoming). "Pressures on Chinese Judges under Xi." *China Journal* 85.

He, Xin, and Yuqing Feng. 2016. "Mismatched Discourses in the Petition Office of Chinese Courts." *Law & Social Inquiry* 41(1): 212–41.

He, Xin, and Fen Lin. 2017. "The Losing Media? An Empirical Study of Defamation Litigation in China." *China Quarterly* 230: 371–98.

He, Xin, and Kwai Hang Ng. 2013a. "In the Name of Harmony: The Erasure of Domestic Violence in China's Judicial Mediation." *International Journal of Law, Policy and the Family* 26(1): 97–115.

———. 2013b. "Inquisitorial Adjudication and Institutional Constraints in China's Civil Justice." *Law & Policy* 35(4): 290–317.

———. 2013c. "Pragmatic Discourse and Gender Inequality in China." *Law & Society Review* 47(2): 279–310.

———. 2017. "'It Has to Be Rock Hard!' Guanxi and Judicial Decision Making in China." *American Journal of Comparative Law* 65(4): 341–71.

He, Xin, and Yang Su. 2013. "Do the 'Haves' Come Out Ahead in Shanghai Courts?" *Journal of Empirical Legal Studies* 10 (1): 120–45.

He, Xin, Luoyun Li, and Yuqing Feng. 2017. "The Mediatory versus Legalistic Discourse in Chinese Courts." *PoLAR: Political and Legal Anthropology Review* 40(2): 326–41.

Hirsch, Susan. 1998. *Pronouncing and Persevering*. Chicago: University of Chicago Press.

Ho, Petula Sik Ying, Stevi Jackson, Siyang Cao, and Chi Kwok. 2018. "Sex with Chinese Characteristics: Sexuality Research in/on 21st-Century China." *Journal of Sex Research* 55(4–5): 486–521.

Honig, Emily, and Gail Hershatter. 1988. *Personal Voices: Chinese Women in the 1980s.* Stanford: Stanford University Press.

Howson, Nicholas Calcina. 2010. "Corporate Law in the Shanghai People's Courts, 1992–2008: Judicial Autonomy in a Contemporary Authoritarian State." *East Asia Law Review* 5(2): 303–442.

Htun, Mala, and Laurel Weldon. 2018. *The Logics of Gender Justice: State Action on Women's Rights Around the World.* Cambridge: Cambridge University Press.

Huang, Hui. 2012. "Piercing the Corporate Veil in China: Where Is It Now and Where Is It Heading." *American Journal of Comparative Law* 60(3): 743–74.

Huang, Philip. 2005. "Divorce Law Practices and the Origins, Myths, and Realities of Judicial 'Mediation' in China." *Modern China* 31(2): 151–203.

———. 2010. *Chinese Civil Justice, Past and Present.* Lanham, MD: Rowman & Littlefield Publishers.

Jiang, Jue. 2019. "The Family as a Stronghold of State Stability: Two Contradictions in China's Anti-Domestic Violence Efforts." *International Journal of Law, Policy and Family* 33(2): 228–51.

Johnson, Kay Ann. 1983. *Women, the Family, and the Peasant Revolution in China.* Chicago: University of Chicago Press.

King, Gary, Jennifer Pan, and Margaret Roberts. 2013. "How Censorship in China Allows Government Criticism but Silences Collective Expression." *American Political Science Review* 107(2): 326–43.

Kinkel, Jonathan. 2015. "High-End Demand: The Legal Profession as a Source of Judicial Selection Reform in Urban China." *Law & Social Inquiry* 40(4): 969–1000.

Kinkel, Jonathan, and William Hurst. 2015. "The Judicial Cadre Evaluation System in China: From Quantification to Intra-State Legibility." *China Quarterly* 224: 933–54.

Kornhauser, Lewis, and Robert Mnookin. 1979. "Bargaining in the Shadow of the Law: The Case of Divorce." *Yale Law Journal* 88(5): 950–97.

Kulik, Carol, Allan Lind, Maurice Ambrose, and Robert MacCoun. 1996. "Understanding Gender Differences in Distributive and Procedural Justice." *Social Justice Research* 9(4): 351–69.

LaFree, Gary, and Christin Rack. 1996. "The Effects of Participants' Ethnicity and Gender on Monetary Outcomes in Mediated and Adjudicated Civil Cases." *Law & Society Review* 30(4): 767–98.

Lam, Raphael, Xiaoguang Liu, and Alfred Schipke. 2015. "China's Labor Market in the 'New Normal.'" IMF Working Paper No. 15/151.

Landes, William, and Richard Posner. 1975. "The Independent Judiciary in an Interest-Group Perspective." *Journal of Law and Economics* 18(3): 875–901.

Lazarus-Black, Mindie. 2001. "Law and the Pragmatics of Inclusion: Governing Domestic Violence in Trinidad and Tobago." *American Ethnologist* 28(2): 388–416.

Lee, Sing, and Arthur Kleinman. 2003. "Suicide as Resistance in China's Society." In *Chinese Society: Change, Conflict and Resistance*, edited by Elizabeth Perry and Mark Selden, 289–311. New York: Routledge.

Lerman, Lisa. 1984. "Mediation of Wife-Abuse Cases: The Adverse Impact of Informal Dispute Resolution on Women." *Harvard Women's Law Journal* 7: 57–114.

Li, Ke. 2015. "'What He Did Was Lawful': Divorce Litigation and Gender Inequality in China." *Law & Policy* 37(3): 153–79.

———. 2016. "Relational Embeddedness and Socially Motivated Case Screening in the Practice of Law in Rural China." *Law & Society Review* 50(4): 920–52.

———. 2021 (forthcoming). *Marriage Unbound: Divorce Litigation, Power and Inequality in Contemporary China*. Stanford: Stanford University Press.

Li, Ke, and Sara Friedman. 2016. "Wedding Marriage to the Nation-State in Modern China: Legal Consequences for Divorce, Property, and Women's Rights." In *Domestic Tensions, National Anxieties: Global Perspectives on Marriage, Crisis, and Nation*, edited by Kristin Celello and Hanan Kholoussy, 147–69. Oxford: Oxford University Press.

Li, Lianjiang, Mingxing Liu, and Kevin O'Brien. 2012. "Petitioning Beijing: The High Tide of 2003–2006." *China Quarterly*, no. 210: 313–34.

Li, Xiangyun. 2009. *Power and Solidarity in Divorce Litigation Discourse: A Gender Perspective*. Jinan: Shandong University Press.

Li, Yedan, Joris Kochen, and Benjamin Van Rooij. 2018. "Understanding China's Court Mediation Surge: Insights from a Local Court." *Law and Social Inquiry* 43(1): 58–81.

Liebman, Benjamin. 2005. "Watchdog or Demagogue? The Media in Chinese Legal System." *Columbia Law Review* 105(1): 1–157.

———. 2011. "A Populist Threat to China's Courts?" In *Chinese Justice: Civil Dispute Resolution in Contemporary China*, edited by Margaret Woo and Marc Gallagher, 269–313. New York: Cambridge University Press.

———. 2013. "Malpractice Mobs: Medical Dispute Resolution in China." *Columbia Law Review* 113(1): 181–264.

Liebman, Benjamin, and Tim Wu. 2007. "China's Network Justice." *Chinese Journal of International Law* 8(1): 257–322.

Lim, Louisa. 2010. "'Lightning Divorces' Strike China's 'Me Generation.'" NPR. www.npr.org/2010/11/09/131200166/china-s-me-generation-sends-divorce-rate-soaring.

Lin, Feng. 2016. "The Future of Judicial Independence in China." Centre for Judicial Education and Research, City University of Hong Kong, Working Paper Series No.2.

Liu, Xuanxi. 2019. "Irrationality and Bureaucratic-Professional Conflicts in the Chinese Bureaucratized Court System." (On file with author.)

Maccoby, Eleanor, and Robert Mnookin. 1992. *Dividing the Child: Social and Legal Dilemmas of Custody*. Harvard: Harvard University Press.

MacKinnon, Catherine. 1989. *Toward a Feminist Theory of the State*. Cambridge: Harvard University Press.

Martin, Patricia, John Reynolds, and Shelley Keith. 2002. "Gender Bias and Feminist Consciousness among Judges and Attorneys: A Standpoint Theory Analysis." *Signs: Journal of Women in Culture and Society* 27(3): 665–701.

Massell, Gregory. 1974. *The Surrogate Proletariat: Moslem Women and Revolutionary Strategies in Soviet Central Asian, 1919–1929*. Princeton: Princeton University Press.

McAdam, Doug. 1983. "Tactical Innovation and the Pace of Insurgency." *American Sociological Review* 48(6): 735–54.

McMillan, Joanna. 2006. *Sex, Science and Morality in China*. London; New York: Routledge.

Meier, Joan, and Sean Dickson. 2017. "Mapping Gender: Shedding Empirical Light on Family Courts' Treatment of Cases Involving Abuse and Alienation." *Law and Inequality: A Journal of Theory and Practice* 35(2): 311–28.

Merry, Sally. 1990. *Getting Justice and Getting Even: Legal Consciousness among Working-Class Americans*. Chicago: University of Chicago Press.

———. 2006. *Human Rights and Gender Violence: Translating International Law into Local Justice*. Chicago: University of Chicago Press.

Merry, Sally, and Rachel Stern. 2005. "The Female Inheritance Movement in Hong Kong: Theorizing the Local/Global Interface." *Current Anthropology* 46(3): 387–409.

Michelson, Ethan. 2006. "The Practice of Law as an Obstacle to Justice: Chinese Lawyers at Work." *Law & Society Review* 40 (1): 18–21.

———. 2018. "Decoupling: Marital Violence and the Struggle to Divorce in China." Indiana Legal Studies Research Paper No. 399. https://ssrn.com/abstract=3245030.

———. 2019. "Decoupling: Marital Violence and the Struggle to Divorce in China." *American Journal of Sociology* 125(2): 325–81.

Minzner, Carl. 2006. "Xinfang: An Alternative to Formal Chinese Legal Institutions." *Stanford Journal of International Law* 42(1): 103–80.

———. 2009. "Riots and Cover-Ups: Counterproductive Control of Local Agents in China." *University of Pennsylvania Journal of International Law* 31(1): 53–123.

———. 2011. "China's Turn Against Law." *American Journal of Comparative Law* 59(4): 935–84.

Mir-Hosseini, Ziba. 2001. *Marriage on Trial*. London: Tauris.

Mnookin, Robert, and Eleanor Maccoby. 2002. Facing the Dilemmas of Child Custody. *Virginia Journal of Social Policy & the Law* 10(1): 54–88.

Moustafa, Tamir. 2014. "Law and Courts in Authoritarian Regimes." *Annual Review of Law and Social Science* 10(1): 281–99.

Nagel, Stuart, and Lenore Weitzman. 1971. "Women as Litigants." *Hastings Law Journal* 23(1): 171–98.

———. 1972. "Double Standard of American Justice." *Society* 9(5): 18–25.

Ng, Kwai Hang, and Xin He. 2014. "Internal Contradictions in China's Judicial Mediation." *Law & Social Inquiry* 39(2): 282–312.

———. 2017a. *Embedded Courts: Judicial Decision Making in China*. New York: Cambridge University Press.

———. 2017b. "The Institutional and Cultural Logics of Legal Commensuration: Criminal Reconciliation and Negotiated Justice in China." *American Journal of Sociology* 122(4): 1104–43.

Nielsen, Laura Beth. 2000. "Situating Legal Consciousness: Experiences and Attitudes of Ordinary Citizens about Law and Street Harassment." *Law & Society Review* 34(4): 1055–90.

O'Barr, William, and Bowman Atkins. 1998. "'Women's Language' or 'Powerless Language'?" In *Language and Gender: A. Reader*, edited by Jennifer Coates, 377–87. Oxford: Blackwell.

O'Brien, Kevin, and Lianjiang Li. 2006. *Rightful Resistance in Rural China*. New York: Cambridge University Press.

Ogletree, Charles, and Rangita de Silva-de Alwis. 2004. "The Recently Revised Marriage Law of China: The Promise and the Reality." *Texas Journal of Women, Gender, and the Law* 13(2): 251–312.

Palmer, Michael. 1986. "The People's Republic of China: Some General Observations on Family Law." *Journal of Family Law* 25(1): 41–68.

———. 1989. "The Revival of Mediation in the People's Republic of China: (2) Judicial Mediation." In *Yearbook on Socialist Legal System*, 145–71. Boston: Brill Academic Publishers.

———. 2005. "Patriarchy, Privacy and Protection: Chinese Law Slowly Gets to Grips with Domestic Violence." In *Forging a Common Legal Destiny: Liber Amicorum in Honor of William E. Butler*, edited by Natalia Erpyleva, Maryann Gashi-Butler, and A L Kolodkin, 786–812. London: Wildy, Simmonds, & Hill Publishers.

———. 2007. "Transforming Family Law in Post-Deng China: Marriage, Divorce and Reproduction." *China Quarterly*, no. 191: 675–95.

———. 2017. "Domestic Violence and Mediation in Contemporary China." In *Mediation in Contemporary China: Continuity and Change*, edited by Hualing Fu and Michael Palmer, 286–318. London: Wildy, Simmonds & Hill Publishing.

Parish, William, and Martin King Whyte. 1978. *Village and Family in Contemporary China*. Chicago: University of Chicago Press.

Peerenboom, Randall. 2006. "Judicial Independence and Judicial Accountability: An Empirical Study of Individual Case Supervision." *China Journal* 55: 67–94.

Peerenboom, Randall, and Xin He. 2009. "Dispute Resolution in China: Patterns, Causes and Prognosis." *East Asia Law Review* 4(1): 1–61.

Posner, Richard. 1990. "What has pragmatism to offer law?" *Southern California Law Review* 63: 1653–69.

———. 1993. "What Do Judges and Justices Maximize?" *Supreme Court Economic Review* 3(1): 1–42.

Resnik, Judith. 1996. "Asking about Gender in Courts." *Signs: Journal of Women in Culture and Society* 21(4): 952–90.

Ricci, Isolina. 1985. "Mediator's Notebook: Reflections on Promoting Equal Empowerment and Entitlement for Women." *Journal of Divorce* 8(3–4): 49–61.

Rifkin, Janet. 1984. "Mediation from a Feminist Perspective: Promise and Problems." *Law and Inequality* 2(1): 21–32.

Runge, Robin. 2015. "Operating in a Narrow Space to Effect Change: Development of a Legal System Response to Domestic Violence in China." In *Comparative Perspectives on Gender Violence: Lessons from Efforts Worldwide,* edited by Rashmi Goel and Leigh Goodmark, 31–42. Oxford and New York: Oxford University Press.

Safronova, Valeriya. 2019. "What Is So 'Indecent' about Female Pleasure." *New York Times,* January 18, 2019. www.nytimes.com/2019/01/18/style/sex-toy-ces.html.

Sapio, Flora. 2008. "Shuanggui and Extralegal Detention in China." *China Information* 22(1): 7–37.

Sarat, Austin. 1990. "The Law Is All Over: Power, Resistance and the Legal Consciousness of the Welfare Poor." *Yale Journal of Law & Human,* no. 2: 343–80.

Sarat, Austin, and Stuart Scheingold. 2006. *Cause Lawyers and Social Movements.* Stanford: Stanford University Press.

Sarat, Austin, and Thomas Kearns. 1991. "A Journey Through Forgetting: Toward a Jurisprudence of Violence." In *The Fate of Law,* edited by Austin Sarat and Thomas R. Kearns, 268–69. Ann Arbor: University of Michigan Press.

Sarat, Austin, and William Felstiner. 1997. *Divorce Lawyers and Their Clients: Power and Meaning in the Legal Process.* Oxford: Oxford University Press.

Schepard, Andrew. 2004. *Children, Courts, and Custody: Interdisciplinary Models for Divorcing Families.* Cambridge: Cambridge University Press.

Shapiro, Martin. 1981. *Courts: A Comparative and Political Analysis.* Chicago: University of Chicago Press.

Shu, Xiaoling, and Yanjie Bian. 2003. "Market Transition and Gender Gap in Earnings in Urban China." *Social Forces* 81(4): 1107–45.

Sigley, Gary. 2006. "Sex, Politics, and the Policing of Virtue in the People's Republic of China." In *Sex and Sexuality in China,* edited by Elaine Jeffreys, 43–61. New York: Routledge.

Silbey, Susan, and Austin Sarat. 1989. "Dispute Processing in Law and Legal Scholarship: From Institutional Critique to the Reconstruction of the Judicial Subject." *Denver University Law Review* 66(3): 437–98.

Sisk, Gregory, Michael Heise, and Andrew Morriss. 1998. "Charting the Influences on the Judicial Mind: An Empirical Study of Judicial Reasoning." *New York University Law Review* 73(5): 1377–500.

Smith, Arthur. 1899. *Village Life in China.* New York: Fleming H. Revell Co.

Solinger, Dorothy. 1999. *Contesting Citizenship in Urban China.* Berkeley: University of California Press.

Solomon, Peter. 2007. "Courts and Judges in Authoritarian Regimes." *World Politics* 60(1): 122–45.

Spence, Jonathan. 1979. *The Death of Woman Wong.* Harmondsworth, UK: Penguin.

Stacey, Judith. 1983. *Patriarchy and Socialist Revolution in China.* Berkeley: University of California Press.

Stern, Rachel E. 2013. *Environmental Litigation in China: A Study in Political Ambivalence*. Cambridge: Cambridge University Press.

Su, Yang, and Xin He. 2010. "Street as Courtroom: State Accommodation of Labor Protests in South China." *Law & Society Review* 44(1): 157–84.

Tatlow, Didi Kirsten. 2013. "China's Most-Watched Divorce Case, 3 Victories, 1 Defeat." *New York Times*, February 5. https://cn.nytimes.com/china/20130205/c05tatlow/en-us.

Trevaskes, Susan. 2007. *Courts and Criminal Justice in Contemporary China*. Lanham, MD: Rowman & Littlefield Publishers.

Trevaskes, Susan, Elisa Nesossi, Flora Sapio, and Sarah Biddulph. 2014. *The Politics of Law and Stability in China*. London: Edward Elgar.

Trinder, Liz, Alan Firth, and Christopher Jenks. 2010. "'So Presumably Things Have Moved on Since Then?' The Management of Risk Allegations in Child Contact Dispute Resolution." *International Journal of Law, Policy and the Family* 24(1): 29–53.

Truex, Rory. 2016. *Making Autocracy Work: Representation and Responsiveness in Modern China*. Cambridge: Cambridge University Press.

Tsui, Ming. 2001. "Divorce, Women's Status, and the Communist State in China." *Asian Thought and Society* 26: 103–25.

Tyler, Tom. 1984. "The Role of Perceived Injustice in Defendants' Evaluations of Their Courtroom Experience." *Law & Society Review* 18: 51–74.

Van Rooij, Benjamin. 2010. "Implementation of Chinese Environmental Law: Regular Enforcement and Political Campaigns." *Journal of Contemporary China* 19(63): 55–77.

Van Rooij, Benjamin, Rachel Stern, and Kathinka Fürst. 2016. "The Authoritarian Logic of Regulatory Pluralism: Understanding China's New Environmental Actors." *Regulation & Governance* 10(1): 3–13.

Wang, Alex. 2013. "The Search for Sustainable Legitimacy." *Harvard Environmental Law Review* 37: 365–440.

Wang, Jian. 2013. "To Divorce or Not to Divorce: A Critical Discourse Analysis of Court-Ordered Divorce Mediation in China." *International Journal of Law, Policy and the Family* 27(1): 74–96.

Wang, Qingbin. 2001. "China's Divorce Trends in the Transition Toward a Market Economy." *Journal of Divorce & Remarriage* 35(1): 173–89.

Wang, Qingbin, and Qin Zhou. 2010. "China's Divorce and Remarriage Rates: Trends and Regional Disparities." *Journal of Divorce & Remarriage* 51(4): 257–67.

Wang, Tao. 2016. "China's Pilot Judicial Structure Reform in Shanghai 2014–2015: Its Context, Implementation and Implications." *Willamette Journal of International Law and Dispute Resolution* 24(1): 53–84.

Wang, Yu, and Kwai Hang Ng. 2020 (forthcoming). "By the Law?—How Chinese Judges Rule on Contested Divorces." *Journal of Comparative Law* 15(2).

Wang, Yuhua. 2014. *Tying the Autocrat's Hands: The Rise of the Rule of Law in China*. Cambridge and New York: Cambridge University Press.

Wang, Yuhua, and Carl Minzner. 2015. "The Rise of the Chinese Security State." *China Quarterly*, no. 222: 339–59.

Wang, Zhiqiong, and Jianfu Chen. 2019. "Will the Establishment of Circuit Tribunals Break Up the Circular Reforms in the Chinese Judiciary?" *Asian Journal of Comparative Law 14(1)*: 1–22. https://doi.org/10.1017/asjcl.2018.13.

Weber, Max. 1954. *Max Weber on Law in Economy and Society*. Cambridge: Harvard University Press.

Wheeler, Stanton, Bliss Cartwright, Robert Kagan, and Lawrence Friedman. 1987. "Do the 'Haves' Come Out Ahead? Winning and Losing in State Supreme Court." *Law & Society Review* 21(3): 403–46.

Wolf, Margery. 1985. *Revolution Postponed: Women in Contemporary China*. Stanford: Stanford University Press.

Woo, Margaret. 2003. "Shaping Citizenship: Chinese Family Law and Women." *Yale Journal of Law & Feminism* 15(1): 99–134.

———. 2017. "Court Reform with Chinese Characteristics." *Washington International Law Journal* 27(1): 241–72.

Woo, Margaret, and Yaxin Wang. 2005. "Civil Justice in China: An Empirical Study of Courts in Three Provinces." *American Journal of Comparative Law* 53(4): 911–40.

Xi, Chao. 2010. "Who Writes Corporate Law Rules? The Making of the 'Piercing the Corporate Veil Rule' as a Case Study." In *The Development of the Chinese Legal System: Change and Challenges*, edited by Guanghua Yu, 159–81. London: Routledge.

Xinhua News. 2009. "Domestic Violence Increases in China." www.chinadaily.com.cn/china/2009-03/07/content_7551147.htm.

Xiong, Hao. 2015. "'Is Court Mediation Feasible?' Quantitative Research on the Attitudes of Legal Professionals in Southwest Grassroots Society of China." *Hong Kong Law Journal* 45(3): 963–86.

Yuan, Lijun. 2005. *Reconceiving Women's Equality in China: A Critical Examination of Models of Sex Equality*. Oxford: Lexington Books.

Zelizer, Viviana. 1994. *Pricing the Priceless Child: The Changing Social Value of Children*. Princeton: Princeton University Press.

Zhang, Everett Yuehong. 2015. *The Impotence Epidemic*. Durham: Duke University Press.

Zhang, Pinghui. 2017. "Why Millions of Chinese People Are Filing for Divorce Every Year." *South China Morning Post*, October 20. www.scmp.com/news/china/society/article/2117424/why-millions-chinese-people-are-filing-divorce-every-year.

Zhang, Taisu, and Tom Ginsburg. 2019. "Legality in Contemporary Chinese Politics." *Virginia Journal of International Law* 59(2): 307–90.

Zhao, Yuhong. 2000. "Domestic Violence in China: In Search of Legal and Social Responses." *UCLA Pacific* 18(2): 211–51.

Zheng, Chunyan, Jiahui Ai, and Sida Liu. 2017. "The Elastic Ceiling: Gender and Professional Career in Chinese Courts." *Law & Society Review* 51(1): 168–99.

Zheng, Ming. 2006. "An Investigation into the Divorce Cases in the Municipal Court of Wugang, Hunan Province." http://belawyer.fyfz.cn/blog/belawyer/index.aspx?blogid=113259.

Zhong, Jianhua, and Guanghua Yu. 2004. "Establishing the Truth on Facts: Has the Chinese Civil Process Achieved This Goal?" *Journal of Transnational Law and Policy* 13(2): 393–446.

Zhou, Viola. 2018. "Chinese Women Are Seeking Divorce—and the Courts Are Stopping Them." Inkstone. www.inkstonenews.com/society/chinese-women-are-seeking -divorce-and-courts-are-stopping-them/article/2139421.

CHINESE-LANGUAGE LITERATURE

All-China Women's Federation. 2010. *Jiating baoli burong hushi* (Domestic Violence Cannot Be Ignored). www.women.org.cn/art/2010/7/13/art_9_134736 .html.

Chen, Min, and Han Xiao. 2017. *Fayuan 'liuren' 'zhaoren'mianlin xinnanti* (The New Difficulty of 'Retaining Judges' and 'Recruiting Judges' in Courts). *Fazhi shibao* (Legal Times), March 31. http://fzsb.hinews.cn/html/2017-03/31/content _1_6.htm.

Chen, Ruihua. 2016. *Fayuan gaige zhong de jiuda zhengyi wenti* (Nine controversial issues in court reform). *Zhongguo falü pinglun* (China Law Review) 3: 211–20.

Chen, Wei, and Qiyu Rang. 2009. *Goujian hexie de hunyin jiating guanxi—zhongguo hunyin jiating fa liushi nian* (The Construction of Harmonious Marriage and Family Relationship—60 Years of Chinese Marriage and Family Law). *Hebei faxue* (Hebei Law Science) 27(8): 43–49.

Chen, Wei, and Qinglin Zhang. 2015. *Lihun susong zhong ertong fuyang wenti zhi sifa shijian jiqi gaijin jianyi—yi mouxian fayuan 2011–2013 nian shenjie lihun anjian wei diaocha duixiang* (The Juridical Practice of Child-Rearing Questions in Divorce Proceedings and Its Improvement Proposals—B). *Hebei faxue* (Hebei Law Science) 33(1): 13–33.

Chen, Wei, and Weiwei Duan. 2012. *Fayuan zai fangzhi jiating baoli zhong de zuoyong shizheng yanjiu* (Can Courts Prevent Domestic Violence?). *Hebei faxue* (Hebei Law Science) 8: 28–38.

Chen, Xuefei. 2007. *Lihun anjian shenli zhong faguan huayu de xingbie pianxiang* (Gender Preference in Judges' Discourse during the Trial of Divorce Cases). *Beida falü pinglun* (Peking University Law Review) 8(2): 384–411.

Chinese Women's News. 2009. *Lifa wei liangxing pingdeng huhang* (Legislating for Gender Equality). www.china-woman.com/rp/fs/cp/140/222/%0A20090916 /4%5C0.html.

Equality. 2017. Zhonghua *renmin gongheguo fandui jiating baolifa shishi jiance baogao* (The Evaluation Report on the Implementation of Anti-Domestic Violence Law of the People's Republic of China). www.equality-beijing.org/newinfo .aspx?id=69.

Fu, Yulin. 2005. Minshi *shenpan jiandu zhidu de shizhengxing fengxi* (A Positive Analysis of the Civil Adjudication Supervision). In *Falü chengxu yunzuo de shizheng fenxi* (A Positivist Analysis to Practices of Legal Procedures), edited by Yaxin Wang, Yulin Fu, Yu Fan, Xin Xu, Mang Zhu, Yingzi Wu, Ying Wang, and Yi Deng, 199–262. Beijing: Law Press China.

Gao, Qicai, and Weiping Zhou. 2006. *Falü tiaojie de shu yu guan* (The Approach and Attitudes of Judicial Mediation). *Falü yu shehui fazhan* (Law and Social Development), no. 1: 59–73.

Gao, Xin. 2016. *Jiabao rending jin yicheng, juzheng buli shi guanjian* (Only 10 Percent of Domestic Violence Was Recognized, Due to Poor Proof). *Jiancha ribao* (The Procuratorate Daily), January 10.

Guangdong High Court. 2018. *Guangdong fayuan shenli lihun an'jian chengxu zhiyin* (The Guidelines of Divorce Cases Adjudication Procedures in Guangdong Courts).

Han, Bao. 2014. *Jicheng fayuan caipan guocheng de fashehuixue fengxi* (A Study in Judicial Process of Basic People's Court from a Socio-Legal Perspective). *Nanjing daxue falu pinglun* (Nanjing University Law Review) (Spring): 99–133.

He, Weifang. 1997. *Zhongguo sifa xingzhenghua de liangge wenti* (Two Problems of Chinese Judicial Administration). *Zhongguo shehui kexue* (China's Social Science), no. 6: 117–30.

He, Xin, and Su, Yang. 2014. *Sifa gongzhen shi yifa zhiguo de jishi* (Judicial Justice Is the Cornerstone of Rule of Law). *Renmin luntan* (People's Forum). 2014.

Hu, Changming. 2015. *Zhongguo faguan zhiye manyidu kaocha: yi 2660 fen wenjuan wei yangben de fenxi* (A Survey of Chinese Judges' Work Satisfaction: An Analysis of a Sample of 2,660 Questionnaires). *Zhongguo falü pinglun* (China Law Review) (4): 194–206.

Jiang, Shigong. 2011. *Sifa nengdong xia de zhongguo jiating—cong zuigao fayuan guanyu hunyinfa de sifa jieshi tanqi* (Chinese Families in the Context of Judicial Activism—Starting with the Judicial Interpretations of Marriage Law by the Supreme Court. *Wenhua zongheng* (Beijing Cultural Review) 1: 24–30.

Kan, Kai, and Jianping Liu. 2017. *Lun fanjiabao fa renshen baohuling de kunjing yu chulu* (On the Dilemma and Solutions of the Personal Protection Order in the Anti-Domestic Violence Law). *Zhi yu xing* (Cognition and Practice), no. 5: 34–40.

Lanzhou Morning News. 2005. *Nügong bukan jiating baoli qisu lihun, sici bei bohui hou zisha* (Female Worker Initiated Divorce Petition Due to Unbearable Domestic Violence, and Suicide after Fourth Time of Divorce Denial). http://news.163.com/05/0803/04/1Q71973A0001122B.html.

Lawsdata. 2018. *Bashou an'li* (Lawsdata). www.lawsdata.com.

Li, Hongxiang, Xiyuan Wang, and Kaibo Zheng. 2016. *Lihun jiating ertong quanyi falü baozhang sifa diaocha fenxi—yi jilinsheng jingji fazhan chengdu butong diqu lihun anjian weili* (Analysis on the Protection of the Rights of Children in Divorced Families). *Zhonghua nüzi xueyuan xuebao* (Journal of China Women's University), no. 3: 14–22.

Li, Xiaoting. 2011. *Shifang bei yayi de shengyin* (Releasing the Repressed Voices). Unpublished manuscript, on file with author.

Li, Xiuhua. 2013. *Renshen baohuling zhunru fandui jiating baoli lifa weidu de kunjing yu duice* (Difficulties and Countermeasures of Including Writ of Habeas Corpus into Legislative Dimension). *Zhonghua nüzi xueyuan xuebao* (Journal of China Women's University), no. 5–10.

Li, Yinhe. 1998. *Xiugai hunyinfa shi yao jinggao daotui* (Be Vigilant Against Regression in the Revision of the Marriage Law). *Funü yanjiu luncong* (Collection of Women's Studies) 2: 4–5.

Li, Yinhe, and Yinan Ma. 1999. *Hunyinfa xiugai lunzheng* (The Debate on Revising the Marriage Law). Beijing: Guangming Daily Press.

Liu, Min. 2012. *Erci lihun susong shenpan guize de shizheng yanjiu* (The Empirical Study on the Rule of Two-Time Divorce Litigations). *Fashang yanjiu* (Study in Law and Business), no. 6: 80–84.

Liu, Sida. 2008. *Shiluo de chengbang: dangdai zhongguo falü zhiye bianqian* (The Lost Polis: Transformation of the Legal Profession in Contemporary China). Beijing: Peking University Press.

Liu, Zhong. 2012. *Tiaotiao yu kuaikuai guanxi xia de fayuan yuanzhang chansheng* (The Appointment of Court Presidents under Tiao-Kuai Relations). *Huanqiu falü pinglun* (Global Law Review), no. 1: 107–25.

———. 2014. *Ge, Zhi, Ji Yu Jingzheng Shanggang: Fayuan Neibu zhixu de shenceng jiegou* (Hierarchy, Position, Rank and Competitive Promotion: The Deep Structure of Courts' Internal Order). *Qinghua faxue* (Tsinghua University Law Journal) 8(2): 146–63.

Lu, Hanyang. 2016. *Shilun renshen baohuling zhidu zai woguo sifa shijian zhong de shitong—yi shiji anli wei shijiao* (A Discussion on the Application of Personal Safety Orders in Judicial Practice—A Perspective from the Adjudicating Cases). *Fazhi yu shehui* (Legal System and Society), no. 36: 44–45.

Luo, Jieqi. 2019. *Zhengwu gushi: jiabao, shiqiu he yibo favu de dansheng* (High-noon Stories: Domestic Violence, Death Prisoner, and the Birth of a Legislation). https://baijiahao.baidu.com/s?id=1633032241856099098&wfr=spider&for=pc.

Luo, Ling.2016. *Caipan lihun liyou yingxiang yinsu shizheng yanjiu: Yi 2010–2011 nian henan sheng de bufen lihun jiufen an'jian panjue wenshu wei yangben* (Empirical Examination at the Factors Affecting Divorce Cases Based on Some 2010–2011 Divorce Litigations in Henan Province). *Zhonghua nüzi xueyuan xuebao* (Journal of China Women's University) 1: 14–23.

Ma, Yinan. 2002. *Hunyin jiating fa xinlun* (New Discussions on Marriage and Family Law). Beijing: Beijing University Press.

Ministry of Civil Affairs. 2017. *2016 nian shehui fuwu fazhan tongji gongbao* (Statistical Report of the People's Republic of China on the Development of Social Services). www.mca.gov.cn/article/sj/tjgb/201708/20170815005382.shtml.

Pan, Suiming. 1999. *Dui xiugai hunyinfa de wuge yiwen* (Five Doubts on Revising the Family Law)." In *Hunyinfa xiugai lunzheng* (The Debate on Revising the Marriage Law), edited by Yinhe Li and Yinan Ma, 103–05. Beijing: Guangming Daily Press.

Panyu Annals. 2006. *Panyu nianjian* (Panyu Annals). Edited by Panyu Annals Editorial Office. Beijing: Fangzhi Press.

Peng, Shizhong. 2011. *Nengdong sifa shiyexia minshi tiaojie gaige de jingxiang xuanze* (Paths of the Civil Mediation Reform from Judicial Activism Perspective). *Jinan Xuebao* (Journal of Jinan University) 1: 52–58.

Panyu Court. 2004. *Panyuqu fayue guanyu gangwei zerenzhi de guiding* (The Stipulation with Regard to Post Responsibility of Panyu District Court, Guangzhou Municipality (Trial)). In *Guangzhoushi Panyuqu fayue guizhang zhidu xuanbian* (*The Compilation of Regulations and Institutions of P. District Court, Guangzhou Municipality)*, 181–88.

People's Court Daily. 2014. *Renmin fayuan "qiguangqixia" daji jiating baoli* (The People's Courts Adopted "Seven-Pronged" Approach to Combat Domestic Violence). February 28. http://rmfyb.chinacourt.org/paper/html/2014-02/28/content_77384 .htm?div1/4-1.

Pu, Xiaohong, Xiaoting Li, and Xi Lin. 2015. *"Sifa nanquanhua" xianxiang tanxi yu jiejue zhilu—yi jiceng fayuan lihun an tingshen wei shijiao* (The Examination on the Phenomenon of "Judicial Patriarchalization" and Its Solution—A Perspective from the Divorce Litigation in Grassroots Courts). *Fazhi luntan* (Legal Forum) 4: 3–18.

Sichuang Annals. 2006. *Sichuang nianjian* (Sichuang Annals). Chengdu: Sichuang Annals Press.

Sina News. 2018. *Panjueshu li 'die bi er'zi da liangsui'* ("Father Is Two Years Older Than Son" in the Judicial Judgement). http://news.sina.com.cn/sf/news/fzrd/2018 -04-09/doc-ifyvtmxe4232696.shtml.

Su, Li. 1999. *Lengyan kan hunyin* (A Calm View on Marriage). In *Hunyinfa xiugai lunzheng* (The Debate on Revising the Marriage Law), edited by Yinhe Li and Yinan Ma, 34–58. Beijing: Guangming Daily Press.

———. 2000. *Songfa xiaxiang* (Bring the Law to the Countryside). Beijing: China's University of Political Science and Law Press.

Supreme People's Court Information Center. 2018. *Sifa dashuju zhuanti baogao: lihun jiufen* (Reports Based on Judicial Big Data: Divorce Disputes). www.court.gov.cn /upload/file/2018/03/23/09/33/20180323093343_53196.pdf.

Tan, Xiaoqing. 2018. *Xinfang ruhe yihua fayuan de shangsu gongneng?* (A Study of Xinfang and Its Alienation of the Appeal System). City University of Hong Kong.

Tang, Weijian. 2016. *Minshi tingshen chengxu youzhi hua gaige de lilun yu shijian* (Optimized Reform of Civil Court Trial Procedures: Theories and Practice). *Guizhou Minzu Daxue Xuebao* (Journal of Guizhou Minzu University) 3: 130–60.

The Paper. 2016. *Haishuo jiachou buke waiyang? quanguo fulian tongji mei 7.4 miao jiuyou yi nüxing bei jiabao* (Do Not Give Publicity to Family Scandals? All-China Women Federation Found One Woman Is Subject to Domestic Violence Every 7.4 Seconds). www.thepaper.cn/newsDetail_forward_1568118.

———. 2019. *Duoyuan huajie jiating hunyin maodun jiufen—dingxi liangji fayuan jiji tuijin jiashi shenpan gaige* (Alternative Resolution on Family and Marriage

Disputes—The Two Levels of Court in Dingxi City Promote Family Judicial Reform). www.thepaper.cn/newsDetail_forward_3253954.

Wang, Lungang, and Sida Liu. 2016. *Cong shiti zhuize dao chengxu zhi zhi: zhongguo fayuan cuo'an zhuijiu zhi yunxing de shizheng kaocha* (From Substantive Responsibility to the Rule of Procedure: An Empirical Study of the Operation of the Wrongful Case Responsibility System in China). *Faxuejia* (The Jurist), no. 2: 27–40.

———. 2017. *Jiceng fayuan shenpan weiyuanhui yali an'jian juece de shizheng yanjiu* (An Empirical Study on How the Adjudication Committee in Basic-Level Courts Makes Decisions on Cases with External Pressure). *Faxue yanjiu* (Chinese Journal of Law), no. 1: 80–99.

Wang, Peng, ed. 1993. *Xing zhishi baike* (Encyclopedia of Knowledge about Sex). Changchun: Jilin People's Press.

Wang, Xiaoling. 2007. *Chongchu weicheng: m fayuan lihun anjian diaocha baogao* (An Investigation Report on the Divorce Cases in Court M). *Sifa* (Journal of Justice), 201–10.

Wenweipo. 2016. *Beijing changping faguan ma caiyun zao qiangji xunzhi* (Beijing Changping Judge Ma Caiyun Killed on Duty). February 26.

Wu, Changzhen, and Yinlan Xia. 2009. *Gaige kaifang sanshinian zhongguo hunyin lifa zhi shanbian* (The Evolution of Chinese Marriage Law during the Period of Thirty Years' Reform and Opening Up). *Zhonghua nüzi xueyuan xuebao* (Journal of China Women's University) 21 (1): 15–21.

Wu, Ruozhi. 2007. *Dangdai zhongguo jiashi fazhi shijian yanjiu—yi huanan r xian weili* (On the Practice of the Family Law System in Contemporary China—South China's R County as an Example). Beijing: Renmin University of China.

Wuyuan Court. 2012. *Wuyuan fayuan qidong er'ji jingqing chuzhi yu'an baozhang lihun an'jian zidong lüxing* (Wuyuan Court Turned on the Second Level of Police Alert to Ensure the Enforcement of a Divorce Judgment). http://wyxfy.chinacourt.org/public/detail.php?id=376.

Xiao, Jianfei, Xinyu Gao, and Yansong Wang. 2014. *Lihun anjian zhong de jihui zhuyi susong xingwei fenxi* (The Analysis of the Opportunism Litigation Behavior in Divorce Cases)." *Shishi qiushi* (Seek Truth from the Facts) 4: 73–77.

Xu, Anqi. 1999. *Hunyinfa xiugai de wuqu—xianzhi lihun* (A Pitfall for Marriage Law Revision: Constraining Divorce). In *Hunyinfa xiugai lunzheng* (The Debate on Revising the Marriage Law), edited by Yinhe Li and Yinan Ma, 182–92. Beijing: Guangming Daily Press.

———. 2007. *Lihun yu nüxing diwei ji quanyi zhi tantao* (A Discussion of Divorce, Women's Status, and Rights)." *Zhejiang xuekan* (Zhejiang Journal) 1: 198–206.

Xu, Chunbin. 2012. *Fenju rending biaozhun anjiu—Yi 2009–2010 nian henan sheng bufen jiceng fayuan lihun jiufen an'jian panjueshu wei yangben* (Standards for Identifying Separation: An Empirical Study on Basic-Level Courts' Granting Divorce in Henan Province in 2009 and 2010). *Zhonghua nüzi xueyuan xuebao* (Journal of China Women's University) 1: 38–44.

Xu, Xin. 2006a. *Faguan weishenme bu xiangxin zhengren* (Why Do the Judges Not Trust Witnesses?). *Zhongwai faxue* (Peking University Law Journal) 18(3): 337–50.
———. 2006b. *Jiufen jiejue yu shehui hexie* (Dispute Resolution and Social Harmony). Beijing: Law Press China.

Yan, Jun. 2016. *Lihun an'jian zhong fuqi zhijian 'qianghaizi' xianxiang ying yinqi zhongshi* (The Phenomenon of "Grabbing Child" Between Couples in Divorce Cases Should Be Focus). http://bjgy.chinacourt.gov.cn/article/detail/2016/03/id/1818486 .shtml

Yang, Shukai. 2014. *Dui lihun anjian tingshen tufa shijian de yuanyin fenxi ji duice jianyi* (An Analysis of the Reasons Behind Unexpected Incidents in Divorce Case Hearings and Suggestions). www.hncourt.gov.cn/public/detail.php?id=152147.

Yang, Xueming, and Zhi Qu. 2001. *Xin hunyinfa redian jujiao* (Focusing on Controversial Issues in the New Marriage Law). Shenyang: Liaoning Huabao Chubanshe.

Yi, Qian, and Li Li. 2017. *Renshen baohuling zhidu de rufa sikao—yi changsha fanjiabao shenpan shijian wei shijiao* (The Legalization of Personal Safety Orders—A Perspective from the Judicial Practice of Anti-Domestic Violence in Changsha City). *Renmin sifa* (People's Judicature) 7: 17–21.

Zhang, Jianyuan. 2018. *Jiating baoli weihe nanyi rending?* (Why Is Domestic Violence Difficult to Recognize?). *Shongdong daxue xuebao* (Shangdong University Journal) 4: 103–11.

Zhang, Xibo. 1983. *Maxiwu shenpan fangshi* (Ma Xiwu Style Adjudication). Beijing: Law Press China.

Zhao, Li, and Yu Ding. 2016. *Lihun an'jian zhong sheji weichengnian zinü fuyangquan guishu cunzai de wenti ji duice—yi nanjingshi liujia jiceng fayuan sinian (2011–2014 nian) lihun an'jian panjueshu wei yangben* (The Problems and Strategies of the Child Custody in Divorce Cases: An A." *Zhonghua nüzi xueyuan xuebao* (Journal of China Women's University), no. 1: 24–34.

Zhao, Xiaoli. 2011. *Zhongguo jiating ziben zhuyi hua de haojiao* (The Horn of the Capitalization of Chinese Families). *Wenhua zongheng* (Beijing Cultural Review), no. 1: 31–34.

Zhou, Bin. 2016. *Jinnain baijia fayuan shidian jiashi shenpan gaige—fang zuigaofa shenpan weiyuanhui zhuanzhi weiyuan du wanhua* (One Hundred Judicial Reform Pilots This Year: Interviews of Du Wanhua, The Full-Time Member of the Judicial Committee in the Supreme People's).

Zhou, Yuan. 2016. *'Jiashi' li 'guofa'—zhuanjia jiedu woguo shoubu fan jiabao fa* ("State Law" for "Family Affairs"—Expert's Understandings on the First Anti-Domestic Violation Law in China)." https://whb.cn/zhuzhan/jiaodian/20160302/50721.html.

Zhu, Jingwen. 2007. *Zhongguo falü fazhan baogao* (China Legal Development Report, 1979–2004). Beijing: People's University Press.

Zhuang, Jinyan. 2014. *Renshen baohuling zai fanjiabao zhong de falü chutan* (The Initial Examination on the Application of Personal Safety Orders in Anti-Domestic Violence)." *Fazhi yu shehui* (Legal System and Society), no. 3: 240–41.

Zuo, Weiming. 2015. *Shengji tongguan difang fayuan faguan renyong gaige shensi* (Reflections on the Appointment Reform for Judges in Provincial Courts). *Faxue yanjiu* (Chinese Journal of Law), no. 4: 23–40.

———. 2018. *"Susong baozha'de zhongguo yingdui: jiyu w qu fayuan jin sanshi nian shenpan shijian de shijian fenxi* (Response to Litigation Explosion in China: Based on Empirical Analysis of the Trial Practice of the Court in W District in the Past Thirty Years). *Zhongguo faxue* (China Legal Science), no. 4: 238–60.

STATUTES CITED (IN CHRONOLOGICAL ORDER)

Supreme People's Court. 1989. Several Concrete Opinions on How to Determine in Divorce Trials Whether Marital Affection Has Truly Broken Down, Promulgated on November 21, 1989.

Supreme People's Court. 1993. Supreme People's Court's Opinions on Adjudicating Issues on Child Custody, Promulgated on November 3, 1993.

Standing Committee of the National People's Congress. 1996. Law of the People's Republic of China on Protection of the Rights and Interests of the Elderly, Promulgated on August 29, 1996.

Supreme People's Court. 1998. The Accountability Regulations on Illegal Adjudication of Judges in the People's Court (Trial), Promulgated on August 26, 1998.

Supreme People's Court. 1999. The Outline of Five Years Reform. *Gazette of the Supreme People's Court of the People's Republic of China* 6: 185–90.

National People's Congress. 2001. Marriage Law of the People's Republic of China, Promulgated on September 10, 1980, Amended on April 28, 2001.

Supreme People's Court. 2001. The First Interpretation of the Supreme People's Court on Several Issues in the Application of Marriage Law of the People's Republic of China, Promulgated on December 25, 2001.

Supreme People's Court. 2003. The Second Interpretation of the Supreme People's Court on Several Issues in the Application of Marriage Law of the People's Republic of China, Promulgated on December 4, 2003.

Standing Committee of the National People's Congress. 2005. Law of the People's Republic of China on Women's Rights and Interests, Promulgated on April 3, 1992, Amended on August 28, 2005.

Supreme People's Court. 2005. The Outline of the Second Five Years Reform. *Gazette of the Supreme People's Court of the People's Republic of China* 12: 8–12.

The Applied Legal Institute of the Supreme People's Court. 2008. Guidelines for Hearing Marriage Cases Involving Domestic Violence, Promulgated on March 1, 2008.

Standing Committee of the National People's Congress. 2008. Law of the People's Republic of China on the Protection of Disabled Persons, Promulgated on December 28, 1990, Amended on April 24, 2008.

Supreme People's Court. 2011. The Third Interpretation of the Supreme People's Court on Several Issues in the Application of Marriage Law of the People's Republic of China, Promulgated on August 9, 2011.

Supreme People's Court. 2014. The News Circulation about the Relevant Situation of Judicial Interference to Domestic Violence by the Supreme People's Court, February 27, 2014.

Supreme People's Court. 2015. Opinions of the Supreme People's Court on Comprehensive Deepening of Reform of People's Courts—The 4th Five-Year Outline of the Program for Reform of People's Courts (2014–2018), February 4, 2015.

Supreme People's Court, Supreme People's Procuratorate, Ministry of Police, and Ministry of Justice. 2015. The Opinions on Dealing with the Domestic Violence Crimes, Promulgated on March 2, 2015.

Standing Committee of the National People's Congress. 2015. Anti-Domestic Violence Law of the People's Republic of China, Promulgated on December 27, 2015.

Standing Committee of the National People's Congress. 2017. The Civil Procedure Law of the People's Republic of China, Promulgated in 1991, Amended on June 27, 2017.

Supreme People's Court. 2017. Notice of the Supreme People's Court on Trying Cases Regarding Marriage and Family Disputes in Accordance with Law and Effectively Safeguarding the Parties' Lawful Rights and Interests and Personal Safety, Promulgated on September 21, 2017.

Supreme People's Court. 2018. An Opinion to Further Reform the Adjudicative Mode and Working Mechanism on Family Issues (Trial). July 18, 2018.

Supreme People's Court. 2019. The Supreme People's Court Annual Work Report. www.npc.gov.cn/npc/xinwen/2019-03/19/content_2084130.htm.

Standing Committee of the National People's Congress. 2019. Judges Law of the People's Republic of China, Promulgated on February 28, 1995, Amended on April 23, 2019.

National People's Congress. 2018. Law of the People's Republic China on the Protection of Rights and Interests of Women, Promulgated on April 3, 1992, Amended on October 26, 2018.

Supreme People's Court. 2020. The Supreme People's Court Annual Work Report. http://www.gov.cn/xinwen/2020-06/01/content_5516480.htm.

National People's Congress. 2020. The Civil Code of the PRC, Promulgated on May 28, 2020.

INDEX

Page numbers in *italics* indicate photos or tables.

access: to Guangdong Court, 19–20; to Shaanxi Court, 20, 22

adjudicated, *52, 53, 54, 55, 57*, 60, 61

adjudicated denials: in Distraught Woman's Case, 184; in Distraught Woman's Case, second petition, 185; in domestic violence and delaying decisions, 135; property division and, 63, 258n2; in routinized approaches, regular cases, 62–67, 85

Adjudication Committee decisions, 76–77

adjudication documents, 16

ADV Law. *See* Anti-Domestic Violence Law

Alcohol Saleswoman's Case, 251; judge's fault in, 72–73; reason shift to impact in, 71–73

alimony, 175. *See also* compensation

All-China Women's Federation, 107, 110, 128, 234, 257n1 (chap. 1)

Alwis, Rangita de Silva-de, 6, 9, 10, 177, 188, 193

Anesthesiologist's Case, 251; female infertility in, 218–20

annual case closure rates, 42, 257n3

Anti-Domestic Violence Law (ADV Law), 6, 7, 15, 111–12; in domestic violence and mediation, 113; enforcement related to, 138

appellate reversal, 164–66

Applied Research Center, 234

assessor, 192

Attempted Rape Case, 251; boy and, 150, 151–52, 156; child custody in, 151–52; compensation in, 119, 207–8, 209, 216–17; cultural biases in, 216–17; domestic violence not mentioned in, 119; facts of, 118–19, 208; inhibited women and, 207–9; intimidation in, 217; judges' inaction and, 211–12; mediation pressure resistance in, 156; reputation in, 208–9, 211–12

authoritarian state: in institutional constraints, 226–28; U.S. compared to, 226–28

Autistic Daughter's Case, 251; in property division, child custody, 180–81

bargaining, 3, 4–5; in Case of Mrs. Li, mediation, 90; in pragmatic discourse, 105–6; in property division, child custody, 179–80

basic-level courts, 18–19

Behr, Edward, 200

Bemiller, Michelle, 142

bidding, 3, 4–5. *See also* property division, bidding loss

bigamy, 158, 259n2 (chap 5)

Bingtuan, 180, 259n1 (chap. 5)

birth-control policy, relaxed, 181

book structure, 23–26

Bourdieu, Pierre, 29, 226

boys, 142, 155; Attempted Rape Case and, 150, 151–52, 156; in Case of Mrs. Li, mediation, 94–95, 98; Case of Mrs. Li and, 89, 199; cultural biases and, 149–52, 156, 158–59, 198–99; Oil Refinery Worker's Case and, 146–47; Railway Worker's Case and, 158–59; Singapore Laborer's Case and, 115, 145